Hornet 33

Hornet 33

Memoir of a Combat Helicopter Pilot in Vietnam

ED DENNY

McFarland & Company, Inc., Publishers
Jefferson, North Carolina

LIBRARY OF CONGRESS CATALOGUING-IN-PUBLICATION DATA

Names: Denny, Ed, 1946– author.
Title: Hornet 33 : memoir of a combat helicopter pilot in Vietnam /
    Ed Denny.
Other titles: Hornet thirty-three
Description: Jefferson, North Carolina : McFarland & Company, Inc.,
    Publishers, 2016 | Includes index.
Identifiers: LCCN 2016041751 | ISBN 9781476666099 (softcover :
    acid free paper) ∞
Subjects: LCSH: Denny, Ed, 1946– | Vietnam War, 1961–1975—
    Personal narratives, American. | Vietnam War, 1961–1975—Aerial
    operations, American. | United States. Army. Aviation Company,
    116th—History.
Classification: LCC DS559.5 .D466 2016 | DDC 959.704/3092 [B]—
    dc23
LC record available at https://lccn.loc.gov/2016041751

BRITISH LIBRARY CATALOGUING DATA ARE AVAILABLE

ISBN (print) 978-1-4766-6609-9
ISBN (ebook) 978-1-4766-2571-3

On the cover: *inset* Hornet 33 (Ed Denny); Yellow Jacket with
Agent Orange spray-rig equipment on board (all photographs are
from the author's collection)

Printed in the United States of America

McFarland & Company, Inc., Publishers
    Box 611, Jefferson, North Carolina 28640
    www.mcfarlandpub.com

To
Kimberly
Allison
Austin
Arthur

my four adult children

For my wife,
Janice Ann Denny,
thank you totally and completely

TABLE OF CONTENTS

The 116th Assault Helicopter Company, known as the Hornets, served in the Vietnam War from October 1965 to December 26, 1971.

In the Gettysburg Address, Abraham Lincoln said, "[F]rom these honored dead we take increased devotion to that cause for which they gave the last full measure of devotion—that we here highly resolve that these dead shall not have died in vain...."

The Army Helicopter Flight School for Warrant Officer Candidates was a volunteer program with stringent admissions standards. Each of these Hornets died a hero; all were willing and clear-eyed volunteers who stepped up and answered their country's call to duty during an unpopular war.

In the American memory, none is forgotten.

Richard Callen	Larry Ricks	Stanley Brown
William Davis	Melvin Morgan Jr.	Charles Danielson Jr.
Merced Gonzales	Dean Bolhouse	Mark Tearl
Carroll Rodgers	Robert Jantz	David Gunderson*
Larry Castle	Charles Sellner	Craig Fox*
David Siverly	William Scott	Thomas McDonald*
Robert Crain	Everett Wilsher	Mark Portwood Jr.*
Raul Villa	Peter Polak	Herman Serna*
Peter Day	Harry Rose	Stephen Chasin*
Richard Allen	Fredrick Follette	Jack Smith*
Gary Humphrey	Michael Goeller	Jerry Martin*
Stanley Stellmach Jr.	James Hopkins	Angelo Larraga*
Thomas Bergren	Ronald Baker	Kenneth Koch*
Joe Reed	Steven Herring	Richard Salmond*
Roger Moore	Jimmy Crisp	James Highsmith
Ross Barlow	Richard Holman	Daniel Dye
Derrell Clemmer	Clifford Wright	Roy Barnes
Kenneth Plavcan	Philip Enlow	Pat Brannon
Fredrick Gruber	Jimmy Harrison	

Killed during Ed Denny's tour as Hornet 33

Whether the war was popular or not, the world's understanding that America will fight to protect its freedom makes our foes think twice before they bother us. If for nothing more than that fact, these men did not die in vain. They showed the world that whatever happens to America, the country will just take it and endure and come back fighting to the last full measure if required.

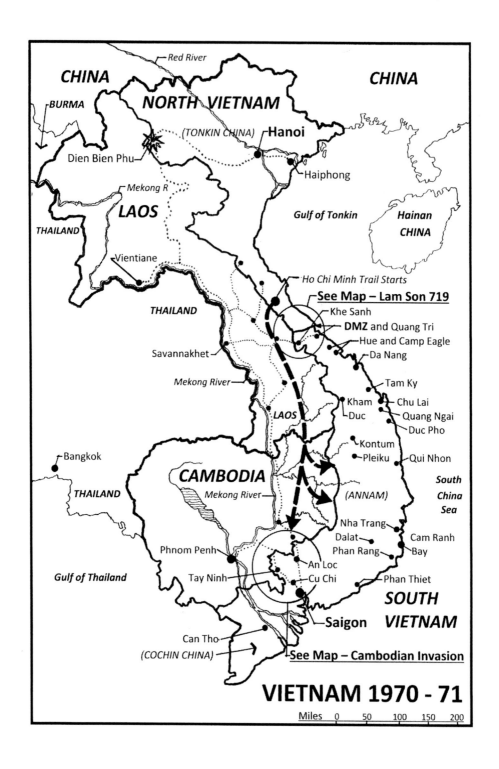

CHINA

BURMA

NORTH VIETNAM

Red River

(TONKIN CHINA) Hanoi

Dien Bien Phu

Haiphong

Mekong R

LAOS

Gulf of Tonkin

Hainan
CHINA

THAILAND

Vientiane

CHINA

Ho Chi Minh Trail Starts

See Map – Lam Son 719

THAILAND

Khe Sanh

DMZ and Quang Tri

Hue and Camp Eagle

Da Nang

Savannakhet

Tam Ky

Mekong River

Kham
Duc

Chu Lai

Quang Ngai

Duc Pho

LAOS

Kontum

Pleiku

Qui Nhon

Bangkok

CAMBODIA

South
China
Sea

THAILAND

Mekong River

(ANNAM)

Nha Trang

Dalat

Cam Ranh
Bay

Phan Rang

Phnom Penh

An Loc

Tay Ninh

Cu Chi

Phan Thiet

Gulf of Thailand

**SOUTH
VIETNAM**

Saigon

Can Tho

(COCHIN CHINA)

See Map – Cambodian Invasion

VIETNAM 1970 - 71

Miles 0   50   100   150   200

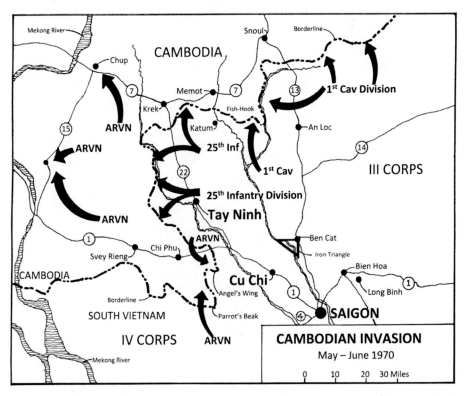

CAMBODIA

Mekong River

Snoul

Borderline

Chup

7

Memot

7

13

1st Cav Division

ARVN

Krek

Fish-Hook

15

Katum

An Loc

14

ARVN

25th Inf

1st Cav

III CORPS

22

ARVN

25th Infantry Division

Tay Ninh

ARVN

Ben Cat

Iron Triangle

Bien Hoa

1

Chi Phu

ARVN

Long Binh

Svey Rieng

1

CAMBODIA

Cu Chi

Borderline

Angel's Wing

1

SOUTH VIETNAM

Parrot's Beak

4

SAIGON

IV CORPS

ARVN

Mekong River

CAMBODIAN INVASION

May – June 1970

0   10   20   30 Miles

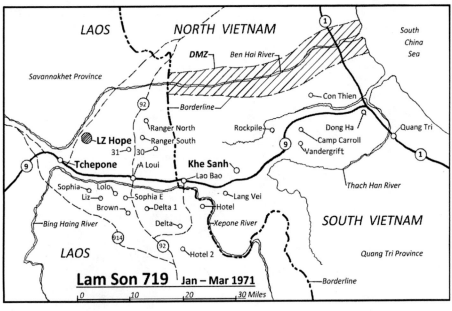

LAOS

NORTH VIETNAM

South China Sea

DMZ

Ben Hai River

1

Savannakhet Province

Con Thien

92

Borderline

Rockpile

Dong Ha

Quang Tri

Ranger North

Camp Carroll

LZ Hope

Ranger South

9

Vandergrift

1

31

30

A Loui

Khe Sanh

Tchepone

Lao Bao

Sophia

Lolo

Thach Han River

Liz

Sophia E

Lang Vei

Brown

Delta 1

Hotel

Bing Haing River

Delta

Xepone River

SOUTH VIETNAM

914

92

LAOS

Hotel 2

Quang Tri Province

Lam Son 719 Jan – Mar 1971

Borderline

0   10   20   30 Miles

PREFACE

In the fall of 1994, I was admitted to the Dallas VA Medical Center for treatment of suspected posttraumatic stress disorder 23 years after I had been in the Vietnam War. My doctor, a PhD psychologist with over 25 years of experience in treating such disorders, submitted a VA PTSD disability claim form on my behalf to the Waco, Texas, Veterans Affairs Regional Office for processing. The VA responded after a (long) time with instructions for me to submit a written account of any purported traumatic events I claimed to have experienced in Vietnam with dates and times of the claimed event(s), the exact place of the event(s), with witness statements verifying what occurred. Events, dates, and places: after 23 years, I couldn't say for sure exactly where or when anything happened. Witnesses: how in the hell could I hope to find or contact anyone I knew back in Vietnam, much less get a written statement from them?

I tried to write something, but I couldn't get beyond the very beginning of any account of my war experiences. I had just spent 23 years of my life doing everything possible to erase any memory of my time in the Vietnam War totally out of my mind. My year in Southeast Asia had not been a single day longer than my year spent in the third grade, and I wanted it to play no larger role in my life and memories than the time I was in elementary school. I guess that was an unrealistic expectation, an apples versus oranges comparison sort of situation. What I wound up with was a useless pile of a few scribbled notes.

Now, 21 years later, in 2015, after a zillion starts and stops, I have finished the story of what I experienced in Vietnam flying Huey's for the 116th Assault Helicopter Company, the Hornets, specifically the Wasp Platoon of the Hornets. At the time I was flying with them, I thought I was lucky to be with such a great helicopter company. The Hornets had been in Vietnam as long as anyone, and they knew exactly how to get business done as safely as possible. The Hornets won every fight we were ever in when I was there. We flew into the mouth of hell many times and came out the other side every time, leaving a sprawling count of dead enemy in our wake. For the enemy on the ground saw that it was the Hornets coming for them, it must have been like seeing terror coming out of the sky to dispatch them to their stinking little afterlife. For any enemy survivors of combat with the Hornets, the PTSD dreams that wake them up screaming in the dark of night has to be the vision of a giant Hornets helicopter coming for them.

From that first pile of scribbled notes, over the years, I eventually stacked up 85 sets of notes of events in Vietnam, Cambodia, and Laos as a form of emersion therapy to at least confront the crap that was bothering me. After a year of intensive PTSD treatment by the VA, my doctor finally told me that my PTSD was in the category of being a case of all the King's horses and all the King's men sort of deal. I was a Humpty Dumpty case. Life wasn't always fair to everyone. For some people, shit happens. You couldn't do anything about what happened in the past. The best thing you could do was understand it, learn everything you could about it, and learn how to cope with the situation. Basically, he was saying, "Just take it." Then we went into strategies about living with PTSD. He said it was like getting your legs blown off in a war. He couldn't give me new legs. The best thing that could be done was to teach me how to use prosthetic legs to walk again, and maybe someday I would run again. Getting my Vietnam experiences out of my head and out into the open was step one in learning to walk on prosthetic legs again. Confront the crap. I eventually worked on those 85 sets of notes until I had a very long set of separate stories.

I have finally distilled all 85 separate stories into a series of 45 interconnected chapters to make a book of a reasonable length. There are still 40 chapters not in this book because they were redundant. How many times can a person say that the bastards tried to shoot me again and missed by a couple of inches one more time, or some damned LZ went hot and turned into pure chaos: that would have been too many times.

In the spirit of Detective Joe Friday from the TV show *Dragnet,* I've tried to give just the facts, sir. And like Joe Friday, I've changed the names of some of the characters to protect the innocent. The following names are pseudonyms given to real people who are included in this book:

1st Lieutenant Sparks	WO Leon Richards	WO Dennis Plumber
WO Gary Newton	WO Randy Walker	WO Austin Scarborough
WO Larry Hood	WO Bob Skyles	Wife, Jane Denny

U.S. Army nurse Captain Bobbie Sue Wolters

Stinger 82 gunship commander Arthur, and Sunny and Bobby Barrera

With the exception of the above listed pseudonyms, the events and details of the story in this book are all factual and as accurate as my memory can recall them. Nothing has been exaggerated, embellished, or glorified. It is just the facts, Detective Friday.

This collection of memories in no way tells the whole story of the Hornets during my time with them: it is just the little role I played as a Hornet. There was so much more than I could start to relate here. Maybe someday someone will tell a fuller history of the Hornets, the 116th Assault Helicopter Company, because they were a great group of "good ole boys" trying to do their best, and it was my great honor to be one of them for a while. For the men I knew who died during my year of flying in Vietnam, I guess I will go to my grave with those men still wandering the darkest reaches of my worst nightmares.

And to the makers of C-Rations: I just want you bunch of sadists to know that I have not opened one single can of 25-year-old spaghetti since I left Vietnam, and I never plan to either.

* * *

My military history is brief. I was drafted (then enlisted) in January 1969 and went to basic training at Folk Polk, Louisiana, and then to helicopter flight school in Fort Wolters, Texas, and Fort Rucker, Alabama. From flight school, I went directly to Vietnam on March 30, 1970, through March 30, 1971, and was discharged when I returned to the States at Fort Lewis, Washington: a 35 month early-out, for which I was very grateful.

Class photograph of Bravo-2 Platoon of the Second Warrant Officer Candidate Company, Class 69-47 at Fort Wolters, Mineral Wells, Texas. Ed Denny is in the front row, second from right.

1

WHISKEY SHOTS, PLAYING SLOTS, COIN TOSS

The day had arrived to leave my hometown of El Paso, Texas, and travel to Vietnam to be a U.S. Army helicopter pilot. Flowers were blossoming in early springtime, toward the end of March in 1970, and I was fresh out of the army's Rotary-Wing Flight School at Ft. Rucker, Alabama, and was a newly minted warrant officer (WO) with only a sketchy notion of what combat flying in Southeast Asia was actually going to be like. My old man had flown in the Second World War for three and a-half years over the South Pacific as a crew chief on B-17 and B-29 bombers to get his wings, and it was my turn to do something to match up to that, even if I disagreed with the Vietnam War. Being an antiwar hippie wasn't an option for me: that would simply be seen as being a coward. The Vietnam War: go to the damned thing and do something that mattered or show yourself as being a yellow-bellied bum. Where was there a choice in any of that?

Up until recently, all of my attention and efforts had been solely focused on successfully completing flight school while I was simultaneously honeymooning with my new wife. Concerns about the reality of going to the war in Vietnam would be dealt with in due time. Well, that time was upon me, and I sort of felt like I'd just finished a high school driver's education class and my first assignment was to go race in the Indianapolis 500 with the big boys. Okay. Guessed we would see how that worked out. All my bags were packed; I was ready to go. Everyone had known this day was coming, and the only thing left was to say good-bye with hugs and kisses given to my wife and family. Then it was onto the jet plane from El Paso, off to San Francisco, and Hawaii next, followed by Guam. Finally, after our long trip, it was the end of the line: Saigon, Vietnam. We'd flown all day and night until we landed Monday morning. With a certain amount of hesitation shown by most of the passengers, we departed the plane to be greeted by a pervasive and horrible stink, our welcome to Vietnam.

Everyone caught a bus to the Long Binh Replacement Center, and I passed the first couple of days there in the Officers' club drinking whiskey shots and spending long boring hours waiting and playing nickel slots. Alone. I remember being alone. Yeah, I recall being totally green and painfully alone.

At an orientation briefing the second day, some army major gave us a little speech: "Gentlemen, welcome to South Vietnam. This may not be a very good war, maybe it's only a little pissant war, but it's the only war we have, so you gotta make the most of it. As army officers, you may never have another opportunity like this to demonstrate your skills, so make your country damned proud of you." The briefing must have been the lifer's orientation. My mind imagined I said, *Hey, Briefer-Man, where's the warrant officer's orientation? Captain America, this isn't a career deal for me. I'm here only because of the draft. I may be listed as Regular Army, but I sure as hell ain't a lifer, or so I hope. Hope this damned Vietnam deal doesn't kill me.*

The third day at the replacement center the long-awaited assignment list came out telling us what unit we were assigned to and where we were going to be stationed. We got on a bus. Hey, there's Smith, and I knew him! A familiar face. I recognized him from flight school back at Fort Wolters and Fort Rucker. We were going to the same battalion, and at a Long Binh Airfield we were put on an outbound helicopter. One of us would go to Cu Chi; the other one would go to Tay Ninh. Who knew anything about anything? Not me! The choice was the 116th Assault Helicopter Company at Cu Chi or the 187th AHC at Tay Ninh. They were sister companies, so the deal was the Hornets or the Crusaders.

My first glimpses of Cu Chi were from our helicopter as we were flying low-level and doing 90 knots: from what I saw, the base looked huge. It was the home base of the 25th Infantry Division, called Tropic Lightning. The place had about 30,000 U.S. military forces stationed there, and from the air it looked like a giant anthill swarming with people. Smith and I tossed a coin, and I won. I shook hands with him and wished him well then jumped off the helicopter and stayed with the Hornets. Smith went on to Tay Ninh, a place up very close to the Cambodian border called Rocket City. I figured Cu Chi couldn't be any worse than some place called Rocket City.

I watched the Crusaders helicopter take off and fly out of sight, leaving me standing on the runway. So there I was, alone, and the die was cast: it seemed that I would be a Hornet, whatever that would be. I shyly walked into the 116th AHC operations shack next to the runway and quietly mumbled, "Excuse me, Captain, but I guess I'm assigned to this company."

The Hornets must have been expecting someone. "Hell, ain't you the prettiest sight I've seen today," a jovial captain at the operations shack said as he shook my hand like I was a long-lost relative. He helped me with my duffel bag while he offered me a cup of coffee or a Coke. I thought he was gonna kiss me. The captain looked at my orders and hustled me to the orderly room to meet the first sergeant and the company commanding officer, a major. Next, the captain took me to a hooch and we put my things in a room, then we went over to the supply shack, where I got a couple of tattered old flight suits, a helmet, a .38 caliber pistol, and a bunch of malaria pills. As we went, he showed me the general layout of the "Hornets' Nest," their great big swimming pool and volley ball court, the Officers' club, the company mess hall, a laundry and tailor's shop, the showers, and the latrine. They even had their own barber shop. He asked where I was from. Texas! Hell, he had a cousin down in Texas. He asked, "Have you eaten? If not, get some lunch, then get into your flight gear, and we'll get you a check ride since our company IP is available today."

The instructor pilot (IP), a warrant officer named Leon Richards, showed up in faded blue jeans, a tee shirt, and flip-flop shower shoes. We flew around a while and did what Mr. Richards called an orientation ride, and then I performed an autorotation back at Cu Chi. We didn't totally crash, and Mr. Richards told me I'd passed my check ride and I'd be in his platoon.

By the end of the day I was unpacking my belongings and organizing my barren little room at my new home. I was getting the bunk and desk straightened away when my platoon mates came in. I tried to introduce myself, but they were too damned tired and not interested in some Green New Guy. Except for Steve Chasin. He was friendly and invited me to join him for supper. The mess hall had pork chops on the menu that evening. I told Steve I was from El Paso. He hollered out for others to hear, "Another one from Texas, pretty funny." He explained that I wasn't alone: "Roger Walker over there is a Texan, too, Arlington, and that guy who is actually named Austin there, he comes from Harlingen, and there's Willie from Mineral Wells, plus Dennis, a town around Galveston, I think, and now you, El Paso."

Austin came over and introduced himself, then sat down and joined us. He and Steve told me they had both been with the Hornets about three months, which made them still New Guys in the eyes of the long-timers, but now they had a newer guy: namely me. They both laughed at my worn-out flight suit the supply guy had issued me. Steve said he was off the next day, so he would swap clothes with me and turn in my old rags to get himself a couple of new flight suits. A lieutenant stopped at our table and said he was 1st Lt. Sparks, my new platoon leader, and I'd fly with him in the morning: "Eat breakfast and be on the flight line at six o'clock sharp. Get to bed early. Dawn comes early."

That first night with the Hornets was a long time ago, 46 years, back in 1970, in a strange place far away. In my room, I wrote a letter home and looked at a photograph of my wife, Jane. It was like she was on a different planet, in El Paso, so far away. Everything that had been the only reality I'd ever known seemed far away. I studied the photograph and recalled sleeping with her four or five nights before. Easy, tender loving till dawn came. We'd been married less than six months. I was 23; she was 21. We'd honeymooned in Alabama in an old pink house trailer just outside the Fort Rucker gate. Long flight school days of flying paired with short, passionate nights soaring in moonlit clouds of romantic intoxication, hours into the night, loving unending, till sleep came from exhaustion. Heaven outside the Fort Rucker gate. So long ago, so far away: another person's life lived in another world.

Jane's dark hair was nearly black, her eyes green. She stood five-feet-five, weighed 110 pounds, with a figure of classical proportions, and moved with trained grace from 15 years of dance lessons, so she had a dancer's perfect control of her body. She could do anything with it that I could dream up. She had the strength, the agility, and the stamina of a young athlete. Hours into the night, lovemaking unending: easy, tender loving, scorching, powerful loving. Recalling El Paso, I heard winds blowing, still saw my wife's smile glowing, and imagined the wonderful smell of her freshly washed hair.

Now, in the hooch, that first night had grown silent, all the lights were out, and everyone had gone to bed. The feeling of being alone in the suffocating jet-black darkness was only amplified by the silence. I stretched out on my bunk and tried to sleep, closed my eyes, and tried to envision Jane hovering over me, loving me slowly, drawing things out. In my fire-hot memories, she leaned back on her arms so I'd have the clearest picture of the display she gave me, like she'd done just last week. Just last week I'd been snatched from my honeymoon bed and found myself deposited in some place called Cu Chi in stinky Vietnam, and I was experiencing the horrible pains of absolute cold-turkey withdrawal from everything I had ever known. I had about 360 more nights to go before I'd be home again. But for those nights, my new reality was being alone and submerged in darkness and silence.

Late that night, I was awakened from my fitful sleep around 3:00 a.m. Outside my door, I'd heard the loud THUD, THUD of someone's feet heavily hitting the wooden floor and then running down the hooch's little hall. Instantly, there were others running. Someone shouted, "Incoming! Incoming!" I sat up and got off my little army bunk.

KABOOM! KABOOM! Two loud explosions shook our hooch. Must have hit somewhere close by. Damn, "Incoming! Incoming!" The possibility of that had never yet occurred to me! Cu Chi was such a big place. How could there be *incoming*? I pulled on my flight suit pants and shirt and my boots, tied the boots, then went down the hall and outside into our small sandbagged bunker. Everyone from my hooch was there in their green army underwear, barefooted. They all laughed out loud at me. "Hey, Texas-New-Guy, you'll look real damned good as a mangled corpse if you get blown up while you're takin' your sweet damned time to get dressed up like you're going to a fancy tea party." I know I must have been shaking like a leaf as I stood there with everyone laughing at me, and I guess I looked funny, looked as Green as anyone could be, but all my mind heard was, *Incoming. Was that Vietcong rockets? Rockets? Really? My first damned night here? Rockets? Really?*

Yeah, I was back home in El Paso last week, just last week. Seemed such a damned long time ago. I'd been having such a sweet dream of my wife, the taste of her kisses, when all the *incoming* commotion started. There I was, and I still had a zillion lonesome nights coming. Had to shake that out of my mind. Stop thinking about home, about my wife, focus on what was ahead of me. I had a full year to survive. Hoped Vietnam didn't kill me. Yeah, I remember feeling alone and scared as hell.

KABOOM! KABOOM! Two more rounds hit. I had the urge to curl up in the smallest possible ball in some corner of the bunker. Green. Scared. That *incoming* was pure crap.

I asked, "How frequently does this sort of thing happen around here?"

No one answered. They'd all busted out laughing at me again.

That was how my journey began: a Green college kid without a clue about what he'd gotten into or what combat flying would do to him, how it would fundamentally remake him into something he never saw coming. He never fully imagined how much death he'd experience there or the Hornets who would die during his year of the Vietnam War.

2

GETTING SHOT AT:
JUST TAKE IT

The Hornets were wasting no time. I was popped into the pilot's seat of a Huey before dawn my first full day with them. I had been driving my wife's car over to the Red Rooster Drive-In on Dyer Street in northeast El Paso for hamburgers only seven days earlier. To be so quickly transported from my familiar and comfortable life back home and thrown into totally different and unknown conditions had my general feelings of anxiety going through the roof. Incoming Viet Cong (VC) rockets the previous night hitting so near our hooch, and within my first few hours of being at Cu Chi, certainly contributed to my apprehension of danger lurking around every corner. My first impressions of actually being in Vietnam made me think the place might just be pretty damned dangerous, and I felt as skittish as a lost cat in a room full of threatening rocking chairs.

First Lt. Sparks, the platoon commander, took personal control of my initial days in Vietnam. That first morning was my baptism into flying out in what he called *Indian Country*, the Hornet Company's primary area of operations. Anyone found out in the Hornet's Indian Country was assumed to be an enemy and subject to being killed on the spot with no hesitation or reprieves. I was getting the lieutenant's special initial orientation process he put New Guys through, I eventually learned. It was day after day after day of flying with him, and he was all business, cold, direct, with no mincing words or sugar coating anything.

Everything started with a helicopter preflight inspection in the dark, before first light broke, and he followed me, watched my every move, to see that all things were done in order by the checklist. When my inspection was done, it was quiz time about everything I'd found, questions about tolerances of every bearing that I'd checked. If the answers didn't please him, he said, "You'll know that tomorrow." Then he showed how he checked items of his special interest and spouted out allowable tolerances and what this or that

Diagram of a UH-1H Model Troop Transport Combat Assault Helicopter, commonly known as a "Slick" due to the lack of outside weapons and often flown with the doors removed. As shown by the dimensions, the Huey was not a small Helicopter, it was about the size of a semi-truck and trailer.

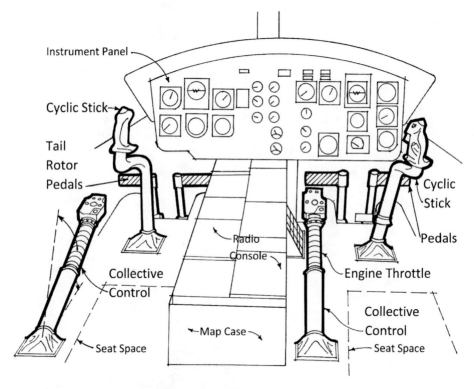

Diagram of Huey Controls. The Cyclic Stick: move it to the right to bank the aircraft to the right; conversely, move it to the left to bank left. The Tail Rotor Pedals: push the right pedal to rotate the Helicopter clockwise: left pedal, counterclockwise. The Collective Control: pull up to go up, push down to go down by changing the Rotor Pitch Angle. Engine Throttle: on the Collective. Now, pat yourself on the head while you rub your belly and hop on one foot jumping a rope and spin in a circle as people are shooting at you, and then you'll know what it is like to operate a Combat Helicopter and head for the great big wild blue yonder.

bearing had. Even when fluid levels were checked and were proper, he actually tasted the engine oil and transmission fluid. Did anything taste burned? No? That was how things were, everything done exactly by a checklist. We'd fly two hours, then go refuel. He'd get out, and I stayed seated in the Helicopter. Two more hours, he'd get out again, and I stayed seated again, and by then my ass was hurting. Had to piss? Well, maybe next stop. In that seat for hours on end, and it seemed forever. My poor ass wasn't hurting anymore, it was screaming bloody murder. It seemed like I flew all day, and Lt. Sparks barely touched the controls except when he flew in the landing zones (LZs). He just watched me like a hawk and listened to every word said on the radio or intercom.

Our fourth day of flying I was copilot on a command and control (C&C) mission with Lt. Sparks: he was the air mission commander who directed the combat-assault-Slicks formation and observed everything happening from overhead, sort of like an orchestra conductor or a play director. We were hovering around in a flooded rice paddy doing Sparks's normal conditions recon for the formation's next LZ, checking it out for potential problems or any Bad Guys waiting there, when some AK-47 automatic rifle fire came from a tree line out my door. Instinctively, I tried to lean away from the source of the gunfire, but my shoulder harness straps and seat belt locked me so tightly into my seat I could lean only the slightest amount. Sparks saw me leaning and went totally ape-shit! He was flying the helicopter and plopped us down right there in the mud. The AK-47 rifle was still working out, pop-pop-pop. Sparks yelled, "You got it!" Then he radioed the Hornet-Stinger gunships and rocket runs. I took the controls and awaited his instructions.

"Hover!" he barked at me. In an instant, he pulled out a pistol, a menacing-looking .45 caliber automatic and displayed it glaringly in my face! Our door-gunner opened up with his machine gun, blazing away, returning fire into the dense green overgrowth of the trees and brush. Stinger rockets began working over the area—*Boom-Boom-Boom*—until the tree line was rapidly turned to splinters.

As we hovered there at a stationary three feet above the ground in the LZ, Sparks hollered, "You'll do your job, and you'll not stop for a damned second. You're responsible for the safety of those two guys in the back. They get hurt from anything you do I'll damned well kill you in a heartbeat! You hear me? Understood? I will kill you. When I'm flying, you ride the controls with me, and if I get hit you take over the helicopter. If we're getting shot at, just take it, damn it! There's no place to hide anyway. Resist your natural reflex to duck away and just take it. I know, sounds insane. There's nothing else to do. Just take it!"

Whoa! My platoon leader had just held his damned pistol to my head! He gave me his speech, and there was nothing I could say about any of that, so I just nodded that I understood. Damn. Damn. Damn. The last thing on earth I wanted was for him to think I was some sort of coward. Leaning in my seat had just been a totally reflexive thing for a split second. Growing up in El Paso, I had long ago learned that it was always better to stand your ground and fight than to run away and show yourself as a coward, which made every bully in your area want to attack you every damned day. But when someone was throwing a right jab at you, it didn't work out well if you just stood still and took it. No. A little bobbing and weaving helped in a fistfight. That was what I was doing: bobbing-and-weaving while I was strapped in that damned seat.

I had decided to fly helicopters for a lot of reasons that conveniently ignored some basic realities. For me, becoming a pilot had been a major accomplishment (since I had a fear of heights to overcome), and being a warrant officer was a source of pride. Hell, by that point in the Vietnam War, the consensus public opinion about helicopter pilots had generally grown to a glowing stature. Also, it was a chance to test my determination and see if I could measure up to basic expectations. Plus, my circle of family and friends looked at me in a whole new light: it was as if they thought that I'd suddenly grown a much bigger set of brass balls than they had ever before suspected. But I ignored obvious facts. Sure, I always knew that being in a war might involve being shot at, even though I avoided thinking about that. Now it was time to face reality: *People were shooting at you!* There was nothing about the war that was hypothetical anymore. Actual bullets were flying in real time.

I was completely amazed to hear from 1st Lt. Sparks that the army's best solution to being shot at was to *Just Take It*. The lieutenant was right—that did sound insane. What were you supposed to do, grit your teeth, toughen up, be brave, and *Just Take It?* In my opinion, if that was the army's answer to a problem, that was a load of crap. I'd been with the Hornets less than a week, and I was still totally green; so everything was still new to me, and I really had no idea how things were supposed to be. If Lt. Sparks was telling me that was the way things were, I had no choice but to believe what I was told. So, my first formal lesson in insanity was to *Just Take It*.

At the same time, I realized that the second lesson in insanity was the fact that, from the way 1st Lt. Sparks had been doing his recon of that LZ, it was clear he'd been trying to draw some enemy fire. He kept poking around that rice paddy so much that anyone who was there had no choice but to shoot at us. Things went way beyond *Just Take It* to the point that it was *Let's Intentionally Make Ourselves Targets*. To a Green New Guy, that definitely sounded like a load of crap. There were a lot of crazy things I was apparently going to have to adjust to. But Sparks didn't treat me any differently after that, just matter of fact, just instructional. He was simply showing me reality.

Everyone around you is depending on you, so do your damned job. And let's kill some Viet Cong while we're at it.

During a single-ship mission I flew with him next, we were working for a 25th Infantry unit doing a sweep-and-clear job (the army PR guys changed the name from search and destroy so that it didn't sound so harsh on the evening news), and we were hovering along a canal, hunting for suspected Viet Cong who were thought to be hiding in bunkers there. If Viet Cong were around, Sparks would flush them out, then our door-gunners could get them. We went up one side of the canal and down the other side, dropping grenades in every damn hole along the banks.

Sparks was a cold-blooded killer. He didn't seem to take joy in what he was doing, no whooping and hollering, no celebrating, and no partying at the Officers' club. Just taking care of his business. The Hornet's policy was kill 'em all, and let God sort 'em out. If they were in the free-fire zone, they shouldn't have been there, gonna be killed if the Hornets find you in Indian Country.

Sparks and I came back to the same area about four or five days later and landed alongside the canal where we'd dropped hand grenades into holes. We got out of our helicopter and met with a group of infantry officer types. Everyone wanted to shake Sparks's hand personally and thank him, and they said he'd gotten 20 total confirmed Body Count for the infantry. Our group walked along a line of dead Viet Cong, seeing our work up close and personal and stinky. There were 10 bodies the infantry tunnel rats had pulled out of holes and lined up neatly. They said, "The other ones were too messy or blown into pieces." Sparks looked at his dead men. They were all just boys, just like us. Wars are fought only by the young. Old men were Senders, and they said, "Hey, kid, you go, you fight, make us proud, be a hero."

I looked at the line of dead VC soldiers, looked at their faces. Did I see any heroes there? They were bloated, puffed up, faces like black balloons about to pop, bust wide open, Michelin Tire Men: grimaces on their faces from death. Their jaws were stretched open in frozen screams with black teeth and engorged black tongues and jellied eyeballs bulged out. They wore black pajamas for the most part, black shirts and black shorts. Big black flies seemed to love the stench. The dried black blood and that smell, that horrible stink, attracted them, and flies swarmed everywhere, doing their nasty little jobs. It all gagged me so that I about threw up. Damned rotting bodies lined up on display. See any heroes? That was the enemy, just stinking dead boys, but boys who desperately wanted to kill us. What could you do? "Kill 'em. God'll sort 'em out."

There was a little South Vietnamese general in our group looking at the corpses and he was laughing, having a big time. The left side of his face was covered by massive burn scars, with his eyebrow totally gone, and his smiling mouth was melted half away into a red smear of scar tissue. He pulled out his .45 pistol, stepped back, fired off a round, a belly shot, *KERPOW,* and a

VC's rounded belly exploded like an overinflated basketball, and goop and maggots went flying everywhere!

Oh, that stink, the horrible rotting meat smell, and the ARVN general was laughing like a crazy man shooting ripe pumpkins while he fired another dozen rounds. What an ugly mess, squirming maggots everywhere and black eyeballs staring up at me. The general kept laughing and shooting, his .45 roaring away. What a damned nightmare scene, but he wanted to leave a clear example of what any other young Viet Cong soldiers could expect to get in the end: bullet riddled.

It had been about a week and a half that I'd been flying, and I'd seen enough to convince me that the Hornets must have been bat-shit crazy. Particularly 1st Lt. Sparks. He was even beyond the bat-shit stage of crazy: playing the role of a giant Loach, poking around the weeds when we were flying a Huey H-Model Slick that was the size of an 18-wheeler truck and trailer. I guessed he was the craziest because he had been there the longest of the Hornets. He was nearing the end of the second year on his current tour, plus I heard that he had done a previous tour as a warrant officer pilot. Three years of flying frontline combat was a bunch. I flew with him for ten or twelve days straight, and we took enemy fire three or four days, but I never leaned away from gunfire again those days. That wasn't easy, just sitting there fully exposed, but Sparks had been right about there being no place to hide. What could you do? You had to *Just Take It!*

Lt. Sparks gave me a little tutorial about being shot at. He said, "Getting shot at; either they miss you, and an inch is as good as a mile, or they hit you. Simple as that. Here's the trick, you *hear* gunfire, rest easy, means you're okay, because they just missed. You'll never hear the straight shot that gets you, because bullets fly faster than the speed of sound."

Okay, well, that explained everything just fine. But I sort of figured that if you heard some gunfire, that probably meant someone was trying to get you, and they were probably adjusting their aim so they could put the rest of their clip into the damned cockpit. I hadn't leaned away from the sound of gunfire. I'd leaned away from what I thought could be coming next: that straight shot I would never hear. I was still unconvinced that serving ourselves up as live bait to entice enemy fire was a good idea. More exactly, I still thought that particular practice was a load of crap, but what could I do about that? Sparks was still the 1st lieutenant and I was still only a brand new warrant officer. My job was to say, "Yes, Sir," and do what I was told. But if Sparks was crazy to put us out as bait, he was still the most experienced man the Hornets had, and he had probably already forgotten more about fighting a war than I would ever know about it. I considered myself damned lucky to have a teacher like him—damned lucky, that was, if he didn't get me shot someday when we were poking around in some landing zone out in Indian Country.

3

WHITE-KNUCKLE FORMATION FLYING

If 1st Lt. Sparks even had a first name, I never heard it used by anyone. As far as I knew, his first name was simply "Lieutenant," and even the most senior Hornets always called him that and nothing else. Everyone in our Wasps Platoon totally accepted his leadership without the slightest question, and that was no more obvious than with our longest-tenured aircraft commanders (AC). I hardly ever heard him give an order to anyone; rather he made only quiet suggestions that were followed to their fullest and in complete detail by everyone without the slightest hesitation or resistance. He certainly exemplified in every way what the army must have desired their greatest leaders would be. He'd obviously decided to be a lifer, an army career soldier, and he probably would run the Pentagon someday. He was punching his ticket, that was for sure.

I heard he'd previously served a tour as a warrant officer helicopter pilot. This tour he'd put in two straight years, '68 through '70, as a combat assault platoon leader, and he would soon be a captain. I also heard he'd spent a year back in the States as a senior instructor pilot down at Fort Rucker, Alabama. He was certainly checking off every box for a good resume: smart, charismatic, respected, tough, and the undisputed leader of all his men. I felt I was damned lucky to have come under his tutelage, even though it was a grueling ordeal every step of the way.

Every minute of every flight mission, whether it was flying as his copilot on a command and control air mission for a combat assault, or single-ship general support mission, he was busy teaching some aspect of what was required of a good pilot. Takeoffs had to be like you were flying Formation Lead: climb rate, air speed, turn rate had to be on the money, 1500 feet per minute, not 1550, and 60 knots, not 59 or 61, and shallow and steady turns. Every approach to a landing zone had to be exact. Every flight course had to be precise and true, no wandering around the sky allowed, because, he said, someday I'd probably have to be a Flight Leader (and every other position in a Combat Flight Formation), so learn to do it right from the start. Because, as a Flight Leader, your tiniest little movement on the controls would be amplified all the way through each ship following you and increased by each ship until the guy flying the last ship would be whiplashed to the extreme.

I tried my best to absorb everything he flooded me with, tried to fly my very best, tried to show I could take it if I heard gunshots directed our way or heard *Taking fire!* But my heart pounded, butthole puckered up, and blood pressure soared off the charts whenever someone called over the intercom, "Taking fire—taking fire! Coming from three o'clock, we're taking fire!" I hated those words, but I hated more the damned ballpeen-hammer sounds of actually *taking hits.* The first time I ever heard that distinctive and blood-curdling sound certainly flash-focused my attention on our flight instruments to watch for any anomalies: RPM—engine and rotor—hydraulic pressure—all holding steady. And I kept checking those instruments and not breathing until it was obvious our helicopter was still functioning basically okay. Out of the corner of my eye, I could see that Lt. Sparks and I were having exactly the same thoughts right then. I could see when Sparks finally took a breath, about when I also did, and I almost heard him let out a big sigh of relief that we were still flying with no problems. It seemed like my grinding days of flying with Sparks would last forever, but after nearly two weeks he told me I'd done okay with him. He turned me loose to fly in the Wasp Platoon and finally start flying in our combat assault formations.

When I'd watched the formations from overhead while flying with Lt. Sparks, I had been fascinated by how precise and orderly they always looked and what a fierce and impressive war machine they were: Helicopters all bunched up like a closed fist coming fast into an LZ with their machine guns blazing and gunships laying down protective curtains of rocket fire on each side of the formation. Every time, it was like watching a spectacular Fourth of July fireworks show, and no matter what I might have ever thought about that war before then, all I could think of was, *Wow! Those guys have to be some of the best there is at this stuff. Who could do it better?*

Then it was my time to join the platoon's Formation Flight, my first day to be integrated fully into the Wasps and become a real Hornet. I was going to be a Combat Pilot. This was what my year was really going to be about. Oh, what a shock that whole deal turned out to be: a long day of tight, white-knuckle formation flying so unbelievably close together. It was like driving down the road at 120 MPH following only two feet off of the surrounding cars. My aircraft commander hollered all day, "Hey, get up closer, come on man, get the hell in there tighter."

If Lt. Sparks was cold-blooded and demanding, he didn't hold anything over the rest of the ACs: the Wasp Platoon he'd created was hot ice. Each one of them was amazing at how they flew tight formations, flying so awfully close together, and they took it all for granted, they were all relaxed, just business as usual. Actually it demanded tremendous concentration and focus, because the Wasps flew no more than one rotor-span separations, and they looked like the navy's Blue Angels or the air force's Thunderbirds flight show teams zooming around the skies of South Vietnam. It was an amazing thing to see and more so to actually be doing it. But at the same time, it was scary as hell.

Sparks had trained all his pilots to be perfectionists. Five, six, or seven ship formations, you could throw a blanket over them. All of their formations worked like a tight, well-oiled machine, each a part of a larger whole that moved as one strong thing. The tail rotor of the ship in front of you sat there about to come through your windshield, or so it seemed, and the rotor blades of the ship beside you were so close to yours that there was zero room for error, so the concentration it demanded was so overpowering I often found myself holding my breath for dizzyingly long stretches of time.

When the Formation Flight Leader took off, all the Wasps' helicopters lifted together, one perfectly coordinated move. Going into an LZ, everyone touched down at exactly the same precise moment with door guns providing densely concentrated firepower. The Wasps were the Radio City Rockettes in the air. Formation flying was so damned exhausting that by the end of the day I was totally whipped. Aircraft commanders, the old timers, laughed and kidded about the sweat on my face after the tension of flying just a few minutes. I had experience racing cars, fast-moving racing in tight spaces, fast stock cars on dirt tracks, bumper to bumper, door to door, but that only taught me how things could turn into wrecks so quickly, a mere heartbeat! But racing stock cars didn't compare to the intensity of formation flying, not even a fraction of it. *Get up closer, get up tighter* was what I heard too often those first days, until I learned to still my racing heart and take it, *Just Take It!*

One day we were landing at a refueling station at a firebase up by the Cambodian border, and as we crossed over the outer perimeter wire on short final, coming in for touchdown, to our total surprise mortars started falling through our flight. There were explosions under us and to our front, crap flying up, hitting us from the ground, *bing, ding, wham, damn.* Then a voice shouted over the radio, "Go round, break-up, break-up." I'd never heard of anything like a *break-up!* I didn't know there was a special maneuver, a Hornets' starburst *formation break-up* where each ship had a set separate path to fly to escape. All I saw was six other damned helicopters flying in all sorts of directions.

I hesitated a second then started to head for the blue of a patch of clear sky and hoped we weren't about to be in some big nasty midair collision.

Then a mortar hit fuel bladders just below us and the explosion rocked our helicopter very violently—damned nearly literally blew us totally out of the sky—but our helicopter flew on through a giant fireball and we were totally engulfed in flames before we came out of it in a few fractions of a second. Our poor helicopter bounced around pretty good, but to our surprise we were still flying, with no red warning lights flashing. However, all the helicopters in our flight were low on fuel.

Then I could feel through the cyclic that my aircraft commander was flying along with me, and he said over the intercom, "I've got it." I released my death grip on the controls and took a breath. Chatter on the radios was fast and plenty excited, the intercom too. Everyone on our ship and in our flight was okay. We soon regrouped and headed for fuel off at Tay Ninh, 30 minutes away. "Can't get excitement like that every day, not even the best ride at Disneyland," my AC said, and grinned at me. My heart was pounding double-speed, but he was obviously loving his adrenaline rush: lessons in insanity—*the crazy Hornets didn't Just Take It, it seemed that they chased danger.*

I looked down between my feet, and there was a gaping four-inch hole in the plastic chin bubble where something had hit us and gone out through my doorway without hitting me. There sure as hell would be plenty of drinks bought that night at the Officers' club, and I'd gladly buy the first round.

Three or four days later, back up near the Cambodian border, same area, northwest of the Iron Triangle, the formation flying empty to a pick-up zone, machine-gun tracers started coming. *Damn, bang, bang, damn!* At least one .51-caliber machine gun was working us and we'd taken a couple of hits. Tracer fireballs were dancing all around us. I plainly felt it when our helicopter was hit, and a couple of other ships called out that they'd been hit also, but luckily we were soon past the .51 caliber.

Crew Chief called out to us, "We've got two big damned holes."

AC replied, "Roger that. All our gauges are looking good."

"Hey, Mr. Denny," the Crew Chief called, "one of those holes was real damned close, about four inches behind your seat."

On the intercom, I laughed and said, "Can't get excitement like that every day, not even the best ride at Disneyland." But my pulse was already pounding hard in my ears, and it got a whole lot faster with that little bit of news.

Getting shot at, *Just Take It!* First Lt. Sparks had told me that before, and he had added, "I know, sounds insane."

But that .51 caliber machine gunner had screwed up royally, and he'd have to pay the price. Our Formation Flight was quickly safely past him, but our Stinger gunships had the enemies big machine gun's location and rockets rained down in a torrent of death coming from the sky to take him out! Hornets didn't ever take any of that crap, and everyone knew that, or they should have! *Charlie shoots, Charlie dies, Hornets' promise.* But I guessed that machine gunner didn't recognize the emblems on the noses of our helicopters, and I supposed that everyone made a mistake now and then. That would be that dumb-assed turkey's very last one.

Still, two .51 caliber bullets coming through our floor and out our roof sure the hell wasn't anything to laugh about. Our fuel cells were under the cargo area, and if you hit that just right with a big bullet, our Huey would've exploded in a giant fireball, a cloud of smoke being the only thing left of us. And for a few minutes it would have rained little specks of Hornet crewmen over that part of South Vietnam, and I doubted that would've improved the aroma of the already stinking place.

But a .51 caliber bullet hitting just four inches behind my seat seemed to push the war idea to the limit. I guessed that if it had hit right under my nylon-sling seat and gone up my ass and out the top of my head, I would've never heard it in the first place, and I'd never have had a reason to be upset about it at all—or anything else, not ever again. But I did hear it, which meant that the damned thing missed me. I didn't like thinking about that particular bullet missing me, because what about the next one? I doubted that would be the only near-miss bullet I'd ever have to deal with during my time in Vietnam. I certainly wanted to buy a round of drinks that night. Doubles.

4

MENTAL DEGENERATION
INTO LOONEY LAND

After about three weeks of flying I started to get an understanding of what was going on, the basic beginnings of one, anyway. It all started with the Hornet gunships, the Stingers, and the ways they worked. The Stingers flew older-style UH1-C Model helicopters: C Models were a short-bodied platform like an old B Model but with a souped-up engine and high-lift capacity rotor blades. The Stingers usually flew in full-rocket armament mode rather than mini-guns and normally low-level, only about 100 feet above the ground. Other companies had newer Cobra gunships, like the Crusaders, but Cobras worked at higher altitudes, usually around 1500 to 2000 feet or higher.

So the Hornets and Stingers were old-school sky warriors and had been since coming to Vietnam back in 1965, which made them some of the combat experts fighting in the Vietnam War if anyone was. When the slicks assaulted an LZ, the Stingers came in with them flying on their flanks, covering them, ready to suppress any enemy resistance and immediately blow it straight to hell with a shower of multiple rockets. The Hornets, and especially the Stingers, didn't take any crap. Their attitude was as simple as could be: *Charlie shoots, Charlie dies, Hornets' promise.*

My first three or four weeks of going out and working in Indian Country we'd been shot at a few times, maybe a dozen, but I mostly couldn't actually hear it or see it. Somebody would radio the warning in or it came over the intercom, the dreaded message that we were taking fire! But when something hit the helicopter, I certainly heard that plain enough, the loud ballpeen-hammer *thumps*. That had happened only a couple of times, and each time the Stingers kept the Hornets' promise: Charlie shoots, well, Charlie screwed up, so he's gotta die.

I'd flown with Lt. Sparks and then about another ten days on combat assault formation missions, enough initial experience that I had a picture of things. It made me feel crazy as hell, but even crazier still I *understood* the twisted reasoning of our Combat Model. First, you went where you thought Charlie was. Next, you landed near them or, even better, right on top of them and offered them no choice: made 'em fight. Then you blasted them straight to hell, and—surprise, surprise—if you were getting shot at you were expected to *Just Take It!*

The biggest flaw I could see with our Hornets Combat Model was the fact that *we'd been shot at a few times!* Oh, yeah, that's the *Charlie shoots* part. There were just two parts to the Model. Second part was *Charlie dies, BUT* (and it was a very big but in my opinion) *we'd been shot at a few times!* That was what I had a problem with concerning our model. We were shot at often enough that I always hoped for the best but planned for the worst. So I feared that every LZ might turn into a hot one, maybe a blazing hot one, and I could only hope that the Hornets always shot best, shot straightest. I *understood* the twisted thinking of our model. The hard part in reality was trying to relax enough that my heart didn't blow out, totally quit! Okeydokey, focus on your flying and forget the LZ because it's gonna be what it's gonna be. *Ya'll do know that the defender always has the advantage in these situations, don't you? I'm from Texas, so just try to think about the Alamo.*

I don't intend to leave anyone with the impression that the Hornets just waited to be shot at. That was never the case at all. We never went into an LZ blind or not knowing what to expect. Lt. Sparks always surveyed every LZ before he ever called a flight in. For the kind of LZ we preferred, our artillery had already prepped the place real hard and our landing would be timed to happen only seconds after the cannons stopped. Slicks would come in hot with Door-gunners blasting and gunships laying rockets. So our objective was to make Charlie keep his head down, leave us alone. But sometimes Charlie was so stupid he had to try to be a hero. Some yo-yo idiot would jump up and let out a blast of AK-47 fire, blazing away at our flight. Maybe the yo-yo thought he had a chance against multiple door-guns and rockets raining down on him. A ticket to hell was all the poor ole yo-yo ever got when he jumped up.

But sometimes Charlie wasn't so stupid, and he *wanted* a flight to come in and was ready to withstand the artillery prep, the gunship rockets, and our door-guns. Instead of a yo-yo kid jumping up, it was organized professional fighting time: hidden bunkers, rocket-propelled grenades (RPGs), multiple machine guns, and deeply buried escape tunnels. Charlie would stay out of sight, wait, hold it, and, when the time was just right, blast out: let hell run loose, ten or twenty soldiers shooting in a fast volley, then Charlie would instantly vanish.

Saw that happen once from C&C flying overhead with Lt. Sparks. On that occasion, the RPGs missed their targets, but all the helicopters took many small-arms fire hits. Then the VC were suddenly gone like smoke through their tunnel networks. So flying combat assault was similar to playing Russian roulette, and you knew you could win only so many times. Eventually, a problem would pop up. Some dumb-assed yo-yo would jump up shooting, or even worse, a well planned and organized ambush was ready for you to fly into their trap.

Now that I was making the rounds flying with different aircraft commanders, I asked how they dealt with the stress, the fear that the next LZ might be a hot one or, worse still, a well-prepared ambush. The common answer was no damned help at all: "You just get used to it, eventually."

Someone said, "You stop thinking about going home. You quit thinking about controlling things you can't control, because there's no such thing as control anyway. Your focus becomes absorbed solely by the present: you're here doing this until you're not. It's just that simple, then you go home, go back to the real world. Simple, right?" The enlisted crewmen had said, "Why worry?" Right—that's what I needed: philosophy plucked out of a *MAD* magazine! "Everyone is dead anyway. Soon enough, death is eminent, today or 40 years from now. In the long picture of time, a human lifespan is like the blink of an eye. Either way, don't worry. Death's coming, yours and mine and real damned soon enough." Oh, so fatalistic and bleak. Then there was the classic line of "Accept Your Inevitable Death, Then You Can Live," but freshman-level Camus and Sartre always bored the absolute crap out of me.

That damned Russian roulette "you get used to it, eventually" was something twisted I could relate to better. Each time I pulled the damned trigger and the chamber came up empty again—*click*—my calmness increased some tiny bit and I dwelled less on the waiting bullet and embraced eventual and inevitable insanity more. The keystone to insanity was in not recognizing there was anything the least bit crazy about what you were doing, so everything always looked just fine. That was the only answer I could find to my questions about fighting that war. The only way to be a combat helicopter pilot was to surrender yourself to pure and complete insanity, where you could allow yourself to keep pulling the trigger of that stupid Russian roulette pistol over and over and over again infinitely. If you flew combat helicopters in Vietnam, you were probably crazier than hell in the first place or you'd surely get there soon enough. I could feel myself rapidly sliding down that shute into the uncharted territory of mental degeneration and into Looney Land. To be only four inches away from taking a damn .51 caliber bullet straight up my ass or being baptized in a huge ball of fire and then get back in another helicopter ever again was the pure definition of being completely bonkers. Thus was my evolving situation: I was falling into the rabbit hole, slip-sliding away to Looney Land where all the normal rules of human existence were turned upside down, where wrong was suddenly considered right, where accepting your own death was considered the way to live, where offering yourself to death repeatedly was just considered a normal part of the day's standard business, and especially where no one saw that insanity ruled everything. Full-blown Looney Land.

There's no use in trying to explain those Vietnam War days now, 45 years later, because all of us helicopter pilots were doing crazy crap everyday back then, and with today's hindsight it all sounds even crazier now. Lt. Sparks had told me the unvarnished truth in the very beginning when he said, "I know, sounds insane." How profoundly accurate he'd been.

When I was drafted, I'd volunteered for the Warrant Officer Helicopter Pilot Program with the written promise that I would be a medevac Dust-Off pilot since I opposed the Vietnam War. Well, so much for lying recruiter's promises. After I'd flown nearly four weeks, Lt. Sparks said that I had an invitation for an audition from the Stingers' platoon, based completely on Sparks's evaluation of me. That was a total surprise to me and what was an even bigger surprise, I said okay. That was certainly the complete opposite of what I had originally planned. If not medevac then why not gunships? I wasn't at all comfortable being a clay-pigeon target in every yo-yo's shooting gallery. So, okay, why not check out the Stingers and try flying with the gunship pilots for a while?

I immediately discovered flying C-Models was a huge challenge. Fully fueled and fully armed they were grossly overweight. They couldn't get off the ground, couldn't even get to a hover, and you had to slide them along a runway until you got enough forward speed that they'd finally get lighter on the skids and you could baby them into the air. But it took forever to get enough airspeed to feel like you were actually flying. Gross-weight takeoffs were absolute white-knuckle flying.

After a takeoff and a couple of minutes of flying, I developed a huge respect for C-Model pilots. They were nothing short of magicians. That first ride we went out to free-fire country, and I made some rocket runs, which I had to admit were great fun. Later that morning we joined a combat assault gunship escort team and prepped a few LZs where we fired plenty of rockets, but we encountered no trouble that day. However, the next day was different. During an insertion, our troops instantly flushed out six Viet Cong who were running away as fast as they could go. In only seconds—it all happened in a flash—there were six dead VC floating face down in an old rice paddy. Charlie screwed up. Then they were dead. The Bad Guys were so caught by surprise that they had never fired a single shot. They were just running away as fast as they could. We had contact twice more that day with the same sort of situations that ended with the same outcomes. That single day we killed a grand total of fourteen Viet Cong. Even by Stinger standards that was considered a pretty big number.

Scotch whiskey flowed plentifully that night at the Officers' club. My

Stinger AC said things were not usually so easy. On my third day as a gunship pilot we killed two Viet Cong who were trying to shoot at us, and later in the afternoon there were two more who were trying to make like rabbits and get the hell out of the general area we had under attack. My fourth day yielded the same results: two and two killed by our rockets. Then the infantry flushed out three more Bad Guys, who then tried to shoot at our gunships. When those guys popped up we were almost directly on top of them and had to make an extremely steep rocket-run dive. After our rockets were launched away we made a last-second pull-out of our dive very close to the ground. A blown-up torso was thrown into the air and splattered on our helicopter's nose, which deposited gore everywhere. At first I didn't know what it could possibly be, but then I had a glimpse of that guy's face as he literally bounced off our gunship. Damn, what a breathtaking shock! Charlie had screwed up, he shot, then, *Boom*, he was suddenly dead. Hornet rules. Yeah, he was certainly dead all right: I'd seen him face to face and he was totally blown to hell! That was the most disgusting and shocking thing I'd ever seen.

Later, in my dreams, splatter nightmares kept waking me up all night. The dreams were worse than the reality of what had happened. In my dreams the dead body smashed through the helicopter's windshield, crashed into the cockpit, and wound up in my lap. Blood-n-guts-n-crap soaked me, but I couldn't get the dead body out of my lap and I couldn't wipe the slime away. Blood was gushing over me, bowel contents smearing on me. Dreams, horrible dreams: mental degeneration into the most morbid side of Looney Land and a chorus of voices screamed to me, "Just Take It! Do your bloody job!"

The next morning I couldn't face my scrambled powdered eggs and biscuits and gravy. My scheduled fifth day of flying with the guns I was paired with Arthur, a young kid, only 19 years old but a senior gunship aircraft commander nonetheless. He said we had the day off, so he was going to give me some gunnery lessons, shoot a few rockets. Arthur said we had twenty-five KIAs during the last three days, a tough stretch for a New Guy, so it was time for a break. We'd go out on the rocket range, relax, and just have some fun.

"Heard about your body strike yesterday. Guess that must've freaked you out, that would freak out anyone, certainly would've freaked me out!"

Told him, yeah, it was certainly a pretty big surprise. Gave me nightmares last night.

"Oh, I bet, would me, too. So, we'll shoot some rockets, relax."

We went out and he showed me how he went about firing rockets. He explained what he was doing, how he aimed by his naked eye using a grease-pencil X that he'd drawn on the inside of his windshield. He said, *"See that hooch over there?"* It looked about 5 or 6 football fields away, a quarter mile, or more, I guessed. The hooch was maybe about 12 feet wide, and he fired off a pair of rockets. I watched them and they looked on target, an impressive shot, and I was speechless when both rockets went in the little doorway. The hooch exploded in a giant fireball. Arthur started doing sharp S turns in a fast run toward the smoking hooch remains and sent off another pair of rockets at the limit of each turn, left turn, then right turn, and they all impacted at the same exact place!

He'd spent about 20 rockets that run, all of them dead on the spot. I was totally amazed by this display. I would have said that shooting like that was impossible if I hadn't just witnessed it. We returned to Cu Chi to rearm. When we refueled we switched seats, and I got to try my skills firing rockets. I did blow up a couple of hooches from less than 100 feet away, close enough I could've thrown rocks at them and been more accurate. Arthur and I joked and kidded, and we spent over three hours with me shooting. The young kid, Arthur, his call sign Stinger 82, was the first really senior guy to act the least bit friendly toward me, and I immediately liked him, felt comfortable being with him.

He said, "If you decide to come over to the Stingers, you'll find it's easier than the Slicks, much more laid back. I didn't like the Slicks. I hated sitting there with a big target on me. At least in the Guns, you have some control, you can fight back, or even better yet, you can take the fight to them."

A feeling of having control—oh, that part sounded so wonderfully appealing! Was Arthur giving me some sort of a sales pitch? That couldn't be. I hadn't flown with the Stingers enough for them to have made any sort of decision about me switching over to the Guns Platoon yet. I thought he was probably just trying to show me that he might have some empathy for my current situation, thoughts, and concerns. Still, I was surprised at how well he was reading some of my mind. Whatever was up, I told him as straightforwardly as I could: "To be really totally honest, I'll have to do some soul searching, ask myself if I have it in me to be able to kill people every day."

That was Looney Land for sure, thinking about being a killer by an overt choice, but that was what I was doing. Arthur had said that we'd killed 25 Bad Guys in the previous three days, and I had ridden along for all those killings. I didn't think I liked the feelings that gave me. I finally understood how right Lt. Sparks was. There was "no place to hide, no place."

The young door-gunner had suggested, "Accept your inevitable death, then you can live." But I couldn't buy that hogwash yet. My answer was still this: "Screw Sartre and Camus and the damn horses they rode in on." Now, I might have to add thinking about the Stingers Platoon to my list of thoughts, along with all the other crap swirling around in my head.

5

New Guy Extra Duties

The next morning after my gunship play day that I'd spent practicing shooting rockets with Stinger 82, I was out on the flight line starting an inspection of the C-Model helicopter we would be flying that day. The first light of sunrise was peeking over the eastern horizon, and I'd just finished a rough night of being awakened repeatedly by bad dreams, so I still felt tired as hell. I was up on the roof of the helicopter checking out the rotor head connecting link bearings when a Spec 5 from the operations office came trotting up and hollered at me to report to the operations shack, that I'd been scrubbed off the mission for that day.

At the office, I asked, "What's going on? On the flight line just now, a guy said I was taken off my gunship mission, said I was scheduled for some sort of New Guy extra duty, officer of the day. He told me it was a 24-hour deal, and that I'd stay overnight in the orderly room."

This was supposed to be my sixth day flying with the Stinger gunships, and they were going up north where the war was really going on: the Michelin Rubber Plantation, Iron Triangle, and the Fishhook area, some really nasty Indian Country up by the Cambodian border.

The operations captain said, "You've gone over your hours limit: you've flown over 140 flight hours in a consecutive 30-day period, so you can't fly for at least two days, and that's it. Yeah, since you can't fly today, you're assigned as officer of the day. I guess you'll be hanging around the orderly room, so go over there and report in for duty."

Well, that sucked big time: operations gave another pilot my damned gunship ride. When I got to the orderly room, they told me, "Come back right after dinner tonight. There's nothing for you to do until then. You better get some sleep today. You'll be up all night patrolling the Company Area every hour, generally being available, and basically just watching the Hornets' store all night. Might bring a good book to read, or maybe write letters home or something."

I could probably handle that. It sounded simple enough: go back to bed. *Roger that!* That was something I could do just fine. So I did! It was great to have a break from flying, a day off for a change. I'd flown nearly every single day since the first day when I started. I'd had only a couple of down days when Lt. Sparks had been busy with other business and couldn't fly those days. Basically, I had been running at full speed in a whirlwind from the time they dropped the starter's flag for me. After a long morning nap, at lunch I checked back in at the orderly room to see what was up, and oh, man, everyone's hair was totally on fire! Some really bad news had just come in: a Stinger gunship had crashed hard! They'd been shot down. Pilots must have been shot or something. They said they went into the ground doing way over 100 knots and exploded in a giant ball of fire.

I raced over to the operations shack bunker. Chatter on the multiple radios was clinical and very matter of fact, very tense, and deadly serious, but the radio calls were coming from the maximum transmission distance and breaking up with a lot of static. Two Stinger gunships had gone in hot, rocket runs on a dug-in gun. They first figured it for a .51 caliber machine gun—deep into Indian Country, up past the Iron Triangle—Two Stingers attacked, and the first did okay, but the second Stinger ship never came out. They found out that it was a twin 20mm antiaircraft gun shooting at them, not the .51 they expected. Stinger 83 was still popping rockets, never pulled out of their dive. A tiny opening in a dense, dark jungle, triple canopy, giant trees, 125 feet tall. High overhead diving rocket runs—a dead man flying with his death-grip fingers still working the trigger.

Stunned to the core and in total disbelief, I looked at the schedule board. There were chalk lines drawn through three names, but what caught my eye was the fact that you could plainly read an erased name, *Pilot—WO Denny*. Anyone could see that it was my damned name that had been lightly erased off the board, and someone else's name, *Pilot—WO McDonald*, scribbled over it. The aircraft commander was listed as *AC—Stinger 83*. Warrant Officer Craig Fox, the man I was supposed to fly with, was crossed out! And my name vaguely floated there in front of my eyes like a ghost name lurking in the background, and it screamed at me with a siren's wail. My mind was so blown away that I couldn't even read the third name. Seeing the ghostly *WO Denny* felt like a bayonet had been rammed through my gut and someone was sawing me in half with the damned thing.

Stunned to the core: that barely begins to describe how I felt to see my erased name up there. Eight or ten Hornets, mostly maintenance or operations enlisted men, were huddled around the radios. A couple of them I didn't know were looking at me, and I knew they'd seen the whole picture the scheduling board revealed. For some irrational reason I suddenly felt guilty and ashamed, felt like I should get out of there, hide myself in embarrassment from anyone's view. My name on the schedule board should never have been erased. I was the one who was supposed to fly with Stinger 83, not some other pilot. Me. Not anyone else. Immediately the question popped into my head that wouldn't everything have happened differently if I had flown that mission? My being there would have affected the flow of time or the flow of events just enough so that the outcome of things might have been altered somehow. Maybe no one would have had to crash if only I had flown that mission. I was sure that was what the people looking at me were thinking: I could see it on their faces, or at least I thought so. The operations captain saw me and came over. I quietly asked him if they could wash my name off the scheduling board. It made me feel like total shit to see it there.

He said, "Sure, sure. Sorry about that. I should have thought of that and already done it."

Stinger 83, Craig Fox. I'd met him a couple of times before at the Officers' club, but I hadn't flown with him yet. The pilot, McDonald, I had never even met him. Not the crew chief, either. I'd never met either one of them, and I didn't even know their first names. I'd never even heard their names until I saw them up on the scheduling board. My name had been erased. I felt horribly sick—and ashamed that someone had taken my place. The thoughts swirling through my head said, *McDonald died in your place. This is your fault. This wouldn't have happened if you had flown, certainly not for McDonald.*

That afternoon around the Company Area most of the people were out flying. Admin folks, maintenance guys, and a few flight guys on days off, ones like me were the only Hornet people around, and they were mostly clustered in groups in the orderly room or in operations or at the mess hall. Gossip, speculation, and rumors went like wildfire, a raging fire that had flashed over and burned white hot for a while then burned out as fast as it started. The word had come down from the top to knock it off, get back to work, quit being like a bunch of old women jabbering like chicken hens with nothing more important to do.

I returned to my hooch, my room, and got on my bed, my mind racing a million miles an hour. Craig Fox. I was shocked hearing how young he was, only 20, but I'd thought he was about 30. Guessed that was what nearly a year of flying guns in Vietnam had done for him. He seemed at least that old. It was the way he carried himself, the self-confidence he projected, the comfort he seemed to have, comfort with himself, who he was. But it was the look in his eyes, too, eyes that had seen a lot of war. That was what made him look 30 years old. I closed my eyes, tried to sleep. McDonald—wondered who he was, what he was like, everyone seemed to like him, spoke very highly of him. He'd been eight months in the Hornets, a senior guy, an aircraft commander. McDonald—the pilot who had taken my place. I guessed it was best I had never met him. I felt like total crap, my damned name being erased.

Guessed I would've felt worse if I'd flown up north, been one of the pilots killed up north where the war was really going on.

I started *Officer of the Day* after trying to eat some dinner. In the mess hall I sat alone. The Wasp Platoon were running late and hadn't yet returned from the day's flight mission. Those in the mess hall were solemn and quiet. In the orderly room, I found basically the same mood. Later, when I was doing rounds of the Company Area, everything was still, "All is well." Yeah, all was well if you didn't count the three newly dead Hornets. The Officers' club was as somberly quiet as a funeral home, very few people in there. In the Enlisted Club a touring band played rock 'n' roll while go-go girls danced, but that wasn't the night for it. There were even empty seats at some of the tables. It was an Australian band with nearly naked dancing girls, but a dark shroud of death hung heavily over the place like a thick black fog, and the gloomy light crowd was seriously involved with staring into their drink glasses and ignoring the band.

Then, about eleven o'clock, while I was making my rounds, a Spec-4 came running up to me, said they needed me at the Enlisted Club. A Stingers staff sergeant was drunk and causing a scene, making the band play the same song over and over again. When we entered, the crowd was pretty liquored up and singing, and the staff sergeant was singing at the top of his lungs at the microphone with a dancer captured firmly in his arm. The band was playing a Creedence Clearwater song as loudly as they could, and the sergeant was swigging a bottle of Southern Comfort as he belted out "Fortunate Son." I approached the band, and the music quickly faded away.

The staff sergeant offered the bottle to me and asked, "A toast, Mister?"

I obliged him, took a drink from the offered bottle and toasted: "Ain't me, no fortunate one, no."

"Is that so, Mister Denny," he asked and poked a finger into the name tag on my flight suit. "Is that so…. Maybe you are … wouldn't you say maybe so, maybe you're the fortunate one?"

If he was asking a question, I didn't answer it. I'd never met this man before, didn't know him, and had never even seen him. I handed the bottle back, and asked him, "Ready to call it a night? Turn in? Go to bed?"

The band was already packing up. After another drink, he answered, "Yeah, bed sounds good."

I asked the band leader, "Can you do one more Creedence number to end the night? Do ya'll know the song '*Long as I Can See the Light*'?"

He picked up his guitar and began. The girls swayed slowly, innocently. With every "I'll be coming home soon" there was plenty of hooting, hollering, and cheering. Everyone joined in and sang real loud.

The sergeant said, "Warrant Officer Denny—I know that name. Saw it on the schedule board last night."

"Really? Yeah, it was there," I replied.

"Saw it when I scheduled the Stingers' crew chiefs. Guess we've both had a hard day," he said and took another long draw of whiskey. Then he added, "At least I won't dream about it any tonight."

"Then you're the fortunate one," I told him.

The band played on. "Hope you blokes are all home, real damned soon. Now, goodnight! Goodnight, and thank you, goodnight! Long as I see the light, goodnight!"

The rest of the night I walked patrolling the Company Area, mind churning. The Officers' club was shut tight as a drum, earlier than normal, everyone turned in. Walked hour after hour, mind churning. Seemed things were locked in a circle. Scheduled for *Officer of the Day*, another pilot took my gunship ride. They told me I was scrubbed, another pilot took my gunship ride, said I'd hit my hours limit, another pilot took my gunship ride. Seemed things were locked in a circle. It always came back to another pilot took my ride.

McDonald—what was he like? Who was he? Married? Maybe not. Heard he was only 21, probably not married. Most people weren't married at 21, mostly not, I tried to tell myself. And Fox, at 20, was he married? Fox, only 20, God, I had pegged him at 30. Was I going to age like that? Well, I was married. I had a wife to take into consideration, and this wasn't just me in the war. She had a stake in this deal too.

Walked, mind churning, full of doubts about everything, full of guilt about someone taking my place, so, what was there to do, accept that I was good as dead? Couldn't do that, no way in hell! I'd had a life back home, a wife, hopes, dreams, plans, a future. I wasn't going to live like I was dead!

I had to decide what I was going to tell the Stingers if they offered me a place flying with the Gun Platoon. Yes or no? The feeling of having some control: that was the attraction the Stingers Gun Platoon had dangled in front of me. But in fact, did McDonald or Fox have control? Apparently not at the time they crossed it up with that nasty twin 20mm antiaircraft gun.

I guessed that if you were living like you were already a dead person, Control or No Control, Illusion or Fact didn't really amount to a hill of beans in the end. Did Fox or McDonald have control of their situation? That question kept recurring in my thoughts, and the answer kept coming up the same: Hell no! Did anything like control even really exist over here in Vietnam? Forget about damn control. The real question I had to answer was whether I could kill people day in and day out without growing to hate myself real damned fast. That was my main question.

By the time I had finished my stint as officer of the day, in the morning, my platoon of Wasps were already gone off flying on the day's mission, and I hadn't seen any of them since all the crap with the shot down Stinger ship had happened. Our hooch was empty and as quiet as a tomb. That was just as well, because I didn't want to see anyone anyway.

I guess I should have been better prepared for the inevitability of casualties: we were in a war, after all. But no one ever said a single word about anything like casualties. The topic had never come up with anyone I had met. I had the feeling that the whole subject was a major social taboo with pilots. It was as if mentioning it could cause it to happen, and who would want that? I knew I didn't.

The bunk in my room looked very inviting, and I flopped on it hard. I was totally worn out, completely exhausted both physically and mentally. My thoughts focused on home, my sweet home El Paso, and my life back there, and my wife, Jane, my dancer, my best friend and lover. I had to stop this swirling in my head, stop seeing movies running through my mind of helicopters flying into the ground and exploding, stop seeing dead men who had died in my place. I had never dreamed I would take this so hard, feel things so damned personally or feel so directly involved in events I couldn't change and didn't have any control over.

When the Wasps came home that night no one mentioned a single word about the three dead Stingers. Everything was just the same as always. At suppertime, Steve Chasin poked his head in my room and said, "It's chow time, let's go eat." We went to the mess hall with Austin Scarborough and Larry Hood (another New Guy who was about two weeks newer than me) to have scorched pork chops. Everything was the same shit, different day. I'd made my mind up about the Stingers. I'd made a few friends in the Wasp Platoon. I didn't want to start all over and feel so damned alone again.

6

HELICOPTERS ON THE MOON, NIXON'S CAMBODIA, FIRST DAY

In the countryside west and northwest of Cu Chi, the terrain looked like the surface of some plain on the moon—barren to the horizon and totally desolate. Bombs had blasted every square foot of this moonscape to the point craters overlapped still others, layers of craters, big ones with smaller ones clustered inside them. This had once been miles and miles of fertile rice paddies, but that was all long gone, destroyed by six years of nonstop bombing. More bombs had been dropped on Vietnam by 1970 than all of the bombs dropped in all of World War II and Korea combined, by a long shot, and the badlands around Cu Chi looked like it.

B-52 bombers had killed the landscape totally, then killed it again, day after day, week after week, year after year. Every living thing out there had died: crops, animals, and people, all dead and blown away. Anyone who ever saw that place could easily envision the disembodied spirits of hordes of dead Vietnamese drifting over the countryside on moonless nights haunting the dead land. Seasonal rains left water ponded in craters, and old signs of canals could be seen, along with vague traces of villages that had previously existed for untold centuries.

The badlands were a free-fire zone, starkly bleak, the surface of some wet and muddy, ugly moon where nothing lived and lingering smoke drifted every day. This was Indian Country, and Death's hand roamed the sky with the B-52s, the fighter jets and the Hornet helicopters, all of them delivering Death. No place on earth had ever been blasted into such a horrible condition. Not a blade of grass had survived. Nothing could live in the badlands of Vietnam. Not one stone out there was left stacked on another. When we crossed the border and flew into Cambodia for the first time, the stark differences couldn't have been stronger.

In Cambodia, the American War hadn't started to enlarge the Vietnam combat zone yet to incorporate the Cambodian areas close to the border into an expanded war that then would include the Cambodians whether they liked it or not. Everyone knew Cambodia had allowed the North Vietnamese and the Viet Cong to use their country as a safe haven for years without any interference from the Cambodians. The Americans couldn't let that go on forever. The time to put a stop to all of that was at hand, and any question about an American invasion of Cambodia was only a matter of when it was coming.

A couple of days before the actual pending invasion, my friend Steve Chasin and I flew into Cambodia on a very strange special single-ship mission: we were ordered to fly a television news crew anywhere they wanted to go on a grand tour of the Cambodian countryside, fly them over farmland, hamlets and towns, schools, churches, highways, and so on. There were actual paved roads with cars and trucks and animal-drawn carts on them, and even little towns with streets, pretty little brick houses with flowerbeds, even the civility of sidewalks and public parks, trees in fenced front yards, tended fields, and perfectly manicured rice paddies with their dressed dikes. There were relaxed people moving normally around everywhere outside, people who had not yet learned to fear Death swooping down on them from the sky. Farmers plowed fields with their water buffaloes, and smiling and joyous little kids jumped for joy in the streets, laughing and flying kites, reaching up to touch the sky, waving at our passing helicopter. They didn't know what we were yet, didn't understand about us. They were just glad to see our mysterious magic flying machine and see us flying so near the ground.

We were directed to fly the television people right over suspected North Vietnamese supply depots, even buzzed them down low-level, their news cameras blazing away and the talking-head news correspondent jabbering. We were made to land in big open fields and watched while the news guys talked to their cameras. Brilliant! We told them that those might be designated landing zones for our American helicopters when they would eventually come! The TV guys said none of that was a problem—by the time they flew their film all the way back to the States, then got it on TV, the invasion would already be happening, like that made everything okay. Great! Brilliant! But they didn't understand that we'd just let the North Vietnamese Army (NVA) know everything about the coming U.S. invasion, where we might be coming by us putting down in those potential landing zones.

The TV guys just said, "Don't worry, be happy, and be sure to look directly into the camera during your interview, instead of at the correspondent." Steve and I were both going to be TV stars when they showed a couple of handsome fellows like us on the Walter Cronkite evening news. Nothing epitomized the Vietnam War more than a brave young pilot sitting behind the controls of a combat helicopter. We would be poster boys. Anyway, they needed to get all the film footage they could get because the war had to go straight into everyone's living room on TV every single night.

A couple of days later it was the much-anticipated real showtime for Cambodia. We'd gotten orders for the invasion; we were going to finally take Nixon's expanded fight across the border. Out on the flight line before dawn, every single pilot and crewman who was fit to fly gathered round in a big circle for a Hornet Company briefing. The CO talked about the coming mission. Our major was actually flying that day, which was totally unheard of, very alien, since he never flew. We were going to be the lead company in a joint flight of three companies. The usual deal, exactly what we expected, tip of the spear as always. The assault flight would be going across the border at the Fishhook, and everyone expected it to be a very dangerous hotbed, an area headquarters for 10,000 to 15,000 NVA regular forces just across the border on the Cambodian side. (See map on page xi.)

We would meet up in Tay Ninh with our sister company, the Crusaders, joined by the Little Bears, a 25th Infantry Division Aviation Company from Cu Chi. We were taking two chase ships from maintenance for crew-air-rescue just in case we had any trouble. But we didn't worry any about that because we'd have six heavy gunship teams with us, both Cobras and our older C-Models.

The CO concluded: "Gentlemen, that's 18 gunships escorting us! That's a damned trainload of gunship firepower! There'll even be a jet fighter cap waiting overhead in case we run into anything our gunships can't take care of. Everyone do a good Hornet job today, kick ass, and take the war to them. So let's saddle up and go to Cambodia!"

Guessed the Old Man wanted his front row seat to the big show, but he got a lot more than he had wished for. Our big three-company flight approached the first LZ, and it turned out to be totally FUBAR from the get-go. There was a big artillery LZ prep, and when the artillery lifted, our 30 Huey Slicks landed on the Vietnamese side of the border, next to a wide river, which was the actual Cambodian border. This was to be the beachhead LZ to secure the crossing point of the river for all the mechanized units that were waiting to get into Cambodia. It would be the entry point and also the safe exit point if our forces needed that. Way over 200 fired-up infantrymen jumped out of our helicopters into the tall weeds, all gung-ho, with their eyes big as saucers! It was a real sight. Here, the war was really going on! But everything was cool so far: the LZ was totally cold. There was no sign of opposition of any kind.

We said, "Thanks for flying today, boys—hope you really enjoyed your flight."

Thick gray acidic smoke hung above the river and cloaked the LZ. Soon as the helicopters were empty, we departed, lifted off to go get another load of troops, but all was cool, the LZ was cold. Then the artillery started up again. It was supposed to be across the river on the Cambodian side, but some fire control officer screwed up royally, made a horrible mistake, and forgot to shift his damned fire coordinates! And the LZ we had just left suddenly exploded into a total hell with American infantrymen trapped there as American artillery shells rained down on them.

From up above we watched helplessly as bodies started flying everywhere. "Holy shit! Stop, Stop!" Couldn't believe the nightmare we saw. Artillery was made just exactly for that: Troops in the open. "Damn! Stop, Stop!" The scene played out in what seemed like ultra-slow motion and went on way too damned long. You know, the army made "friendly fire" sound like it couldn't really be anything all that bad—after all, it was friendly. But to me the only name for it was fratricide: the killing of your own. That was what was going on down in that hellhole LZ: fratricide, no matter what the army's public relations people called it

Our combat assault mission just became a giant Dust-Off for injured survivors. As soon as we were sure that the stupid artillery crap was over, we swooped back into the LZ to help anyone we could. Soon our ship was packed full with gravely wounded infantrymen, only live ones, and quickly our chopper was roaring toward the hospital at Tay Ninh, maxed out flying at 120 knots. We couldn't make our old Huey go any faster, and it was a long way to Tay Ninh and any medical help.

A river of blood, brains, and skull-bone chips flowed across the floor, between my feet, collecting in the chin bubble. *Stop, Stop!* I couldn't make that bird go any faster; she was shaking nearly to pieces already. Oh boy, here the war was really going on!

For over 45 years now, I've tried NOT to consciously recall those haunting, sickening events, but I've never stopped the damned nightmares.

Leon Richards, our aircraft commander that day, turned in his seat and offered his advice to the crew chief and door-gunner as they tried to tend to the wounded grunts. Before going to flight school and becoming a pilot, Leon had been a Special Forces Green Beret, and from his Green Beret days he had extensive first-aid training. If anyone could offer good suggestions, Leon was the man.

I listened to him over the intercom pointing out men who needed attention: a tourniquet here, a pressure bandage there. Over my shoulder I saw a soldier trying to stuff lengths of intestines back into his ripped-apart abdomen. From the terrified panic in his eyes, I could see that he knew full well he was already dead and there was nothing he could do about that fact. But he had his tongue stuck out, biting it to keep himself from screaming as he hopelessly tried to pull himself back together. Another kid sat and rocked as he cradled the tattered remains of his shattered left arm that hung from his shoulder attached by only a few ropey strands of tendons and strings of ripped muscle, but there was no bone left, no substructure.

Amazingly, only a couple of the grunts were whimpering, crying in pain, and even they were trying to be quiet. It was like they all tried their best not to add to the burden of their wounded friends, their buddies, their brothers-in-arms. There was no one begging not to die, and no crying for momma, no last prayers or confessions, no pleading to God for his help, and no cussing God for his absence. One by one, they each stilled in their own time, and one by one they became silent. Then there was nothing but the silence—all crying had stopped, just the silence stayed and hung heavy and sour in our helicopter. There was just our rotor blade slapping the wind, screaming out, the engine roaring, straining at its peak, screaming out a painful mourning song, scream-ing out to drown out the silence, screaming out to make the wounded cry some more. Just cry a little longer—please cry, cry, try, goddamn it, try.

At the hospital helipad in Tay Ninh there was no hurry, there was no rush. It was way the hell too late for any of that. We'd brought in thirteen blown-up GI grunts, but all of them were dead, everybody was dead, dead and silent; their friendly fire wounds were just too damned severe. It was too damn late for anyone to hurry about anything. Leon and I had flown them as fast as we could, and our helicopter couldn't go any faster, but that hadn't been enough. Now they were all dead. Our own artillery had done a fine job of fratricide.

Our helicopter was awash in blood from all the men who had bled out, plus their vomit and the stinking mess from shredded men. I had to sit there in the helicopter and hold the controls while it ran at flight-idle and the med-ical orderlies carefully removed the corpses from our cargo bay and put them on gurneys one at a time. The hospital people were very respectful and rev-erent in the performance of their duties, but it seemed to me that the night-mare scene took forever. I guessed that this was far from being the medics' first rodeo. I watched as each man was put on a gurney and a sheet was cer-emoniously pulled over them. Then they were rolled away toward the hos-pital. A medic came up to my doorway and held out his hand to give me something. He said, "Take these tonight, and they'll help you sleep." Then he handed over two pills to me. There were no words I could say. I just nodded to him an acknowledgment and put the pills in my pocket.

Our two stunned crewmen had jumped out of our helicopter there on the hospital helipad to escape as far away as they could from the horrible sit-uation, and they were walking around so covered in blood, soaked in blood, that medics rushed to them thinking they were gravely wounded. *Gotta find a water hose somewhere, spray them down, get their bloody clothes off,* ran through my head. *Gotta find water, buckets, and a brush.*

That was obvious. There was so much blood that it was running out of our helicopter everywhere. But it was early morning, and we still had to fly all day until dark. There were four of our Hornet helicopters at the hospital, all terrible messes. But we were called on the radio to rejoin our flight ASAP. We went to the Crusaders' maintenance hangar and did what we could to wash out our choppers as quickly as possible. Our crewmen had to fly in wet flight suits. We still had a day's worth of troops to haul to the invasion in a ship that reeked of recent death.

As soon as we were back in the air our snake-eater aircraft commander turned on the FM radio and dialed up Saigon, the Armed Forces Vietnam rock 'n' roll station blasting out American music. He turned it up loud, very damned loud, and flipped the switch so the guys in back could listen. At least he was able to wash out the painful silence. The lingering stink—we would just have to adjust to that.

Oddest thing, the DJ on the radio was the same guy I had listened to on KELP radio in El Paso all through my college years. It seemed the draft had snared him, too. Hearing him on Saigon radio instantly flashed my thoughts back to those less troubled times. My mind needed to be anywhere except where I was right then. I closed my eyes briefly and felt myself driving my '65 Fastback Mustang—man, how I loved that car—or my old '59 Chrysler New Yorker before that. In my wandering memories, my former girlfriend and I drove that old Chrysler down to the Rio Grande River levee to park a while, and it was a nice starry night, a warm summer night. I was in love with the young, blue-eyed, blond woman in the sundress. Recalling the smell of her unique perfume filled my consciousness. The memory that flooded my mind was so overpowering I could taste her kiss and feel her softness. Saigon radio was playing those same oldies songs that I had heard for years, and it blocked out the horrible silence of the Dead. And my memory furnished the beautiful girl to block my visions of the infantrymen who had died in our helicopter such a short time before. It was Caroline and me and the Rolling Stones at the Rio Grande…

Back to reality, back to flying: out on the horizon, artillery shells were exploding, prepping another LZ, ripping up everything. Maybe ten seconds from our touchdown, a white-phosphorus shell exploded that marked the end of the bombardment. Saigon Radio blasted out Chuck Berry's "Johnny B. Goode" while the Stingers started their hot runs with a long string of rockets that walked down the shrub lines, *Boom, Boom, Boom…* We were in the LZ only a few seconds, rockets coming the whole time, *Boom,* till we were out and clear. A very impressive sight to watch: three bad-to-the-bone Attack Companies of Huey Slicks.

Back to the staging field again, then on to another LZ, again, and on and on. As the day got hotter and hotter, with the sun beating down, the smell in our helicopter didn't get any better. Quite the contrary. The pungent aroma of bowel contents, vomit, urine, and blood all mixed together was anything but pleasant. Every olfactory receptor in my whole being screamed at me, *Concentrate on the aroma of Caroline's wonderful perfume.* When I had tried to lay her down on the front seat of my old Chrysler, she said, "No, wait, it'll wrinkle my dress, and I can't go home like that. My mom will notice that right away." My heart sank with a thud, until she turned her back to me and said, "Get the zipper for me, will you?" All of my 19-year-old's dreams were coming true.

Our last LZ was after sundown, and then it was back home to the Hornets' Nest in the dark. We spent well over an hour cleaning out the helicopter. Luckily, the crew chief had gallon jugs of degreaser, disinfectant, and wire brushes. We all provided the elbow grease. Then it was on to cleaning the stench of Death off of me in the shower, scrubbing myself raw for a half an hour.

A week later we watched Nixon on TV talking about the Cambodian invasion's first day—oh, how well it all went, and how surprisingly light the U.S. battlefield casualties were. No, no, no, no, *friendly fire* victims weren't battlefield casualties. They were *accident* victims, that's all. No one wanted our battlefield numbers to be inflated, did they? We wished we'd had that son-of-a-bitch Nixon washing out our bloodied helicopters after that first day of going into Cambodia. God, I hated watching Nixon, his smugness, and his way of lying with a straight face, sure that America would believe it all! Oh, he had a secret plan, all right: he was gonna end the war with honor. Yeah. BS.

No one ever heard anything about that sorry LZ that our American artillery blew up when it was full of American infantrymen: there were no questions asked of any of the Hornets who watched the whole thing happen. The army wanted to look the other way, brush everything away, far away, and pretend all was good. I often wondered how deep in Alaska the army had buried their forgetful artillery fire control officer, and I hoped that he hadn't been planning on making the army a career deal or anything like that. But intestines wouldn't go back in a young man's ripped-up belly, no matter how hard the dying kid tried. And Richard Nixon didn't have to watch thirteen gurneys slowly roll away with sheets draped over the dead young infantrymen. While we were watching Nixon on TV there must have been thirteen caskets somewhere back home in the United States with American flags draped over them awaiting burial. And their families would have been told, "No, Ma'am, your son wasn't a battlefield casualty. He was killed in an unfortunate accident, and you have our sincere condolences for that."

Right after all that went down, the latest hot rumor floating around the Hornets' Nest was that the army didn't give out Purple Heart Medals for "accident victims." Purple Hearts were only for *real* heroes who were wounded in *real* combat and not the accident prone or the careless. Most of us said that had to be a BS story. The army might have had a bunch of oddball regulations, but surely they wouldn't do that. But who knew for sure? After all, the army did try to classify every single fatal helicopter crash that they could as a case of "Pilot Error, and therefore an Aviation Accident, Noncombat related." Yeah, you mean "pilot error" like the outrageous act of allowing your aircraft to be in the wrong damned place at the wrong damned time sort of error?

Well, tomorrow was another day in the Vietnam War. Before dawn, the Hornets had to ride the Pale Horse of Death into battle again. It was back to Cambodia. Everyone knew it would be the same ole crap—just a different day in Paradise.

7

MORE NEW GUY
EXTRA DUTIES

Just two or three days after the "friendly fire" fiasco at the riverside LZ up at the Cambodian border, I was assigned to fly again with Steve Chasin being our aircraft commander on the Hornet Company's biggest mission yet into Cambodia. The 25th Infantry Division was being totally tight-lipped about what was going on. They just told us to bring the whole Hornet Company, everything we had that would fly, and report in at Tay Ninh at the Crusaders Aviation Area no later than 6:30 hours, and we would be briefed as needed when we got there. The 25th wouldn't say anything else other than it was something big happening in Cambodia that had a "Maximum Effort-Broken Arrow" battle designation, which I was told meant to drop everything and come right now with whatever you had ready for a fight. Hell, the 116th AHC Hornets were looking for a fight every morning when they woke up. At least that was the whiskey talk every night from the Stingers gunship pilots in the Officers' club.

Okay, so it was a Broken Arrow deal (someone from Oklahoma must have cooked that up as a code phrase they thought sounded really cool). Well, whatever. The important thing to me was that I was getting to fly with Steve Chasin again. Steve was not only the best friend I had made in the 116th, I'd learned more from him than any other aircraft commander I'd flown with (not counting 1st Lt. Sparks of course, because Sparks might have been the best AC there ever was). Steve had some screwball hippie ideas about flying that he called "the Zen of Helicopter Flying," but when I had tried his kooky suggestions, damned if they didn't work as well as he advertised!

Feeling like I was still half asleep, at 4:30 hours I was on the flight line in a helicopter that maintenance had just rolled out of their hangar. I was checking the logbook to make sure they had really signed off on all the red-X problems they'd repaired. A Spec-5 I recognized from flight operations came up and said, "Mister Denny, the captain needs you in the office ASAP."

So, what's up, did I screw up some paperwork, or something? In the operations shack, about a half-dozen people were talking loudly all at once to the operations captain. I walked up to present myself to him as instructed and he pointed a clipboard at me and said, "Denny, you're grounded for at least two days—you're over the hours limit again. I think you're gonna be assigned as Bunker Line Duty Officer. You know the drill for New Guy Extra Duty by now."

I objected: "Captain, I was on a New Guy Extra Duty detail just a little over a week ago, and I'm perfectly able and ready to fly today, so can't you forget about the hours thing…"

He interrupted me and said, "Mister Denny, can't you see that I'm busier than a one-legged man in an ass-kicking contest, so the only goddamned thing I expect out of you is a sharp 'Yes, Sir' and a snappy salute when I tell you something. You understand that, Mister? Now get your shit in a pile and get the hell out of my flight operations center—your young butt is grounded, so go report to the orderly room for your extra duty assignment when there's somebody there."

All I could do was come to attention and bring up a salute and say, "Sir, yes, Sir." I snapped off my salute, but then I couldn't help myself and added, "But, Sir, aren't there other guys newer than me in the company…"

He started hopping on one leg and pointed his clipboard toward the door. I guessed he was showing me what a talented one-legged ass-kicker he could be. Everyone standing around was laughing and from the twinkle in the captain's eye, I could see that he was halfway joking around with me. I saluted again and said, "Yes, Sir," and headed for the door while everyone laughed. From behind me, the captain called out, "Come back when you're done tomorrow and let me know how you liked Bunker Line Duty: it's a 24-hour straight-through gig, and you'll love trying to keep those knotheads awake all night out in those damned perimeter-wire Guard Towers."

The flight operations captain was basically a laid-back, good-natured guy with a big sense of humor who was always quick with a joke. That was why I was comfortable enough with him that I could take the liberty to banter with him the smallest amount, even though he was a captain. And that morning I could tell he was halfway joking, but it was clear he was halfway NOT joking. He looked like he was busy as hell, so that's why I did what he said without any more questions.

At the orderly room the guy who was playing at officer of the day was a Yellow Jackets Platoon New Guy who didn't know any more about what the Bunker Line Duty Officer job was than I did. He answered my first couple of questions with, "Beats the shit out of me." Then he real quickly showed that he had grown bored with me and rudely laid his head back down on the desk to go back to sleep, which I took as his way of saying to leave him the hell alone. So I left to go to the mess hall and get some breakfast since some of the Wasps might still be there finishing up their chow before hitting the flight line.

All of the pilots who were flying that day had already left the mess hall to go to the flight line. There were just a few aircraft commanders still there, since ACs technically didn't have to report for duty until a half-hour after the pilots. Steve Chasin was there, and he was the only one I was looking for anyway. I set my food tray down at his table and told him I'd been grounded again for being over the hours limit so I'd been scratched off the day's mission and wouldn't be flying with him. No, I didn't know who the pilot would be. He said he'd never heard of *Bunker Line Duty Officer* and didn't know anyone in the Hornets who had ever caught that particular extra-duty assignment before. So, he was sorry, but he couldn't shed any light on the topic.

We walked together out to the flight line, and man oh man, the whole damned place was lit up by floodlights like a movie set. Big lights were coming from a hundred sources, and it was brighter than high noon. There were Hornets scurrying around everywhere taking care of the last-minute preparations that were normal before the orders to begin to fire up the engines. We made our way to Steve's helicopter, and Jack Smith was up on the roof doing an inspection of the rotor head. Jack was another New Guy who had joined the Hornets only a few days after I had. It seemed that he had taken my place flying on the upcoming mission.

There was a tremendous electricity in the air, and it was obvious that this mission was going to be something bigger than anything I'd seen in Vietnam ever before, at least as far as the whole Hornet Company was concerned. Something was coming that was going to be even bigger than the first day we had invaded Cambodia, but anyone who might have known what was really happening wasn't talking. The CO probably knew, and I imagined that Lt. Sparks knew. Whatever it was, I was going to be the son of a bitch who missed out on the whole damned day.

Jack Smith was a really quiet guy, kind of standoffish, and I hadn't really gotten to know him very well. He didn't live in our hooch, so he sort of mixed with a different crowd than I did, and I didn't run into him very often since he didn't go to the Officers' club. I thought there was some sort of religious deal with him that kept him away from the booze scene. I wasn't burdened with that sort of affliction, and I guessed that my particular set of morals might have been a tad bit looser than his.

I hollered up to him, "Hey, Jack, I'm not flying today. Tell you what, I'll switch with you. I've got something called 'Bunker Line Duty Officer' today, and if you'll switch with me, I'll give you thirty bucks. You know I was supposed to fly with Steve on this mission, but they scratched me off at the last minute. What do you say? Thirty bucks of easy money?"

Jack laughed and said, "I think I'd better do what they told me. I don't want to get in trouble."

"Nobody will get in any trouble. Hell, probably no one will even notice that we switched. Anyway, have you ever heard that it's a whole lot easier to get forgiveness for something than to get permission? If anything at all comes up about it, I'll tell them that I made you do it and that you didn't want to, so any blame for anything will be all mine," I shouted up to him, but I already knew he wouldn't do it. He was too damned straightlaced for any scheme like that.

He hollered back to me, "No, I don't think so, Ed, but now that I know you have extra cash just floating around, maybe I'll work out a deal with you for a loan. You got more than just a little ole thirty bucks to lend out?"

Damn, ole Jack had a sense of humor I'd never expected. I replied, "Hey, I just thought I'd try about the switching thing. Any loan deal, come see me in my loan office at the Officers' club tonight. No, scratch that. Not tonight. I'll be on the bunker line tonight, so make that tomorrow night."

"Yeah, sure, sure. Roger that. Just hold your breath and wait for me at the Officers' club," he said and laughed again, and even I knew that was another joke.

That was the longest conversation I'd ever had with Jack by a long shot, and it was the first time I'd ever had the feeling that he was opening up some. It looked like Jack was someone I was going to become friends with after all. We'd have to get him into our little New Guy's group: me and Steve Chasin and Austin Scarborough and Larry Hood. The only thing was, we all lived in the same hooch and Jack didn't. That didn't really matter. I'd make it a point to talk to him more whenever we did cross paths, maybe invite him to join us at the mess hall. I saw him around there some times.

Anyway, Steve was officially no longer a New Guy since he'd made aircraft commander, which he did shortly after I had joined the Hornets, and Austin would be an AC soon. But they were my friends, and they had treated me well since my very first day. Hell, in the first few minutes after I had met Steve he was literally offering me the shirt off of his back—in fact, the whole damned flight suit he was wearing, plus a second flight suit to boot. And I was wearing those clothes right then. The shirt I was wearing had "S. Chasin" written inside the collar with a black laundry-marker pen. Of course, he was willing to trade flight suits with me so he could trade in the old worn-out stuff I had so he could exchange them at supply for even newer flight suits than he was wearing back then. I just saw the whole thing as a win-win situation for both of us. Maybe we didn't really have a New Guy's group anymore, just a friends group. I would have to adjust my thinking on that.

"Since you won't give me my damned ride back, Jack, I guess all I can say is have a good safe day out there today, whatever the hell you guys are going to do," I told him and waved good-bye.

Jack said, "And you enjoy your bunker-line duty."

Then I went over to Steve, who was in the helicopter going through his startup checklist, and patted him on the helmet and said, "Since it looks like I'm not going with you today, I'll see you sometime later, I guess, and you guys have good luck and real good hunting."

"Yeah, well, I hope we don't get into any deep shit that's bad enough that we need luck to enter the ball game," Steve told me, and as usual, he'd hit the nail right on the head.

Steve was two years younger than me, but sometimes he'd come out with something that made him sound wise way beyond his age—and mine. I hit him on the helmet again and nodded that I fully understood he was right, then I jumped down off the skid and started walking toward the operations office to get a cup of hot coffee. Out on the runway, I saw a tight cluster of men: there was the company commander and the executive officer, the chief maintenance officer, who was an older captain, the flight operations captain, and all three of the Hornets' platoon leaders. I guessed that the old man was telling them what this whole deal was about, if he knew.

The operations shack was totally empty when I walked in, not a single soul was there, and the place was eerily silent. It was normally as busy as a beehive in the early mornings. I got my coffee and then studied the schedule board. Virtually every aviator in the Hornets was listed up there. My name was still on the board paired with Steve Chasin, and Jack Smith was shown with Leon Richards. But Jack had been reassigned to Steve to replace me, and I had no idea who was actually flying with Leon. It must be some really New Guy I didn't know about since Leon was the instructor pilot and the number two man behind Lt. Sparks to break in New Guys if Sparks was already training someone.

Obviously, the schedule board hadn't been updated yet to reflect last-minute changes. Things had been so hectic around there earlier that I could understand that some things like the schedule board still needed to be taken care of when things calmed down. It was no big deal. Damn. I wished I'd seen the board before I talked to Jack. I would have just told him that since someone was replacing him for flying with Leon Richards, it was because HE was actually the one over his hours limit and he was supposed to have the Bunker Line Duty Officer assignment and I was still assigned to Steve. Go look at the schedule board for yourself, Jack. Damn. Too late then. If I tried that, he would know I was just trying to con him, and that was no way to treat a future friend. Oh, well, maybe *Bunker-Line Duty Officer* wouldn't be so bad.

From outside, I could hear the throaty whir of the helicopters' turbine engines starting up. I just had to face it. They were going without me. Suddenly, I was feeling totally alone. I hated that feeling. Standing there in the silence, actually alone, I nearly jumped out of my skin when the operation's radios crackled with the sounds of pilots starting to call out their communication (commo) checks. Resigned to my situation, I walked over to the orderly room and sat on the front steps. I didn't want to wake up the guy who was sleeping inside again, since he had been such a butthole earlier. Anyway, I wanted to see the helicopters as they departed the Hornets' Nest to fly off to Cambodia for something big and hairy—I assumed. After a little while, one at a time, eight Stinger C-Model gunships lumbered into the dark sky, followed by two flights of Slicks: First Platoon, the Yellow Jackets, and Second Platoon, the Wasps, and they totaled sixteen troop transport Hueys altogether. They were headed to Tay Ninh, and then—I didn't know what.

Three or four minutes after they took off, our whole company of Hueys came back right over the Hornets' Nest flying in formation: the Stingers were in a delta vee of seven ships with one more in the slot, followed by the two Slicks platoons flying side by side in paired, staggered configurations. It all looked very damn impressive. The roar of 24 combined helicopters coming over at a relatively low altitude was tremendously loud. Everyone in the sprawling Cu Chi base who was still asleep at that early hour certainly got jolted out of their beds. At the east end of the Cu Chi runway, the Little Bear helicopters had also started taking off, and it sure seemed that the war business in that part of Vietnam that morning was certainly brisk.

I'd fallen asleep waiting for someone to show up at the orderly room. I was leaning up against a handrail newel post on the stairsteps when the 1st sgt. kicked my boot to wake me up and asked me what I was doing out in front of his orderly room? Was I sleeping off a night of drinking? Shouldn't I have gone with my flight platoon earlier?

"Well, Sergeant, they told me that I was assigned to pull 'Bunker Line Duty Officer' today and for me to report here. So, what am I supposed to do?"

We went in the orderly room, and he gave me a set of keys to a Jeep and told me to go over to Division: they would give me my instructions there. A Jeep? Hot damn! I was going to have the use of a Jeep for the next 24 hours! That was sweet!

At Division, they went through a whole speech, but the most important instructions were about making sure that each guard tower had the correct inventory of ammunition and flares they were supposed to have and restocking them as needed. I was going to have three towers, numbers seven, eight, and nine. I asked the guy why they called it Bunker Line Duty if it was actually just guard towers involved. You could tell that the guy had been asked that question a thousand times, and he gave me a canned answer about the whole thing being the perimeter defense system and it comprised a series of guard towers that were backed up by a whole, sophisticated network of bunkers that were not normally manned unless there was enemy activity attacking the perimeter wire, and needless to say the bunkers were not being manned right then. Okay?

Then it was off to inspect my kingdom, my three towers. I was a helicopter pilot, not some infantry officer, and in flight school they didn't teach me a single thing about commanding enlisted men on the perimeter wire. I was a warrant officer and there was no training about commanding even a damned fence post, so I decided to just play the John Wayne role from the movie *The Green Berets*: "So, Pilgrim, is everything nice and secure at your guard post this morning, son?"

When I climbed up the first tower, they all jumped up to wobbly attention and saluted me, at least the ones who weren't sleeping on guard duty. The daytime guards were from the night before. There was pot smoke wafting heavily in the air everywhere, and they thought they were in the crapper for sure. They were not used to warrant officers, but they saw the wings on my chest and they seemed to relax some. I introduced myself and shook their hands. Every one of those kids looked about 15 years old. I just ignored the pot. I didn't want to get involved in anything that was going to turn into a time-consuming stink involving me, and I wasn't interested in getting anyone in trouble for something that would only involve me for that one day.

Over the course of the morning, I saw the reason for the Jeep. I was just a glorified gofer chasing all around Cu Chi getting crap for the three towers. But I had to admit that I loved to be driving the Jeep. I didn't realize how much I missed having my car, missed being able to jump into it anytime and drive down to the corner 7–11 convenience store for a pack of cigarettes whenever I wanted. And I got to see a lot of Cu Chi other than just the Hornets' Nest and even found the base PX. I stopped in there just to check it out and probably stayed way too long.

When I got back to the Hornets' Nest for lunchtime, the Company Area looked like a ghost town. There was hardly anyone out and about. Hell, everyone was off flying except me, it seemed. When I went in the mess hall, it was full of raging wild talk of a Hornet bird shot down! Oh, shit! Not again! It had been only about ten days before when Stinger 83, Craig Fox, had been shot down, killing everyone in the helicopter. And now there was another damned ship shot down? I listened to what I was hearing in total disbelief: "Bad exploding crash—all KIA, everyone—load of troops on board, and they were killed—everybody killed! Who? Nobody knew anything yet, nothing!"

I immediately headed out for the flight operations office to find out the details. I'd been in-country five weeks, but I was so tired I felt like I'd been there forever and ever. Five weeks and we had three dead Hornets: that much is exactly what I knew. And the last time I had extra duty another man had died in my place! That, I also damn well knew! Mark McDonald: that was his name. All of my horrible feeling about that incident instantly came flooding back to me. I was just starting to get to the point where Fox and McDonald weren't exclusively on my mind totally around the clock. And now we had another ship down within just ten days. Could that really be true?

When I walked through the door at operations, some kid who hadn't even started shaving yet was shooting off his mouth loudly, "Hell, what does it matter, anyway? We're all crazy. We're all dead. You just gotta get crazy, and finally accept your eminent death." Yeah, right, you stupid little son of a bitch, why don't you run your mouth about something you may actually know about, like how much fun you had in high school last year. I walked up to the little knot of young enlisted guys who were jabbering, running their mouths, and I asked them, "Is what I heard in the mess hall true? Did we lose another ship shot down?"

The kid who had been blabbering about eminent death said, "Yes, sir, it's true."

I asked the obvious, "Who was it, a gunship again? Was it Stinger 82?" I was afraid I'd hear that it was my new friend, Arthur. But I should have known that it wasn't a Stinger. In the mess hall they'd said there were troops on the helicopter, but my mind wasn't processing that sort of information.

"We don't know for sure yet. The Crusaders radioed over to us that we'd lost a ship, but they had only a partial tail number. But from the partial number, if it's right, we're pretty sure it was Chasin and Denny, Serna and Portwood. We're still waiting for better information," the kid said.

Oh, my God! The breath went out of me like the kid had hit me in the stomach with a goddamned baseball bat! Not Steve! Not Steve Chasin! No. No. No way in hell could it be Steve!

When I was finally able to breathe again, I said in an elevated voice, "Well, that sorry bullshit must be wrong. It must be somebody else, because do I look like I've been in a helicopter crash?"

"Well, no, sir, I guess you don't."

In a full shout, I told the specialist, "So, it isn't Chasin and Denny then, because I'm standing right here, and I'm Denny! I'm Ed Denny, so it's not me and Chasin! Now you got that straight or not?"

"Yes, sir."

I looked up at the scheduling board, and there it was bigger than life: AC—Hornet 34 Chasin. Pilot—Denny. Crew Chief—Serna. Door Gunner—Portwood. A line had been drawn through the names. My damned name was still on the stinking board! The damned scheduling hadn't been changed from that morning!

The operations captain came out of his office and said in a steady voice, "Erase Mister Denny's name from the board and wash it off so you can never see that it was ever there and put Warrant Officer Smith's name there—he was the pilot. Then erase Mister Smith's name from Leon Richards's crew and put the XO's name there. Now, Mister Denny, will you step into my office?"

In his office, he said, "I've just gotten off the landline with Tay Ninh and they confirmed to me that the lost ship was the one we thought it was, and it was confirmed that there were no survivors. It was Steve Chasin's ship, and I know he was a good friend of yours. He was a friend of everyone who had ever met him here in the Hornets, and that includes me, and a lot of people are going to be very upset about him being killed, just like you are right now. Just like I am right now. People get killed here sometimes. That's the rude truth. And when that happens, there's nothing anyone can do to change it. Whatever is done can't be undone. You have to just accept it and put it behind you and go on with your duties the best you can. You can mourn what happens here while we're in a war situation at a later, appropriate time, but for now you just have to put this out of your mind and get up tomorrow and get on with the war."

I asked, "Why didn't you just let me go with the flight this morning? You knew I wanted to fly. I didn't care how many hours I had. If I had flown with Steve instead of it being Jack Smith in my place, things might have gone down differently, and none of this would have had to happen to anyone."

"You know, you're right about that. I'm one hundred percent sure that if you'd flown, things wouldn't have happened this way. You being there would have changed everything. I'm totally sure of that. But instead of it being just one ship shot down, you and Steve Chasin might have been shot down and another ship or two shot down along with you. Things would have been different alright, but they may have been a hell of a lot worse because you were there. Hell, you could have been flying and taken a bullet and jerked on the flight controls and crashed into the helicopter beside you, and both of you crashed into other helicopters in the formation, until you had a whole chain reaction of crashing helicopters going on so that the whole damned formation fell out of the sky into seven or eight crash sites. You think about that. Now, go to your hooch and get some sleep," the captain instructed.

"I've got Bunker Line Duty Officer today, so I can't do that. I'm supposed to be on duty right now, in fact," I reminded him.

"I know, I know. Consider what I said as an order. When the CO and the XO are gone off flying for the day, I'm the temporary company commander around here, and I can decide whatever I want my Hornets to do. I'll send someone to wake you up at the right time, don't worry. So, do what I said and don't make me tell you twice, like you usually do, Mister Denny. Now, get the hell out of my office and close the door behind you and let me have a few quiet moments to myself, please," he said as he set a bottle of Wild Turkey whiskey and a glass on his desk as an exclamation point.

8

THE GUARD TOWERS,
BEING INSANE

I walked in a trance back to my hooch and collapsed on my bunk. God, Steve Chasin killed, Jack Smith killed. How could I ever believe such a horrible thing? Steve Chasin was gone. *Poof.* Just like that. Dead. And it wasn't just Steve on my mind: seven Dead Hornets in ten days. How could I ever believe THAT horrible thing? And it easily could have been me in either of those crashes, and for some stupid reason I was feeling that it SHOULD have been me and not McDonald or Smith. I certainly didn't deserve to live anymore than they did! I had to stop my mind, get some sleep. I was apparently in some sort of a state of shock. I forced my eyes shut, gonna be herding cats all night out at the perimeter-wire towers. There was nothing I could do about those deaths right then except sleep and escape Vietnam for a short time.

Soon enough, I was carried away by jumbled dreams, but it was NOT my wife's arms I encountered. Oh, no. I couldn't be that blessed. Naturally, it was seven goddamned dead Hornets calling me, demanding answers I didn't have. All I could do was say, "I don't know, I don't know, I missed that 'cause I was somewhere else, doing something else," to everything. Then the scene transformed and swirled into a tiny hole in dense jungle, and I was riding along on a gunship dive, rockets, rockets, firing away, but there's a twin 20mm gun pumping back, *Whomp, Whomp,* tracers big as basketballs. Inevitably, giant balls of fire swallowed up our gunship, fire everywhere, and in the fire, the dead left-seat pilot laughed and laughed, a grinning skeleton roaring with laughter, and said, "Man, that's so much fun, do it again, do it again," until it became a repetitive chant. Came back around into another steep rocket-run dive… One nightmare rolled into another one, and then it's Chasin standing there, and I was wearing his old clothes, but he was a dead man, and he needed his flight suits back. I tried to work buttons and zippers, but with fingers that'd been burned off into useless little crispy-black nubs. "Come on, goddamn it, Denny: I've got places to go, appointments to keep." I hand him the shirt, but he wants the damned pants. He flashes in and out of focus and his head thrashes side to side in apparent waves of pain, but he is very polite and thanks me. I stood there naked, nothing on at all, totally damned buck naked for all the world to see, and I found I was burned to a withered-up hard shell everywhere and all my appendages had been burned away into the vague hint of remaining stubs.

Steve was there in my room, calling out to me, and he was surrounded by a chorus of dead men all calling me: "Denny, Denny, Denny." Then Steve was shaking me by the shoulder. I woke up some and heard, "Denny, get up, wake up. You've got guard duty."

I sat up on the edge of my bunk and rubbed the sleep from my eyes. The damned bed was soaking wet, as was my flight suit, and I was shivering cold. I didn't think I had ever felt more alone at any time in my life than I did right at that moment. And I'd never felt so ashamed of being alive as right then. I looked around. There was no Steve Chasin there. Just me, all alone. There was nobody in my room. There was only the silence of an empty hooch. So who woke me up? It must have been someone from operations, I guessed.

Up in a guard tower, at 04:00 hours, I was blasting into the black Cu Chi night with a nicely mounted M-60 machine gun blazing away, spewing out my personal frustration and disillusionment and crushing depression (although I didn't know what to call it back then). I was going totally nuts that night. First, it was poor Mark McDonald dying in my place. Then poor Jack Smith dying in my place, and Chasin and the crewmen and all those troops, all of them dying that day. That totaled seven dead Hornets in the five weeks. In my mind, I was all tied up with those dead men and I would be forever. Even if I lived to be a hundred years old, I would have to carry those deaths in every fiber of my being, and they would always remain a part of me, like an inoperable cancer.

Everything was a ball of confusion. An outburst of anger had me in its clutches for the moment. Since I'd met the new shift of enlisted men at the changing of the guard, I'd been internally consumed with a battle of competing emotions: anger at the entire situation that I was in by being in Vietnam, the turbulent and often ugly period of time in which I was living, and the role I was generally playing in it. That was two years after the Tet offensive, and well into Nixon running the war, and everyone who even read a newspaper or saw the news on TV knew that the war was fully decided, was totally over—but it just hadn't stopped yet, that was all. The complex military machine that occupied Vietnam was huge and deeply entrenched and marched on like a perpetual motion machine fueled by its own massive momentum. There were hundreds of thousands of soldiers, nearly a half-million, to be brought home, with all their tools of war, big and small. Disengaging and withdrawing from that war was going to take years more: at least two or three. We were the foreign occupiers in Vietnam, and the country was their home. Were there any occupiers who had ever really won in the long run in all of history? We would lose in the end when we grew too damned tired of the war and of spending America's money and blood, sweat, and tears on it, and packed up and went back to our homes. And the North Vietnamese would win because they were willing to fight on their home ground forever, even if it took that long. They would win or die trying. The general American goal was to survive, get out of Vietnam alive, pure and simple. The other side's goal was to have America gone from Vietnam at any price of human sacrifice. It was not an even match of wills: no possible comparison at all.

The Hornet pilots I had talked with were all of the opinion that the only thing we were doing in Vietnam in 1970 was trying to manufacture the required conditions so we could get out of the war without getting the living shit kicked out of us when we were headed for the doorway out of that country. And that's all the whole Cambodia invasion was: the American army trying to set the stage for their soonest possible disengagement. Our only option at that point in time was to stand up the South Vietnam Army to take over our part of the fight while we stood down and bowed out of this party, our backs covered and protected by the South Vietnamese as we departed. Then they would settle everything with North versus South. A familiar theme to Americans, since we'd already been through that once ourselves and everyone knew who won that one, except for maybe a few hillbillies who thought the Civil War was still not yet decided one way or the other.

I had been shooting the damned stinking Vietnamese countryside all night long, ever since it had gotten dark. I fired M-79 grenade launchers, machine guns, M-16s, and even my .38 pistol. The sky was crowded with flares all night: I was shooting something every second of that horrible night, and it all sounded like there was one hell of a battle going on in my perimeter sector. My ruckus had TEN towers worked up, all of their guns screaming along with mine and flares floating down all along the line. Oh, what a concert I had created. On the radio, the 25th Infantry Division people were hollering loud, wanting to know what the hell was going on? Was there a ground attack happening over there? No, no ground attack. Just someone who thought they saw movement in the wire, but it was probably a stray dog or something. (I couldn't very well say that it was ME who saw ghosts of dead pilots dancing in the wire. That was all. Just ghosts, nothing else.)

Everyone said you either had to be totally crazy to fly a combat helicopter in the Vietnam War or have a real damned serious death wish. I felt in the middle of that night that I had crossed over the last threshold into crazy land. And there would never be any returning from crazy land. It was a one-way trip, and whatever person I'd been before was forever gone, left behind all alone. All of that guilt, anger, fear, self doubt, fate—was there any such thing as fate—there was a load of what felt like pure crap swirling in my head that all at once left my damned brain just liquefied, and I felt like I was having an out-of-body experience. I was flooded with the realization that, if we had seven men killed in five weeks, by the end of a year the total number of dead Hornets would be a big number, and I surely would be in that group somewhere. How could I not be? The kids in our company ran around saying, "Accept your death, then you'll be set free, and you could begin to live." Okay, I would give in and accept it, goddamn it. I saw it all clearly then: I was dead meat.

By morning's first light we'd shot up all the ammo in three damned guard towers, everything, even all of my pistol ammo! When there was nothing left to shoot, I said good-bye to the boys in the towers and got in my damn Jeep and drove all over every square inch of Cu Chi until breakfast. I was like a drunken Paul Revere as I drove, shouting into the wind, "Oyez, Hear Ye, Now Hear This, stinking Vietnam: no one should have to die for a war we've so clearly given up on!" That seemed rather obvious, but not enough people were saying it out in the open! If I was already a dead man, didn't that mean there was nothing left to live for? Wasn't suicide the only logical answer? Wouldn't that be the ultimate demonstration that you still had control of your own fate in the end? But even with the unexpected death of a close friend, hadn't I chosen to be where I was? Wasn't that control?

Coming back from perimeter guard duty, I found the Hornets' Nest totally empty again. Everyone was off flying. I guessed it was another Maximum Effort day, and the company had left before dawn again. I was alone in my silent hooch, left behind and alone. My head was spinning, and I felt as if I was drifting through some sort of horrible negative hallucination and I felt just like hell. I was exhausted and flopped on my bunk, tossed, turned, and wondered why things had gone the way they had. I needed to get some sleep after being up all night, if I could, if sleep would ever come to me again. After about an hour, I finally drifted off, but immediately sleep brought oddball crazy dreams all over again.

My nightmare started off with the funeral-dirge sound of a song by Steppenwolf, "Desperation," playing in our hooch. Worn out, the flight guys came dragging in at the end of a long black day, a sad day. Everyone's head downcast: Steve Chasin was Dead. The brass hadn't been around yet to put Steve's personal things away. On his bunk, waiting, was his unopened mail. His precious letters from back home, from his young wife, back in Georgia. From Mom and Dad down in Atlanta. On his bunk, waiting—unopened mail and a little package, Steve's Cu Chi address done in crayon.

They told me that three NVA .51 cal's shot 'em down. Flew into a nasty crossfire, couldn't get away. NVA .51 cal's locked on 'em until a blazin' fireball fell from the sky, into a jungle, rolling, hilly, like north Georgia, and now—a little package done in crayon.

Since the brass hadn't done it yet, we packed Steve's things up. He usually won at poker, but not today, no—not today. And there was this little package. No time for tears, no time for mourning. Hornets fly again at dawn like every day. Packed his footlocker, his clothes, the picture of his young wife and his 3-year-old twin sons, Jimmy and little Stevie Junior.

Unopened mail—love letters from home, from his young wife back in Georgia, from Mom and Dad down in Atlanta and innocent kids at Sunday school. No tears, 'til the little package addressed "Dear Warrant Officer Daddy." Ripped it open—found a cassette recording. On the tape player we heard, "Happy Birthday, Daddy" sung by two joyful little boys. On his bunk, waiting—unopened mail. On his bunk, waiting—a little package. No time for tears, no time for mourning until we heard, through pained silence, "Happy Birthday Daddy" from his boys. No time for tears, until we heard, "Happy Birthday Daddy" from his boys. And Hornets fly again at dawn like every day. Every day, new dawn, new mission. No one will call his name, not for a long time, maybe years.

So, New Guy, don't ask why there's no Hornet Three-Four. It's because there's no time for tears, no time for mourning. No one ever wants to hear Steve's call sign on the radio, and there won't be another Three-Four while any of us are still here. If you got a wife back in Georgia, we really don't want to know. Birthday in three months, you say, if you stay alive until then. Buy us all enough Scotch whiskey, we'll show you a little package we have, play you a little sad birthday song, tell you about unopened mail, and bring you to tears. Unopened mail—love letters from back home, from his young wife back in Georgia, from Mom and Dad down in Atlanta and innocent kids at Sunday school. On his bunk, waiting—unopened mail, on his bunk, waiting—a little package—

It all folded into another dream, another nightmare I couldn't escape.

Three NVA .51 cal's blowing big holes in our helicopter, fire breaks out, engine goes quiet, holes keep coming, flames in the cockpit, burning, screaming. We fall out of the formation, going down burnin', "Three-Four going down." NVA .51 cal's got us locked, shredding us, and the inside of the cockpit is a cloud of blood and flames. "Three-Four going down," and bullets keep hitting us.

Everything coming apart, breaking to bits. Steve's quiet, Dead now, bullets still coming. Bullets still coming, crew Dead now, inside the cockpit, clouds of blood, big bullets keep ripping through me. We're falling out of the sky, dead weight, controls won't work. My body's Dead, but brain won't stop. Brain won't stop, NVA .51's won't stop. See my face melting away from the fire. Big bullets keep ripping through me, left hand is gone, leg shot off, guts in the floor, sizzling, crackling, I'm totally Dead, but brain won't stop. On the intercom, little boys singing, "Happy Birthday, Daddy, Happy Birthday." Ground is screaming up at us, coming fast, coming hard, getting close. "Happy Birthday, Daddy, Happy Birthday."

My young wife held my face, kissed me, brushed away my tears and took my face to her bosom as the Warrant Officer Cadet Choir began singing "If I die in the combat zone—Box me up—Send me home. Pin my wings upon my chest—Tell my Mama I did my best. Sound off, one, two, sound off, three, four." Stupid damned brain wouldn't stop, wouldn't let me be Dead...

"Denny, Denny, Denny. You're screaming! Denny, Denny," wake up, wake up, wake up, you're having a dream! Opened my eyes, for an instant, I thought it was Steve Chasin. Shook my head, it was someone else.

I said, "Dream Hell, a damned nightmare that we lost a ship, had one shot down."

Guy said, "Yeah, we did. Yesterday. So you weren't having just a dream. Steve Chasin's ship was shot down."

I asked, "Did he have any kids? Did he have little twin boys?"

"I know he was married, but kids, I don't know. A friend of yours?" he asked.

"Yeah, a friend of mine, a good friend." I mumbled.

"He just got to go home early, that's all it was," he said.

I never knew who that guy was or even what rank he was or how he knew my name or who I was or where he came from to be in my room like that, and I never saw him again after that one brief encounter. But I was thankful that whoever he was he'd pulled my ass away from my dreaming.

I sat there on the edge of my bunk and so wished that when I had just awakened, I would have realized that everything that had happened in the Hornets for the last two weeks was just a part of a very elaborate nightmare that had captured me. But the real nightmare was that reality was reality, and it was as bad as the worst dream I ever imagined, and I wished I had some damned place where I could go hide away and allow myself to simply sleep peacefully for a while: a place where dreams didn't exist. But there was no place to hide. That was a time to *Just Take It!*

9

Dead, First Day,
First Minutes

My mind had hoped that Vietnam would make sense somehow, that things would be logical and understandable, and cause would always yield predictable effect, like two plus two would always equal four. That night I'd spent out at the guard towers causing such a ruckus, I released my grip on any hope that I could control anything, except maybe my own suicide, and that wasn't for me. Flying in Vietnam would either kill me eventually or it would not. When I had extrapolated our death rate since I'd been in-country into a year's worth of Hornet deaths, I came up with about 80. Hell, that equaled more than the total number of pilots that we even had in the whole Hornets Company, and I sure didn't believe that ALL of our pilots would be killed in my year. Since pilots seemed to be superstitious about the topic and never talked about previous Hornet casualties, I just bluntly asked the operations captain about the issue. He assured me that before we had lost the two helicopters just recently shot down it had been six months since the Hornets had anyone else killed. Naturally, there had been a lot of Hornets killed over the years, but there were also periodic long stretches of time during our history when no one was killed. The most recent deaths could be attributable to the Cambodian invasion. That had certainly stirred things up for the Hornets, and not in a good way. But losing two ships in ten days was unusual, and it was just a freak thing, the captain said. I tried to believe that reassurance.

Three or four days after the guard towers night, I was up at Tay Ninh visiting the Crusaders Company Area. The aircraft commander I was flying with for that day was Dennis Plumber, and we had been given a couple of hours off from our single-ship general support mission when an infantry unit had not been ready for us to come in, and they asked us to give them some time. Two hours would do. With some time to spend on our own, we headed to Tay Ninh so Dennis could stop in to visit an old friend of his, a former Hornet pilot who had transferred over to a medevac unit to fly Dust-Off.

When we landed at the Crusaders Company Area, we stopped in at the operations bunker to tell them we would be parking our helicopter at their place for a little while. While we were talking to the operations guys, I asked about the fellow I knew—Smith was his name, "Smitty," the one I had flown with up from our battalion headquarters down in Long Binh on our first day. The name Smith just drew blank stares from the Crusaders: no one had heard of a "Smitty," and they said he was not with the Crusaders. I again told them how Smitty and I had flown together from Saigon, told them we'd tossed a coin back in Cu Chi, and I won the coin toss and chose to stay with the Hornets, and Smitty had gone on to Tay Ninh to join the 187th AHC, the Crusaders.

They just looked at me like they didn't know what the hell I was talking about, until I could see a lightbulb turn on over one guy's head, and he said, "About six weeks ago you say? Oh, man, oh, yeah, you must be talking about THAT damned New Guy. Hey, man, I hate to tell you this, but he was blown up by a rocket the same minute he got here. Yeah, was a totally freaky deal. This New Guy was walking from the helicopter out on the flight line to the operations shack, and halfway in between a damned rocket hit right next to him, and he was completely blown to bits, along with all of his paperwork, and no one ever even knew that guy's name. Smitty, you say, Warrant Officer Smith?"

Damn, damn, damn! My ears couldn't believe what I was hearing! A zillion thoughts were firing in my head all at the same time. McDonald, then Jack Smith, and now another Smith, Smitty. Don't tell me there's another guy who has died I was somehow connected with. This whole Vietnam War crap was turning into an episode of the TV program *The Twilight Zone* for me.

The Operations guy said, "So, you two guys tossed a coin, and he came up here to Rocket City. Guess that makes you feel a little spooky, huh. Something so simple, a coin toss. Almost makes you believe in fate, doesn't it, but if you're gonna get killed, that happening on the first day has gotta be better than putting in a full damned year in Vietnam and then buying the farm on the goddamned last day. That would suck."

Smitty, I didn't really know him. We were in flight school together but not the same platoon, and I didn't even know his first name, and I'm sure he didn't know mine. We just ran into each other that one day at Long Binh, just took that one helicopter ride from Battalion up to Cu Chi together, and yeah, that whole thing made me feel spooky, all right. But I was feeling so much more than just a little spooky. My whole mind was spinning about a million miles an hour, and I just had to stand there and take all that in and keep quiet. I couldn't very well say anything like, "Shit, another dead guy!

That's the third time now that I'm connected to someone who got killed, and believe it or not, this is twice now that it has been someone named Smith. What are the odds of shit like that happening? I ran the numbers in my head: something happening three different times goes to one in goddamned zillions! What the hell was happening to me?' Spooky, you say? This was so far beyond just spooky!"

All I could say was, "I think that getting killed, no matter what the damned day it was, first or last, would suck big time."

Everyone laughed and agreed with that assessment.

Four days ago I was so totally upset when my friend Steve Chasin was killed, but this day I was troubled that I felt so *ambivalent* about poor Smitty's death. Naturally, I was very shocked when I heard the news and I felt sorry for the poor guy. But my main feeling was a sense of relief that I really didn't know him and I'd never crossed paths with him very much. At the same time, I felt guilty about being somehow associated with the events that led up to his unforeseeable death. I was bothered that I'd played any role where HIS FATE could've been MY FATE, based solely on a heads-or-tails coin toss, even when logic said, *His death was a product of pure randomness! Nobody had any role in his outcome except the guy who shot the damned rocket in the first place!*

We were in Tay Ninh because of the limited free time we had, so we left the Crusaders operations shack right away and hurried over to drop in and visit with Dennis Plumber's old friend, who had finished with his flying. His year was up, and he was soon going home, just a couple more days until he would be gone. I was really interested to meet a real live medevac pilot, someone who knew the real poop on what flying Dust-Off was all about. He had transferred out of the Hornets and moved over to a medevac unit. Maybe I could do that, too.

We found him in his underground bunker home, a cozy little place to live and hide from rockets. It was the middle of the day, but he was still dressed only in his dirty old boxer shorts, and he was drunker than a skunk, stumbling around. It was impossible to know if this was just that day's drinking session or if he'd been drunk for days on end. It looked to me like the guy had been on a three-or-four-day bender. He sure looked like he hadn't slept in at least that long. Lord, he was skinny, just skin and bones, looked like a heroin junky or a World War II death camp survivor. He was tall, well over six feet tall, but he couldn't have weighed over a hundred pounds, a mere skeleton-man.

He was mumbling to us about being tired of flying wounded men to the Tay Ninh Hospital, just boys, and they didn't have enough manners, the common decency, to not die in his damned helicopter. We didn't stay long because the guy was too burned out and so completely used up, and it was painful to see him in that totally spent condition. I could see that man eating his pistol someday, probably soon.

My life's viewpoint had changed in just weeks. Inevitable mortality or eminent mortality was the filter everything passed through. Medevac-man I'd just met looked like his condition might qualify for the eminent-mortality category, and he was a painful example of how crazy things could be in lousy Vietnam! I had thought I was going to go to the war and keep my hands clean while I got through things. I was going to be a helicopter pilot, all right, but I was going to be one of the good guys and fly Medevac Dust-Off and join the circle of Angels of Mercy that saved wounded men. It was going to be rotary-wing ambulance time for Ed. But the army put me where they needed someone instead, so I wound up in a combat assault company. I tried to accept that turn of events and not let it make me too angry or flipped out. I hadn't tried to fight the big army machine about that deal because what could I do to change things. But after seeing Medevac-man in his condition, I could see that Dust-Off wouldn't have been any good for me anyway. Dealing with the consequences of America's being involved in a war, the steady stream of battle casualties, would have worn me down very quickly, and I would have probably wound up just like Medevac-man: totally used up and screwed up to the max limit. So, the only available choices were: stay with the assault Slicks and be a big fat target sitting in a plastic helicopter in hot LZs where the lead was flying everywhere or go to the Stinger gunships and be a full-time gung-ho killer or try for a transfer to Dust-Off. Damn. Being a target with the Slicks seemed to be the least objectionable of the choices, even though they all three sucked in their own way.

That day was turning into a downer, and my head sure hurt like Hell. *Goddamned Vietnam: looked like I was going to have to grit my teeth and Just Take It.*

10

FLIGHT HOURS CLERK

Lt. Sparks never mentioned anything about the two ill-fated fatal missions I'd been scrubbed off of. Instead, he did something else. He assigned me an extra duty: Wasp Platoon "Flight-Hours Accounting Clerk." The pilots' running 30-day flight-hour's tally had been kept by our operations personnel, but they hadn't been doing the job well enough to please Lt. Sparks because they'd kept letting people go over and bust the 140-hour flight limit (like had happened to me two times already). So it'd be my job from then on for the rest of my tour of flying with the Hornets. And that job was to collect all the logbook data every evening when everyone was finished flying and update their running hours totals BEFORE Lt. Sparks posted the next day's flight schedule. I became the Wasp's brand new flight-hours accounting clerk. Lt. Sparks must have known that I was the only guy who would want to accept that particular nightly chore. With that job, I was never going to get scrubbed off another flight at the last minute, not ever again. No one else in our platoon had any sort of permanent extra duty, but I was glad to get that one.

So every night I was out at the operations shack at least one or two hours updating the running-hours totals. I set up a spreadsheet calendar and posted a big erasable whiteboard where everyone could see their accurate hours status and predict when they would be getting some time off from flying.

Pretty soon, I had a handle on the situation, identified potential problems and got our pilots' availability evened out. I quickly discovered that 1st Lt. Sparks was the biggest problem of all. As far back as I could see, he'd been flying way over his limit, and I told him about what I'd discovered. I showed him where he'd have to *NOT FLY* for about 10 days straight to fix things to get to the point where I could have any hope of managing his limit, because he was running at 200 hours flown in the previous 30 days. He had his own solution: start him back at zero with a fresh start, and he would be better about watching the limit in the future. Okay, boss, if that's what you say.

The most satisfying part of being the flight-hours clerk was that I had

60

a job where I was able to be in control, to some extent, of what was happening and not just be a pawn tossed around by random chaos all the time. I also got to see all the after-hours work that Sparks had every night, the work that went into scheduling the next day's missions, and the meetings with aircraft commanders to evaluate pilots, particularly new-guy pilots. Also got to see Sparks operating out of the cockpit: he was all business but relaxed. I saw how the senior aircraft commanders worked with him, accepted his leadership, and I got a detailed look at the behind-the-scenes inner workings of a Vietnam War Assault Helicopter Combat Platoon.

Days of flying slipped into weeks, and things settled into something of a routine. Most of the time our missions were combat assaults in Cambodia, where we got shot at more than when we were in our normal area of operations around Cu Chi. But no one was wounded or killed, and we had no ships lost. My flying got more and more solid as time went on: just visualized where I wanted to go (like Steve Chasin had tried to teach me), and the chopper usually took me there sorta automatically. I eventually got to where I was able to consistently stay mentally ahead of the helicopter and always generally knew what the next few moves were going to be. It was comforting to feel I knew what was coming rather than just reacting to unforeseen things always popping up. Often, I could look at an LZ as we approached and guess if we'd be shot at or not, and those instincts were too often proved right.

Still, every time we took enemy fire my guts tied completely in knots; but I took it and when we were taking hits I did my damned job, just gritted it out and took it, but I never got comfortable with it. I hated it, and it scared the hell out of me every time it happened. Still, the Hornets always somehow found their way out of any trouble that came along.

Then, after a few weeks of hanging out around the flight operations bunker, where I had my own little work-desk area set up, one night Lt. Sparks and Leon Richards were talking in operations in quiet voices, over in the corner, for about a half hour, and then they came over to me. Sparks said, "Leon is going back stateside soon, in a little less than two months, actually, and then we won't have an instructor pilot. And I'll be leaving soon, also. We talked it over, discussed everything, and we'd like to know if you'd accept a slot at IP school? The 1st Aviation Brigade IP School is at Long Binh, down at Saigon. We'll put you on the list. Your class date will be in two or three months, if you want. What do you say? Wanna be an instructor pilot?"

Needless to say, I was more than a little surprised, totally shocked was more like it, and I asked, "Instructor pilot? You're kidding, right?"

Leon Richards was a nice guy, always relaxed, easygoing and laid back with a quiet voice. He smiled at me, gave me a wink and said, "You won't have to teach anyone to fly. Won't be teaching knucklehead asses, no new beginners, nothing like that. The job is evaluating experienced pilots, doing check rides every 90 days with all the Hornet pilots and working with the New Guys some. Ride with them while they practice the standard emergency or crisis maneuvers, autorotations, stuck tail rotor, hydraulics off, standard stuff, you know the list of things. It's a chance for them to practice and get the rust off, keep themselves sharp. All you'll have to do is ride along with them. That's all."

Sparks said, "Now, understand that this will be in addition to your normal duties of flying as an aircraft commander on missions. You'll be an AC by then, of course."

I stood looking at them, dumbfounded.

Sparks asked, "What do you say?"

Richards said, "I'll be gone home. We need someone to take the job. We'll both be gone, you'll be here, and someone has to take the job."

Sparks said, "School only lasts two weeks, and the instructors: the army's very best of the best. Long Binh mess halls are good, and the Officers' club is something to behold. Get into downtown Saigon on the weekends, if that's what you might like. So, what do you say?"

I thought a second—two weeks with no hot LZs, no getting shot at. What's the worst I could do? Bust out of the IP school? Embarrass myself?

"Okay, if this isn't a huge practical joke, sign me up I guess," I answered.

Sparks said, "One more thing: Scheduling. Are you ready to learn that? When I'm gone, I want you to take over pilot scheduling for the platoon. It's the obvious next step from hours clerk, and you've done that okay. It just happens later at night when the missions come down from Division for the next day, usually around midnight, sometimes later. We'll get that done before I go."

If I was going to take all this on, becoming an instructor pilot and doing the scheduling, could I still accept the generally popular philosophical sentiment that "Vietnam don't mean nothing"? In the beginning, Lt. Sparks had held a damned .45 caliber pistol to my head, but now he and Leon Richards were offering me the instructor pilot's job. How could something that strange happen? I spent some time thinking about that. In the end, I concluded that I happened to be the one pilot who fit most neatly into their time scheme for the coming months. I could go to IP school just when Leon Richards would be leaving to go home, and then we'd have a basically seamless transition in the company. I was also the one who would have more time left on my tour than the other pilots in the company. In the two-month time frame Sparks and Leon were talking about, all the pilots in the company who were senior to me would be nearing their downhill run and getting short. It was all a fluke of timing much more than it was anything to do with any positive attributes I might have displayed. Being the platoon flight-hours clerk certainly had nothing to do with becoming an IP, and crunching hours totals was still a giant leap away from actually doing scheduling, deciding which pilot flew with which aircraft commander on which mission.

Instructor pilot AND scheduling officer, BOTH, on top of what I was already doing. I needed to talk to management about a pay raise if I was going to take on all of that. Nights spent drinking in the Officers' club looked like they were going to be reduced to about zero, but I had been hoping for a long time to find some control over the randomness of the chaos of events swirling around everything in Vietnam, so I was willing to trade my social evenings in exchange for a chance to feed my delusions that anything resembling self-determination even existed in a war. But delusions of all sorts and sizes thrived in an environment like a combat assault helicopter company, so why not pamper mine.

Anyway, all the things Sparks and Richards were talking about were off in the future, and lately I'd been spending all my time trying to focus on existing in the current moment, trying to learn to live life like I was expecting to be gone to Glory Land just any ole time. My only concern at the time was for the LZ we were landing in right at the moment and forget about worrying about if the next LZ was going to be the hot one or not. If I was going to start thinking of future things, being back home in the World with my wife was certainly more appealing to ponder than army matters.

11

ACs Flew Left Seat:
Hello, Americal Division

You had to have 300 hours of combat flight time logged before you could become an aircraft commander. I was nearing that milestone, so I was started on AC training. That meant I moved over from flying in the right seat to the left seat because aircraft commanders flew in the left seat.

First Lt. Sparks started me off first. Initially, everything seemed sort of backward and awkward, but after a couple of days with Sparks, I got over the feeling that things were uncomfortably placed. Then I moved on to Leon Richards and spent a couple of days flying left seat with him. It was formation flying on combat assault, and after the missions, we practiced a few autorotations and the gamut of the book of emergency maneuvers.

Then it was a round with every other AC in our platoon, day after day. Each offered advice and gave plenty of criticism. It was an intense rite of passage that every prospective AC went through, and it was grueling and certainly stressful. It was expected that you would fly all day, no matter how long, 8 hours, 10 hours, 12 hours, and handled all radio communications, all crew instructions, all of everything, just the same way you would if you were having to fly alone with no other pilot there to help you with anything. All of the ACs wanted to have total confidence that you could handle every situation on your own, because there might come a time when the second pilot in your helicopter was knocked out of commission and you would have to fly him to a hospital.

Some ACs liked to screw with me when I was flying. While we were in formation, they'd chop the throttle to simulate an engine failure over jungle then scream about where you gonna autorotate, where you gonna land? Hard questions with no good answers available, because truth was over the jungle with no motor we're going in, going to crash in the trees. Might as well kiss your ass good-bye. But, hey, crashing "don't mean nothing," because you're already Dead anyway, remember, now or in 40 or 50 or 60 years, max.

Twenty-three-year-old Ed Denny in May 1970 as he began his transition training of flying in the left seat, the Aircraft Commander's seat, as he took the last steps to becoming the latest incarnation of a long line of men to carry the radio call sign of Hornet 33.

When I was about halfway finished with my AC training, Lt. Sparks gave me an assignment to ferry an old worn-out helicopter to Da Nang with a pilot from maintenance and exchange the old one, then bring back a nice new chopper from the depot. They needed someone who was left-seat qualified because the maintenance officer was not left-seat experienced. Lt. Sparks was pressed too tight with Maximum Effort missions to be able to let an aircraft commander go away for that long, because it would surely be at least a three or four day round trip. So Lt. Sparks decided to send me as his best available solution to the problem. And if he decided that I was left-seat qualified, then I was. He called the shots about things like that.

When we started our trip, we had barely flown the 40 miles to Saigon before the maintenance officer said we had to stop for required repairs and we'd have to lay over for a while. Poor pitiful me, that was definitely too hard to take, stuck in Saigon overnight, but what could a body do? We spent the night in downtown Saigon and had a dinner of Vietnamese food and whiskey, then went to see some go-go girls in a nightclub. At the end of the evening, buzzing pretty good from all our drinks, we went to bed at a bachelor officer's quarters (BOQ), but after curfew there was a frantic banging on our room door. Our door-gunner was there, and he was nearly in tears: our crew chief was missing in the Cholon District of Saigon. He had gone off with a woman, but he never came back to meet the door-gunner as he promised. The two enlisted crewmen agreed to stay with the girls just a couple of hours, but by then he'd been gone a couple of hours longer than that. I flashed a picture in my mind of our guy sprawled out in some garbage-can filled alley with his dumb-assed throat cut from ear to ear or worse.

We had to dodge patrolling MPs the whole time we chased around pitch-black Cholon alleys riding in bicycle-powered rickshaws looking for our missing man, and I had plenty of pictures dancing around in my head of all four of us Hornets found at dawn with cut throats. It took over an hour before the door-gunner recognized the place where they'd split up. From there, we started a search and went door to door calling out, "Come out Joe." I figured he was probably already deader than a damned doornail, but to my surprise and great relief, finally, there he was, naked as a jaybird and wrapped in only a little bitty bath towel, staggering drunk, out of his head, with his arm draped around a young party girl, and grinning like a possum eating grapes. Obviously he'd been having a big ole party.

The girl giggled and said, "He so used up. Which of you take his place 'til morning? Me tighter than 12-year-old girl, and me love you long time, G.I., and give you everything you ever wanted from girl, G.I." Oh, yeah, I was sure all of that was true, Sweetheart, but we had an early-morning call coming, so it was our beddy-bye time. Yeah, I understand; we number-ten G.I.; berry bad customers.

Our trip to Da Nang took nearly a whole week. Maintenance issues followed wherever we went. There was a night spent in Phan Rang, and another layover in Nha Trang. Finally, we arrived at Marble Mountain on the south side of Da Nang. Then there were three days at Marble Mountain waiting around for our new helicopter. Marble Mountain was an enclave where the Hornets had a sister company that we shared nothing in common with. The "Black Cats" had once been a combat assault company just like the Hornets, but by 1970 they were strictly a VIP outfit that flew generals, both American and South Vietnamese, and other VIPs around the battlefield. They weren't very likely to get too close to any hot action when they were hauling General Westmoreland or Secretary of Defense Robert McNamara or curious members of the U.S. senate.

Their helicopters and equipment were all brand new. Their living quarters and the Officers' club would have pleased Conrad Hilton. Flying troops into combat was no longer their game. Considering they were pilots in a war, they had a pretty sweet Georgia peach, as good as anything to be found in Vietnam, just flying generals around. Plus, there were plenty of nurses at China Beach, right next door. Every single night at the nurses' Officers' club it was the same scene: young, beautiful, intelligent, lonely women needing a strong shoulder where they could rest their head, find companionship to remind them of home, or maybe a little affection if a guy got lucky. A nurse might be looking for a handsome man with silver wings and maybe they could use a Black Cat. At least that was everyone's fantasies about the nurses: lonely, horny, and needing a pilot to help them through the dark night.

The funny part about the Black Cats, they all looked like someone's clone project, all perfect, sent over from central casting: Robert Redford, at the least a young Paul Newman. Not one Tweedle-Dee or Tweedle-Dum in the whole outfit. And they were every one of them great pilots, at least that's what they all professed loudly with plenty of nonstop talk about flying in the *"WAR!"* Every story always topped the previous one. You wanted to talk about invading Cambodia? Couldn't compare to the A-Shau Valley. A-Shau been the shits since '66, and Khe Sanh Valley, God knows, worst sort of hell since '68. That "friendly fire" chaos at the river at the Cambodian border—guess what, same sort of shit happened on the DMZ at Con Thien, but a lot worse than anything that happened in Cambodia. There was this B-52 strike, 6 airplanes instead of just a little bit of artillery fire, and a whole battalion of Green Marines caught out in the open, but their commander was a New Guy and he didn't know how to call the forward air controller, so bombs fell on American Marines for a very long five full minutes. By the time the bombing was ending, every damn general in I Corps was on the radio cussing, screaming: Marines, air force, and army, all of 'em. That very same day, everything went quiet, and nobody ever heard a peep about the mistaken bombing! Getting to know the Black Cats was a trip into the heart of crazy land where everyone had delusions of some sort, about nurses or something else.

But when we got back to Cu Chi after being away, on our landing approach we could see all the Hornet helicopters were there at the Hornets' Nest in the middle of the day. There were people scrambling around, scurrying everywhere, and we wondered what the commotion might be. Obviously, this was something very unordinary. On a normal day, anything flyable would be flying. We hovered our new helicopter to maintenance and landed it over at the hangar. The Hornets' Nest at Cu Chi was totally ablaze with wild rumors!

But before I could shut our helicopter down, a maintenance captain came out and said, "Leave it running. Gotta service it then turn it around for a long trip."

We asked what was going on.

"Packing up. The Hornets are moving."

Where? Nobody was saying. Brass was totally mum. Just that it's I Corps, that's all. Maybe "Hot Dang" or "Poon Tang" up by Da Nang. Supposed to leave in a day or two.

With the big Cambodian adventure done, we were expecting something, so the Hornets' leaving Cu Chi wasn't that much of a surprise. But we weren't expecting such short notice or the other big news: the 25th Infantry, the whole division, was leaving Vietnam totally, going *HOME, back to the Hawaiian Islands!* If they were sending the whole 25th Division home, Washington was serious about getting out of this quagmire war soon!

So the Hornets were going up to I Corps, oh, yeah, always the stepchild and always the damned expendables. In Cambodia, we were first in, leading every combat assault, and we cut the path for everyone the whole damned time for the duration of that invasion. That had cost us two crews, seven KIA Hornets. Tip of the spear, that lot in life was okay; we wouldn't have had it any other way. The going gets tough, call the Hornets. You need some ass kicked, call the Hornets. But leaving home, leaving the Hornets' Nest behind us? The 116th AHC had been based at Cu Chi for five years and had made everything homey: hooches broken into little cubicles, TVs, air conditioning, a big swimming pool, sofas, refrigerators, stereo reel-to-reel tape machines, and even a volley ball court. Believe it, if it could be had the Hornets had it, all the comforts of home.

The Hornets going to I Corps, wow, and flying in the mountains, wow! We were rice paddy experts. We could dig 'em out of rubber plantations or chase 'em out of spider holes and make 'em run out of tree lines. But mountains—let's think that over. I'd just flown hundreds of miles all the way up the coast to Da Nang and back, and we didn't see too damn many places that looked very good for the Hornets' sort of flying. There wasn't much flat land, and it wasn't natural Hornet Country.

The biggest shock of all, 1st Lt. Sparks was gone from the Hornets! He had left the day before. We were going to I Corps but without Sparks. Gone? Sparks was gone: you could have knocked me over with a feather. We all knew Sparks had to be getting short, but no one really knew when he would actually be leaving. What would our platoon do without someone like Sparks around to run everything? He had been so short he was given the choice of moving north with the Hornets or going to Long Binh to finish his last few days at the First Aviation Brigade Headquarters. In Vietnam, the only constant was that everything changed when you were least expecting it. So Sparks was gone and I never even had the chance to say good-bye or anything. I just stood there breathless and tried to process the information and all the implications for the Wasp Platoon.

Who's the new platoon leader? Nobody yet! Everything was happening too damn fast, and the brass couldn't handle every little thing all at once. A new platoon leader would be named in a few days after we got relocated.

Okay, word's out: *Chu Lai was our destination,* and we go tomorrow. *Chu Lai:* flew over it just after dawn that day, right on the coast, right smack on the beach. The 23rd Infantry, the American Division, was located at Chu Lai. If that was where we were going, God help us. The American had been caught shooting women and children in ditches at My Lai. We wouldn't fit in. The Hornets' kills were always clean. Bad Guys, yes, but women, no, and children, never. If you were shooting women and little children in ditches, then put me in the goddamned ditch with them. If that was what this sorry damned war had become, put me in the ditch with the women and let me stand with them.

I questioned the Vietnam War before I came, and I still philosophically opposed it; but there I was in the middle of it and trying to do my best. But none of that was what I thought about. I was there and I had my job, my responsibilities, my friends, my buddies. Each of them was a good guy, and there was no one I disliked. I look back now, 45 years later, and they were each a special breed of man. We would be the American's new red-headed stepchild, since that choice was already made for us. But the Hornets were clean and had always been clean, totally clean. Killers, we were killers for sure, no way to deny that. But ditches? We wouldn't turn a blind eye to that stuff. Shooting women and children in ditches, every Hornet that I knew would line up between any damned infantry and innocent children or women, and you would have to go through them to get anyone to shoot—and good luck with that sort of crap.

Flying for the American may not have been our first choice, or even on our short list, but the army wasn't about choices. Following orders was the organizational foundation of the whole army, every aspect of the military rested on that fundamental and basic premise. Follow Orders, give a Sharp Salute, and loudly say, "Yes, Sir!" No questions, no "Why" or "What for?" If the military wanted you to have an opinion, they'd give you one. If they wanted any damned questions, they'd tell you they wanted questions. Did you hear anyone requesting questions? American Division, I Corps, Mountains, Chu Lai: "If I die flying the mountain zone, box me up, send me home. Pin my wings on my chest. Tell my Momma I did my best."

With our helicopters loaded to the roofs we looked like a bunch of gypsies escaping from the dust bowl in Oklahoma back in the '30s. The Hornets were a big swarming flock of helicopters filling the sky and blotting out the sun. We flew from Central III Corps down in the south up the long length of South Vietnam to coastal I Corps and landed at Chu Lai proudly and brazenly trailing red, yellow, green, and purple smoke.

Our new Company Area had formerly housed an engineering outfit and—talk about being picked clean to the carcass bones—the engineers had left nothing of any use. Man, oh man, all the buildings had been stripped totally bare, but out the backdoor of our future homes a sandy beach was just a few steps away, the South China Sea right there, all our own. Only problem was, we were a zillion miles from our flight line, which totally sucked. How would we get out to our helicopters to fly every day? What sort of a damned idiot came up with that idea? Yeah, the Americal Division.

The Company Area had nothing: no showers, almost no latrine, just a solitary two-hole outhouse, and no Officers' club or Enlisted Club. There was not even a damned mess hall for us, nothing. Just bare hooches with bunks, but nothing sandbagged at all. The word "bare" didn't accurately convey the conditions of the hooches we had. Outer walls: just thin plywood on two-by-fours with wire screens for the upper portion of the walls and shutters that closed over the screens. A kid's damned BB gun could blow holes through it. The interior of the hooches were open-bay single rooms with eight bunks. The mattresses were thin bags of wadded-up lumps of some sort of stuffing.

A mortar shell or damned rocket hitting anywhere nearby would totally shred anyone inside those flimsy hooches, and there was only one single sandbagged bunker for the whole area that maybe could hold 20–25 people, and that was it. One little bunker, when what we needed was shelter for a company of over 250 men. Any damned incoming at night, and we were totally screwed.

Larry Hood and I were nearly finished with our aircraft commander transitioning, so we were put in the AC hooch with Leon Richards, Roger Walker, Dennis Plumber, Gary Newton, Austin Scarborough, and a real short-timer guy, his name gone in my old age. We had three or four other ACs, but they were all short-timers, too, going home soon, and they were given quarters in another hooch that actually had a few rooms that had been added on to the building. Seniority had its privileges.

We were given two days to get the place whipped into shape before our aircraft commanders were supposed to start flying orientation flights with other Americal helicopter units. So we had two days to get the new Company Area transformed. Red-headed stepchild didn't come close to describing how we were being treated by being quartered in such a skeletonized Company Area. No mess hall? Sorry. A unit nearby, some rear-echelon infantry unit, would "allow" us to eat at their mess hall. Thanks for the offer, but it didn't take long to figure out exactly how screwed we were on that deal!

They must have thought we were idiots who wouldn't notice a big problem the first time we saw the operations hours for the infantry mess hall. It didn't seem to be a problem for the Americal Division that their mess hall didn't open until after we were long gone flying on our day's missions or that it closed before we returned at night. Their hours might've worked for our ground support people who were around the Hornet Company Area all day, but our flight crewmen were left out in the cold to go hungry or fend for themselves. So if you were planning on a mess hall meal, sorry, but you were totally screwed on that deal. At lunch, obviously, we were many miles away.

That meant the aviator Hornets depended on C-Rations for every meal multiple days, or even a week, at a time. That situation never changed, not for the rest of my tour, although it was complained about endlessly. Long Range Recon Patrol (LRRP) rations became a favorite treat, and packages of food from home seemed like Christmas morning, when they came, which was not often enough.

At the American Division Officers' club, supper was probably just a toaster item, maybe a grilled ham-n-cheese sandwich, but it was as good as Thanksgiving Day's dinner when you'd had nothing to eat but C-Rations for five or six days straight. Craziest thing was, on single-ship missions, we were often flying hot meals and iced beer to the infantry grunts out in the field, while we ate C-Rations dating from the Korean War. Bless the Army Supply System, 20-year-old cold Spaghetti, yuck, not so good! Hey, Mr. Jangles, please, pass that Tabasco hot sauce over here, one more time.

Getting back and forth to the flight line? Our brass had a simple answer for that: Shuttle truck service. Better not be late for the morning truck, or if you came in late in the day and missed the last evening truck you might be stuck on the flight line a lot longer than you wanted.

The only positive aspect of our Chu Lai Company Area: merely a few steps out the back door of our hooch the ocean surf broke on a sandy beach. Everyone thought that was a great deal, man, oh man, our personal tropical resort, our own personal beach, and no one else was there crowding things up after a hot, miserable day of flying. Wouldn't it be great to just jump into the breaking waves? Where could we get surf boards? Wouldn't a speed boat flip everyone out? Hell, just rubber inner tubes! We all ran and jumped in the surf for the first time, then we found out that the *water was oilier than a damned can of Pennzoil!* We looked out in the harbor and saw an oil tanker sitting there, evidently offloading a shipment of aviation jet fuel that day. Guess they had a small spill. Then we learned that those tankers were out there every single day, one after another. The offloading stopped only long enough to hook up a new tanker. Our damned ocean surf was oily most days for our stretch of beach. There were only three levels of pollution for any given day: standard pollution, heavier pollution, and maximum pollution. The oily ocean sucked. Our Company Area being so far away from our flight line sucked. Having no mess hall sucked. Just about every item you could think of about being in Chu Lai sucked, but it didn't matter because "Vietnam don't mean nothing."

So, here we were in Chu Lai, Vietnam, and the creator of our little universe was gone. He had made everyone into his own image some ways. For a few days, the Wasp Platoon was leaderless and lost. First Lt. Sparks was gone. Still, the Wasps coasted along on the path he'd set us on. We'd be okay.

12

Shoot at a Hornet, You Die

O ur gunship platoon, the Stingers, had a rule: "Shoot at a Hornet, you die." The local Bad Guys—the damned Viet Cong, and some North Vietnamese Army cadres around Chu Lai—had no experience with us, none, and they knew nothing about us or the Hornets' rules. We realized that it would take them a while to learn.

Our ACs had taken orientation rides, and seen the countryside, seen the mountains. They flew a couple of days with some different American Helicopter Units, Missions out in Indian Country, and they made the rounds of the Firebases and some of the LZs in our new operating area. Then our full Wasp Platoon had our first mission, and we flew to a village south of Chu Lai, a little Infantry extraction, just pick up some troops and bring them back to Chu Lai—that was all, real simple stuff. But when our Wasp Formation Flight touched down in the landing zone, some VCs started dropping damned mortars right in the middle of our helicopters as we sat in the LZ waiting for the infantry guys to get aboard our choppers. The grunts seemed to be taking forever! The goofy American grunts were shooting into the bushes in every direction while they were backing up toward our helicopters, blasting away with all of their guns at once. Some of them were doing their best John Wayne and firing from the hip, shooting at nothing—because there was nothing there, only ghosts! Damn mortars falling in pairs; that was the PROBLEM, not ghosts. And we needed to get out of there before the Cong actually hit something. We could see the guys firing at us about 150 yards away, working two tubes, half-a-dozen guys firing as fast as they could go—Whomp, Whomp! A Stinger gunship rolled in on them, rockets away. The mortars were still briefly flying, but it would be the end of that little story real damned soon.

The trail ship called out over the radio when he was loaded, and the flight leader immediately lifted off for the sky. The whole Hornet flight was up and out as a single unit, gone, but six American infantry grunts were still back in the goddamned LZ, shooting the hell out of their imagined ghosts in the bushes. The damned fools hadn't gotten on their helicopter when they should have because they were having too much fun playing Sgt. York or Audie Murphy or something. At that moment, all of the Hornets had a collective opinion of the Americal grunts who were still in the damned LZ: dumb son of a bitches. We were going to have to go back into a stinking hot LZ to pick them up. We wondered what else besides mortars the Bad Guys had in the way of armaments to blast away at us?

Okay, we had to circle back around, land again, and pick the Yahoos up. One ship could have done it alone, but the whole flight went in hot, door guns roaring. Twelve door guns were sure a lot better than a single ship landing alone. Okay, Audie Murphy and his buddies were onboard, damned LZ was finally empty, so let's fly. The mortar boys had all been dispatched. There were just some smoking holes where the Bad Guys had been firing from. They were sure brazen, right there in broad daylight on the edge of this little ordinary village. It was amazing how they showed themselves out in the open when there were gunships circling overhead above their location.

As we were returning to Chu Lai, a radio message instructed us to land back at our Company Area after dropping off the infantry guys. We were finished flying for the day. Roger that. One sortie and done? What's up? *What's up?* Americal's brass had absolutely blown up, and every bigwig around was totally out of their mind. You'd have thought Hornets had killed the Pope! Or rocketed tourists in St. Peter's Square! Or taken a collective dump on somebody's altar!

That little piece-of-shit village, that was My Lai? Really? Are you kidding me?

You mean the same My Lai where the Americal Division killed all those civilians? Something like 450 women and kids, and now your panties are in a wad just because our Stingers' gunships put a few rockets on some Bad Guys who shot at us from that village? The Stingers killed only Bad Guys, no one else, no BS *"Collateral Damage."* Bad Guys, broad daylight, out in the open, shooting mortars at a Hornet flight! Doesn't matter what village they're in, *shoot at a Hornet, you die, asshole.* Sounds just like a war, doesn't it? They shoot, we return fire, someone dies. Sounds like that's how war is done. That's how Hornets did their war. But at Americal, evidently, generals were fainting, and full-bird colonels were crapping in their pants. Since feces rolled downhill, it was piling up all around our commanding officer, our New Guy major.

So what if it was My Lai? They were shooting mortars at us from out in the open, and that made them Bad Guys. Case closed. Anyway, no one ever told us specifically that the Bad Guys had a free pass for the duration of the crazy Vietnam War at that stupid little village.

Hornets *GROUNDED*. That was case closed. Anything happening at My Lai required an investigation! Court-martials—you ever heard of that? That's one possibility for you cowboys, yeah, maybe! Ever heard of the Long Binh Jail? You can't go around killing people, without permission, just because you claim they're shooting at you! Gotta get permission! So, that's how it was, huh? That's bullshit! The Americal Division was in the middle of its own mess, and we'd stepped in it the first day we did anything. Grounded. Let's see how long that lasts.

We had plenty of other things that needed doing without flying. So we could use the time off. There were things like we had no showers or toilet facilities. Things like our platoon didn't have a small thing called a platoon leader, not since 1st Lt. Sparks had departed. No one had been officially appointed, so we were running around leaderless. Without our longtime platoon leader, Leon Richards was uniformly looked to as our unofficial leader since he was the company instructor pilot and the senior aircraft commander and a reformed Green Beret. What scheduling had to be done Leon pointed a finger at me and said, "Sparks told you that was your job."

We were in an awkward situation. We had 1st and 2nd lieutenants in our platoon, but none were aircraft commanders yet, so they really couldn't become our platoon leader. All of our ACs were warrant officers, and we had no captains in our platoon because Sparks was a 1st lieutenant and he couldn't be commanding a captain.

When Sparks left, we had no one to take over in his place. The Hornet Company had lots of captains, but they were all in other jobs. So during our "Grounded Time" we needed to get the company sorted out and some captain appointed to move into Sparks' old job, as the new Wasp Platoon leader. Spark's leaving had left a big hole. Three captains from our 1st Platoon (the Yellow Jackets) moved to new jobs, one as executive officer, another to full-time Air Mission commander, and a third to our platoon to be "Temporary Platoon Leader" because he wasn't an AC. I was named scheduling officer. No one complained about my becoming scheduling officer because, frankly, none of them wanted to do it, be at the operations shack every night till all hours of the night. Worse still, the job required that someone had to stay sober every night.

While we were grounded, the Stingers ACs had to get some Americal Division manners training with hours of "Rules of Engagement Orders" lectures. They even got little cards with the written rules for them to use: "Hey, Charlie, time-out, okay? Can you give me a minute to check this situation on my card?"

Rules? Stingers didn't need no stinking rules! They had one rule, a good one: "Shoot at a Hornet, you die, asshole." Want me to write that on an Ace of Spades, leave it for you, then you'll have your own card, Charlie?

The Stingers actually did operate under rules:

1. Protect yourself.
2. Protect your wingman.
3. Protect your unit.
4. Kill only the enemy, but kill all of the assholes, every damned one of them!
5. Let God sort them out.

Stinger Rules, easy to remember, worked well, and they saw no reason to change them. Worked well everywhere, all occasions, even rocket runs in downtown Saigon, 1968, during Tet, chasing Charlie through the streets and blowing their scrawny asses to hell.

America's Number One Rule that the Stingers hated the most: "Even if you're fired on, DO NOT ENGAGE ANY TARGET, unless you had prior approval from an American general officer—no exceptions." Oh, yeah, Yes, Sir, Salute *Real* Sharp to that one, Sir. *What were you gonna do if the Stingers chose to ignore that dumb-assed rule, send them to Vietnam as a punishment?*

The third day the Hornets were grounded the Americal-Division brass decided that the best way out of our little My Lai mess was for them to pass out decorations and awards for everyone from our platoon who flew that mission! Gallantry, Bravery, Service Above and Beyond! A big ceremony at our Hornets' Company Area! The whole Hornet Company in their best clothes and standing at attention in a full company formation, the proud heroes out front, standing tall, cameras flashing, medals pinned, hands shook, sharp salutes, congratulations, and thanks said. Distinguished Flying Crosses for the ACs. Air Medals with a V-device for the pilots. No court-martials, no Long Binh Jail. The little formal ceremony became an Official Welcoming Ceremony to bring the Hornets into the Americal Division. We'd be flying under the historic and widely decorated Southern Cross, and they loved getting the 116th AHC!

I was still flying left seat transition during that mission, practicing the AC role, but on the roster I was listed as *Pilot*. The mission aircraft commander never touched the controls once that day, but you can guess who got which medal. Our guys were very damn offended getting those medals in that way. A DFC had special meaning to pilots, and we felt that particular PR stunt stained them. The whole thing was a farce, a giant joke, and it sure proved *"Vietnam Don't Mean Nothing."*

The Americal brass were all decked out formally with their best clothes, their shiniest shoes, all of their fruit-salad ribbons, and their most photogenic and broadest smiles. There was plenty of punch and cookies, but no mess hall where we could sit someone down. Our CO, the major, walked the head Americal bigwig over to inspect our lone two-hole outhouse to see if we could get anything out of Americal. He started his sales pitch: "It would be nice if the Hornets didn't have to stand in line for 15 minutes waiting to take care of their business, only to find that they had just sat down in somebody else's wet-and-fresh sweaty butt-tracks." We were glad to get TWO more new outhouses, thank you, very much (we needed SIX). We were lucky to get even that much. We were not a part of the Americal Division. We were First Aviation Brigade and the 269th Combat Aviation Battalion, the Black Barrons, and we were only *attached* to the Americal, not *assigned* to them and thus not an organic part of the division. So they didn't really care much one way or the other about where we took our dumps.

But we were glad to be back in the better graces of the Americal Division so the Hornets could start flying again, because being stuck on the ground made all our pilots start getting real jumpy.

New Platoon
Leader *Temporary*

Our platoon, the 2nd Platoon "Wasps" had a new platoon leader, even if only temporarily. He was a captain, formerly of the 1st Platoon "Yellow Jackets." Of all the captains the Hornets Company had, he possessed the most senior date of rank, so he was king of the hill. He was a super nice guy, and everyone who came into contact with him found him to be a personable man, which was not always the case with career army officers, not at all. The only problem with him was that he had not yet achieved AC status, which was an important problem. As merely a pilot, he couldn't lead the Wasp flight on combat missions, which meant he couldn't lead the platoon in general. When we were on the ground, there was no problem with his being in charge, but not in the air. The army had ranks for people and we all understood where everyone was in the hierarchy of everything. But aviators had their own hierarchy for how things stacked up when it came to flying. In a helicopter, a warrant officer could be an aircraft commander flying with a captain as his pilot, and the warrant officer would be the one in charge: he was the commander. Having this transferred captain as our new platoon leader created an awkward situation, but we soon found that he was a very smart guy, someone we could look up to generally.

The very first day that he was a Wasp, he called a meeting with our aircraft commanders and told them that he was the new platoon leader and he was in charge, but that as a pilot he still had a lot to learn—a lot. And it was each of their jobs to take him as a student, be a tutor to him, teach him, and make him as good as they were. His little sales pitch impressed all the aircraft commanders, and he won them over, each and every one. They had never seen a hard-bar officer be so honest, so grounded that he could admit that he needed some sort of help. At least he wasn't trying to pull off any of that "fake-it-till-you-make-it" bullshit. They embraced him on first impression and took him in, so the rest of the platoon had to follow their lead.

Okay, he was a smart guy, someone to look up to. Probably someone had told him this was the way to get things done. So the rules were plainly laid out for everyone. On the ground he was the boss. But in the air the warrant officers would be the bosses. The Wasps could comfortably work with that. They would teach him "Combat Flying," flying Hornet style, flying Wasp style.

Now back at Fort Wolters, in Mineral Wells, flight school for warrant officer candidates was a two-prong deal that involved simultaneous basic officer training, along with helicopter flight training. In either one, if you screwed up you were gone fast, buddy. No slack, screw up any, and you're gone. If you couldn't fly, sorry, you were gone. Didn't catch on to things quick enough, you were gone. On the basic officer training side, if you didn't look quite right, polish your shoes just exactly the right way, display your locker completely perfectly, you might be gone. At Fort Wolters, they took whatever they were given, pressed them through a very fine screen and passed along the best and ditched all the rest. Except, maybe, just maybe, commissioned officer flight students had things easier. After all, they were already army officers, men already proven, lifer career men, good men just out of OCS, hot young stallions. They drove Corvettes, lived off base, and had all of Mineral Wells' young women at their doorstep around the clock.

At Fort Wolters there was a little bit of the attitude of don't mess up the young officer's career and he'll probably catch on farther down the road. So, after a few days, our ACs figured out our new platoon leader was one of those guys. No matter how much he might have wanted, flying wasn't his deal. He had two left hands and two left feet. He was obviously a very smart guy and someone to admire, and he was clearly trying his best, but in formation flying he jumped around like a grasshopper on a very hot rock. Going Point A over to Point B, he couldn't stay very straight and level, no matter how hard he tried. Within three or four days, our ACs saw why he hadn't gotten his AC status before. He would have been fine in the infantry, artillery, armor, any army branch—because he was a very smart guy—but why aviation? It was tough for anyone who was a pilot when flying came hard to them. He wanted to learn, was an eager student, but he had no natural ability.

But this was a hard time, with everyone learning new ways to do things, learning mountain flying. Mountains, mountains, everywhere mountains. The LZs were all on tiny little pinnacles. There were no nice big rice paddies, no flat land, and no big formations of Hornets coming in tightly grouped with all their guns blazing away, unless we were somewhere right along the coast. In the mountains, it was one-at-a-time daisy-chain formations and single ship landings. And the mountains around Chu Lai weren't little, but big and tall, high up, real mountains covered in totally dense jungle.

So the situation we were in was stressful for everyone, including our new platoon leader. At first, I never fully understood why he was appointed to our platoon with the title "Temporary" Platoon Leader. That seemed to automatically undermine his authority, but nothing had to make sense to me, because I was at the bottom of the chain of command and the brain pool. Then in a short time, we got three New Guys in the company, and they all came to our platoon. They were all hard-bar officers: a young captain and two 1st lieutenants. It appeared that the newly acquired young captain was in line to take over the platoon as soon as Captain Temporary was gone.

Then it was apparent what the brass wanted. They had some job for our Captain Temporary, and they wanted someone to bestow aircraft commander status on him since 1st Platoon wouldn't do it. What our Captain Temporary needed was simple: four or five days of flying with Steve Chasin. The captain needed to learn the "Zen of Helicopter Flying," Steve's wacky hippie crap that worked. However, none of our ACs had ever flown with Steve when he was the teacher. They'd flown with him only when he was the student, just a pilot learning from them. There was also the slight problem of Steve's being dead, so he couldn't help anyone with their flying.

Our company instructor pilot, Leon Richards, flew with Captain Temporary day after day for a solid week then gave him an AC check ride, pass-or-fail. Leon bypassed the traditions of having each aircraft commander fly with a potential new AC candidate or even having any vote on the issue. Leon passed the guy. It was his decision, and his name was on the line on the army's paperwork, and, just like that, Captain Temporary was out of our platoon. Next step was to find out what the deal was with our new young Wasp captain and what sort of platoon leader he intended to be. He looked just like a kid who was in my high school chemistry class, and he looked about that age, too.

Now that the Hornets were Heroes again (with all their new medals) and welcomed back into America's good graces, we were flying missions daily, doing combat assaults into the valleys, or on the top of the mountains, landing one ship at a time. Out in the boondocks, we were still getting shot at way too much. The Chu Lai territory Bad Guys hadn't learned about the Hornets: "Shoot at a Hornet, you die, no exceptions."

Their Americal Manners Lesson did nothing for the Stinger gunship pilots, who stayed the same as they ever had been: Gunships did their work, *then* a Stinger might call for permission if the situation allowed that, and the Americal Division pretended they didn't know Hornet Stingers had been shooting up their whole area of operations. The Stingers couldn't help being raised as shooters more than talkers. So the Hornets were maintaining an uneasy balance with the Americal Division when we heard the whole company was to attend a briefing the next day. We figured it was to hear about court-martials and going to the Long Binh Jail again, the sort of saber rattling over something the Stingers had done that had pissed off Division. Let 'em bring it, we don't care, "Vietnam don't mean nothing."

KHAM DUC BRIEFING,
LETTERS HOME

Kham Duc was a place I'd never heard of. I suppose that was for very good reasons, because during the Tet Offensive of 1968—the widespread attacks launched by the Viet Cong all across South Vietnam—the battle for Kham Duc was the only clear victory for the North Vietnamese Army forces and their local allies. A full division of NVA soldiers attacked Kham Duc and quickly captured it in a lightning-fast two-day-long battle, killing about 300 Americans and over 1,000 South Vietnamese troops and civilians. Two C130 Air Force planes were shot down trying to get in and out of Kham Duc, one that had 150 evacuees on board and all of them killed in the crash. At the height of the battle, the air force pilot of the last plane to land at Kham Duc to rescue evacuees took off as crazed NVA soldiers overran the airfield and he was awarded the Medal of Honor. Altogether, the air force and army combined lost nine aircraft shot down in the two-day battle and evacuation. The next day, B52 bombers filled the sky over the Kham Duc Airfield and dropped a zillion pounds of bombs on the area. I imagine that the NVA victory party turned into an unexpected visit to the Pits of Hell when the B52s came and rained death on every Bad Guy near the place.

Kham Duc was located basically due west of Chu Lai, way out next to the Laotian border, an airfield runway and base camp in a little valley surrounded by tall mountains. Tall, like seven- and eight-thousand-feet tall. In many ways it was like Dien Bien Phu, but no one liked that comparison at all. It was a particularly dangerous place, with mountains much bigger and taller and nearer than the mountains I later saw around Khe Sanh.

But I'd never heard about any of that until the Hornets were given a briefing by some Americal Division bigwigs. For over two years, Kham Duc had been in the hands of the North Vietnamese, from 1968 till then—the summer of 1970. Americal was going to take it back, take back control of that large section of southwestern I Corps along the border that was supposed to be under their general purview, take it back with a combat assault of a combined group of helicopter companies. Guess who was going to *lead the charge*? For the Hornets, everything was clearly the same as ever: we were the first to go in. If the Hornets got through the initial landing okay, the American could then relax and push some of their own units in. If the Hornet's assault went sour, they could simply cool their jets and pull back from any battle. For the American it would be no harm no foul because the Hornets weren't on their books anyway. The Hornets would be just some more 1st Aviation Brigade losses, so no worry.

We had this briefing team comprised of full-bird colonels, lt. colonels, and majors. American brass were everywhere, some even with silver aviator wings, but mostly our briefers were straight-legged infantry guys. They had easels, maps, big photographs, and poster boards with written information galore. They were sure that any NVA at Kham Duc would be unprepared since total military surprise was assured for our side. But the American Division didn't really know what to expect, because they had no good current intelligence on the situation around Kham Duc. They hadn't done any reconnaissance there for a good long while because they didn't want to tip their hand about the pending attack. So the extent of resistance waiting for us was an unknown.

Now the NVA probably expected that someday an American attack would certainly come. After all, the U.S. wasn't going to allow them to stay there forever. But they had no way of knowing when an attack might come. So surprise was on our side. Not one Hornet believed a single damned word of the Americal Division's BS. The briefers said Americal might not know what to expect but resistance should be only "light" to "moderate" and the Hornets should expect nothing more than basically acceptable losses. Now that they were talking expected losses, the Hornet attention level perked up immediately and immensely. Just exactly what did Americal consider "basically acceptable losses"? We knew what the Hornet level was! *Zero!* Anything above that, NOT acceptable! None of the Hornets was willing to die for damned South Vietnam and not for that damned war. We were perfectly willing to make Bad Guys die for their war. That was okay with us. But Hornet aviators dying—nope, no way in hell. Anyway, this damned war was already over. We knew that. The war was OVER! It just hadn't stopped yet and would not for at least two more years. But the U.S. was already actively leaving as soon as they could. Everyone also knew that. Hell, it was all over the damned TV every night. (Even if we got programs on a one-week delayed basis, we had our TV.)

So what the hell was "light" and what the hell was "moderate" to the Americal Division? The officer giving the briefing wouldn't give a straightforward answer to that question, but he had a chart on an easel that said equipment losses could be 10 to 30 percent and personnel losses were forecast at between 5 and 20 percent! Holy crap! Twenty percent was an acceptable personnel loss? *NOT okay* from the Hornet perspective! You people are frigging crazier than hell! Damned D-Day losses on the beaches at Normandy weren't 20 percent! Kham Duc, a place you'll totally abandon as soon as the weather turns bad, but you wanna take it anyway, just because Americal got whipped there? Got your asses totally handed to you, and Americal fled the battle in two days. Now you don't want to leave Vietnam without getting some payback for that loss that's been stuck in your craw for two years now. Guess you want to come roaring in there with a big air assault, all guns blazing and flags waving.

If you wanted the place so damned much, why didn't Americal put B52 strikes on Kham Duc for three days, then a solid carpet of napalm and artillery around the clock, nonstop a couple of more days, then maybe—maybe— helicopters bringing in infantry troops to finish the deal. So I wondered at the time why anyone would want to initiate that battle with a helicopter assault inserting infantry troops without first prepping the landing zone area with bombs and artillery. But Americal wasn't wanting to chase anyone out of Kham Duc. Just the opposite. They didn't want them out, they wanted to catch them there. Americal was willing to take losses, OUR losses, on an initial combat assault in order to catch the NVA and lock them into a big bloody infantry fight.

Some of the Hornets asked those sorts of questions, but the Americal mind was made up. They said they'd considered everything for months, and a combat assault was what they were going to do. Months, you say? And you think the NVA didn't know every detail about your plans by then? You people are frigging crazier than hell!

They had a chaplain close the briefing with a Warrior's Prayer and some warm-n-fuzzy advice: "Boys, be good and write a letter home, what might be a last letter, to Mom, or your wife, or your best girlfriend." That was a sobering dose of reality: those Americal gentlemen really did think that there was a chance for the Hornets to receive "basically acceptable losses"! During the combat assault they would all perform their battlefield duties and listen to the radio chatter or any battlefield status reports from the comfort of their leather chairs behind their desks in the Americal Division headquarters offices back in Chu Lai. But their concern shown for us was touching. However, their chaplain jabbering on about "Writing Last Letters Home" was over-the-top melodrama that wasn't comforting. Hey, back at home they would figure out that it was the last letter when no other letters ever arrived. Then I guess there would be a knock on the door, with two military officers there delivering a sad message from the army about your family member. It just sorta worked that way, friend.

I sleeplessly tossed and turned most of that long night, guts tied in a hard knot, kept awake wondering what morning might bring. I hadn't written any "Last Letter Home" or any sort of that nonsense to be mailed only in the event of my death, but the chaplain did succeed in making me dwell on home and my previous life with my wife, contemplate the course of my life up to that point in time, and wonder what would be in my future, assuming that I had a future beyond Vietnam. After being a warrant officer in the army for a while, I could see that playing the role of a little pawn in someone else's larger game wasn't going to be anything I could be happy with for the long term. Being in a situation where you had no control whatsoever over anything that was happening all around you was also an extremely unpleasant existence, and I wanted to escape that as soon as possible. I thought about dead men I felt had died in my place: McDonald and Smith and Smitty. I wallowed in my emersion bath of survivor's guilt and self-doubt about my worthiness to even be alive or my potential to make something out of myself and to add to the overall improvement of mankind or even as much as a single person. Things would have been so much easier if I could have just explored memories of making love with my wife, but that wasn't my luck. So I just tossed and turned, and the night slowly passed.

Coffee and hardtack C-Ration crackers and Vienna sausage served as breakfast. The sun would be coming up soon. The eastern horizon was glowing yellow and pink, and it was time for everyone to fire up their choppers to go take Kham Duc back from the damned Bad Guys.

In the cool predawn air, the two Hornet Slick flights, Wasps and Yellow Jackets, were flying in signature Hornet formation style: super tight, very close, and very concise. We'd put up every flyable helicopter, seven Wasps and eight Yellow Jackets, plus six Stinger gunships, two heavy gun teams. We didn't know what we were flying into, but we were going out to Kham Duc and the U.S. Army was going to reoccupy that place one way or another. If the NVA were waiting there fully prepared for us and ready for a fight, we were bringing it to them.

To avoid having a single large armada spotted headed out west, the three separate assault companies approached a rendezvous point from different directions. The Hornets were to be the first going in, and the two Americal companies would follow right behind us. We were winding around mountain peaks, weaving down the valleys, and getting closer and closer to the Laotian border, pure Indian Country. Americal infantry forces hadn't been out here in a long time. This area wasn't contested. The NVA controlled this area and had for the last two years.

We were flying at 3,000 feet and mountain peaks still rose up above us on both sides. It had been triple canopy jungle everywhere for many miles already, no place for a forced landing without going into the trees, a hard crash assured. This was not a place conducive to helicopters. We were well past Firebase Siberia going west, and the Americal didn't call it Siberia for no reason. It was the last American outpost, the final frontier before flying up to the Laotian border. If you went down out there, the jungle would just swallow you up, unless your crash burned a hole big enough that it could be seen in an aerial photo. Otherwise, there was no hope of your remains ever being found. If you survived the crash and wanted to survive the total ordeal, you'd walk out however many miles you had flown in to that nightmare.

On the radio, the air mission commander told us we were four minutes out. "Begin an approach descent, and you'll see Kham Duc in two more minutes."

I was flying with Roger Walker that day, a pure Texas good ole boy from Arlington. Even though this was an AC check ride, Roger wanted to be in the left seat. He'd said that he felt more secure flying there. As we neared Kham Duc, I looked at him and saw he was unhooking his seat belt harness. I wondered what the hell he was doing. Then he threw off his shoulder straps and started climbing out of his seat. God, was he gonna jump out of our damned helicopter?

Asked myself, *You kidding me? Don't do it! What the hell am I supposed to do?*

He started to stand up in the doorway.

"Hey, Roger, don't jump, man, don't jump!" I yelled into the intercom in a panic.

His first foot stepped out onto the skid. Roger answered back, "I ain't jumping out."

Now he was fully out on the skid, the wind whipping furiously in his flight suit. I fought the helicopter to hold it in our spot in the formation while trying to watch Roger outside. He was out there with his 8mm movie camera, hanging on with one hand, shooting his camera with his other.

"I'm gonna film this," he said.

Lord, hang on, Roger!

We were flying at the back of the formation, descending through 2,000 feet, the Hornets flying so tight, so exact, and concise. Kham Duc was nestled in the valley spread out in front of us. We were approaching aligned with the runway on a steep descent, fast airspeed, going about 110 knots, really hot. The Yellow Jackets always loved this stuff. They were a bunch of cowboys at heart, hot-rodders, blitzing into LZs fast. Fast and steep, and I guess if an LZ ever called for that, obviously Kham Duc was the prime example.

With the Slicks on short final, the Stinger gunships started their rocket runs. Our flight leader called for Door-Guns Hot. Hornets were rocking and rolling then, full-blast mode. I looked over at Roger standing outside in the wind. He was filming me, and I gave him a salute. Damn, this was off the chart craziness. Rocket explosions filled the landing zone. They were intended to ensure the elimination of any booby traps. Nobody wanted to sit down on a mine. My guts were tied in knots. I'd been holding my breath for nearly a minute already, and every muscle in my body was tensed to the max. If any crap was going to hit the fan, it would be then, and Roger would have a great film of it.

We were landing both platoons simultaneously, heading for touchdown to the right side of the paved runway in the red dirt, because the Stinger rockets could eliminate traps better in the dirt than the pavement. *Boom, Boom, Boom, Boom,* rockets galore. The tail of my skids touched down, and we slid a few feet to a stop. The infantry grunts jumped off damn fast. The LZ was a chaos of explosions, incredibly loud, with a wall of rockets hitting on both sides of us. We barely came to a stop before we were already lifting off. I'd pulled in full power and we nosed over gaining speed fast, banked hard into a sharp left turn, and I was barely able to keep up with the formation. The flight climbed out at the power limit since everyone wanted to be out of the damned bowl we were in surrounded by mountain peaks.

Radio calls came from the grunts on the ground: "LZ cold so far. Say again, cold, cold."

I worked into my place in the formation. Roger was coming back in the helicopter. I was finally breathing again, deep breaths. "LZ cold" was the best news I could have expected to hear.

"Wow, what a ride!" Roger hollered. "What a fantastic movie I got!"

"Roger, you scared the shit out of me. I thought you were jumping out," I said in complaint.

He only laughed and said, "Didn't have a skydiving parachute or I might have."

I looked at him and said, "I didn't have heart attack pills, either."

Roger had always been crazy, a daredevil, but I never in my life expected such an over-the-top stunt as that. As he was buckling back up, I watched the Dolphin Company lifting out of the LZ, and the Third Company was on short final. Reports from the ground were that the LZ was still cold, no resistance. If there were any NVA there, they hadn't shown themselves yet. Still, we were departing using a different valley than the one we came in through. We didn't want to fly back over a track we had already flown over, and we were still far from safer territory. We needed to get away from that heavy jungle, away from the mountains around us as we were zipping through the valleys, avoiding the peaks above.

I was tremendously relieved: no resistance from any enemy on the ground, no RPGs or machine guns, no small-arms fire or mortars and rockets. The LZ was cold. There was hardly a phrase in pilot's language that was as sweet as "LZ cold." The Hornets had been in and out without getting shot all to pieces. I was also sure the Americal was totally disappointed that we had not caught a bunch of NVA at Kham Duc with their breakfast fires going, rice cooking, and their pants down, taking a morning dump, and their AK-47s stacked in little piles. If any were there, they weren't in the Kham Duc base proper, not out in the open. If anyone was there, they were probably in the close-by jungle and mountains. Anyway, we'd seen nothing to indicate that a large force of NVA was there, certainly not a division or anything like that.

But we were still not out of the woods altogether. We headed back to the staging area at Hawk Hill to refuel, reload, and then go back. We still had more loads of troops waiting for us, and we'd be hauling people and stuff to Kham Duc the rest of the day until dark and probably for days to come. We flew again way out over all that jungle, and on our second landing at Kham Duc Airfield we had a chance to look around some.

On the south side of the runway there was the tangled wreckage of a large air force plane. Couldn't tell what it had been, a C123 or a C130. There was just a shredded pile of aluminum and recognizable scraps of an aircraft: a tail section, burned-out bones of engines, and the outline of a fuselage. And there were piles of ashes that had been helicopters, one big enough to have been a Chinook. This had obviously been the site of death, American death, army, and air force.

The red-dirt dust kicked up by our rotor wash swirled in eddies that seemed to be ghosts twirling, dancing because someone had come to visit. Finally, some American brothers had come back! I could understand a little why Americal had been wanting this to be a fight, to have Bad Guys to kill for this. No number of dead NVA bodies lined up along the runway would be enough. So if it was not that day, someday soon there would be dead bodies for sure. Americal was at Kham Duc for blood. There would be blood, blood of dead NVA, with maggots crawling from their mouths and ears and eyes just like the dead VC I'd seen along the banks of that canal with Lt. Sparks my first few days of flying in Vietnam, which seemed to be infinitely long ago by this point in my tour. There was no doubt that there would be blood. The Americal Division had just put a large plate of bait out there in the middle of the jungle to try to draw the NVA into a fight: "Come on dudes, let's get it on!"

In the long run, the combat assault of Kham Duc Airfield served as an unfortunate template for future such operations. The fact that North Vietnam was not wanting to fight a big battle at Kham Duc just to please the Americal Division didn't mean they would behave the same at other places or at different times. What the template of Kham Duc did was to embolden all of the American and South Vietnamese war planners to envision future big combat assaults. The U.S. still wanted some payback for the siege American forces endured at the hands of the NVA at Khe Sanh in 1968. That big payback day surely would come. But this peaceful and quiet day at Kham Duc, the LZ was cold. What outcome could be better? We Hornets considered the assault of Kham Duc to yield "basically acceptable losses": *ZERO!* That was how the Hornets liked things: zero damned losses for our side.

15

AC TRANSITION, FINAL RIDE, DENNIS PLUMBER

Dennis Plumber was a hard-ass, old school and trained by 1st Lt. Sparks like all our ACs. He was getting to be a short-timer, so he tolerated no BS, no kidding around, all about business. That must have meant no pilots standing on the landing skids of the helicopter during combat assaults.

Around our hooch, in Chu Lai's sweltering heat, he sat in his army-green boxer shorts waxing his long handlebar mustache, which was bushy and magnificent. I pictured him as an English master sergeant serving in Zulu country in 1800s Africa. He never joined us playing tackle football out on the beach: crashing, smashing, brutally hard football. A bad enough broken leg was a sure-fire ticket out of Vietnam, maybe a hospital in Japan or the Philippines, maybe even stateside! But Dennis didn't play football; it might have messed up his mustache without yielding a broken leg.

Dennis smoked a Sherlock Holmes curved pipe while sitting in his boxer shorts, skinny as a rail and totally untanned, pale as a dried-up corpse in a funeral home. With all his personal quirks, he came off as an oddball eccentric—but, man oh man, could he ever fly a helicopter. He always flew with his seat lowered to the very bottom adjustment stop, and I often wondered how he could even see over the instrument panel he was so low. He looked like an East L.A. low-rider driving a cut-down 1949 Mercury. He was an oddball unique character and the last aircraft commander I needed to pass to finish my AC transition.

So starting our flight day at dawn, I treated him just like he was actually 1st Lt. Sparks and did everything exactly like Sparks had drilled into my head: preflight inspection, just like Sparks. Engine run-up and radio commo check: I channeled my very best Sparks. Dialed up the Saigon rock-n-roll station and put it on Plumber's radio monitor, made sure he saw me turn it off for me and the crew in the back. We'd take care of business with no Rolling Stones to distract us.

We were in the combat assault flight flying trail ship so Plumber could screw with me all he wanted: chop the throttle, simulate an engine failure out over the jungle, in the middle of No-Man's Land, and then he would holler about, "Where's your landing spot?"

We were doing an assault into a single-ship LZ on top of a mountain ridge that was so small and the ridgeline so narrow the helicopter skids hung over the front and back edges of the bare rock. It was like teetering on the edge of a knife blade 5,000 feet up, hanging there on the rock while the infantry troops jumped off the helicopter. Mountain winds buffeting the aircraft, updrafts, downdrafts, crosswinds swirling: my first landing was very conservative, 60-knot approach speed, slowing to a stop, touch down on the rocks.

Plumber blew his top, "Flight School flying like that will get you killed. Don't hang in the air so damned long being a big fat slow moving target."

Next landing I hung back and loitered over the valley until the ship in front of me was on very short final for his landing, then I nosed our helicopter over hard and started a dash for the little LZ. We passed through 110 knots doing hard banking S turns, with the power maxed out, and our ship finally shuttered to 120 knots. Continued with the sharp S turns, screaming toward the ridge with every drop of speed I could get out of that helicopter. Last turn threw the aircraft into a huge flare, collective all the way down to the stop, and I was pretty sure I could catch the ship before we splattered all over that tiny LZ. The wind would be the final arbiter. A landing or a hell of a crash: it was a tossup which way things would work out.

That little hotshot maneuver was the very far edge of what I could do, what anyone could do. My heart was racing, my breathing stopped. The wind gods gave me a free pass that time. We came to a stop perched perfectly on that little knife blade of rock. That was the dumbest thing I'd ever done flying in Vietnam. Soon as I started it, I realized that. Plumber didn't say a word. The infantry troops were hooting and hollering as they jumped off our chopper, some patting me on the helmet and giving me grins and thumbs up. I looked at Dennis, and he reached over and flipped the switch on my radio console and brought up Saigon radio. Steppenwolf was blasting their song "Born to Be Wild" about shooting all your guns at once and exploding into space. I pulled in all of our power, took off and had the helicopter nosed over hard.

Barely off the ridge, Plumber chopped the engine throttle for my being such a wiseass. He was teaching me a little lesson. An impenetrable cloak of vegetation covered the mountainside that fell steeply away below us and covered the valley at the bottom. There was nothing but jungle, no open spot anywhere. But instead of lowering the collective, the standard procedure for an engine failure, I pulled the collective to the top stop and pulled the nose up hard and we shot up into a steep climb, but our rotor RPM was dropping as fast as a rock dropped in a river. When the rotor slowed to the point that we stopped climbing at all, I did a pedal turn and nosed back over, lowered the collective and aimed back toward the ridgeline LZ that was maybe 500 feet below us. Our glide path looked okay to me and we probably could make it, but I was stealing rotor RPM too fast and we wouldn't have enough left to get there and have anything for a landing, just a controlled crash.

Looked over at Plumber and said, "There's my spot. Better to crash there than the damned jungle."

Dennis rolled the throttle back on. Our RPM came back and we started flying under power.

Dennis said, "Better catch up with the flight."

He twisted up the volume on Saigon radio, and they were playing a whole Steppenwolf album. Knew that album by heart. We had a copy of it at Fort Wolters in flight school: it was our secret contraband that we had to keep hidden away, totally against the rules, totally taboo, but my California Hell's Angel roommate loved it, and he was the one with the big balls who had the outlaw record player. "Your Wall's Too High" filled my earphones and my thoughts went back to my old girlfriend, Caroline, and the levee down at the Rio Grande.

Late in the afternoon, returning to Chu Lai at the end of our combat assault mission, Plumber called Leon Richards on the radio and asked if he was in the mood to give a check ride that evening. Then Plumber asked what call sign I'd chosen.

"You know you can't take 34. That was Chasin's number, so it's off limits, and only 32 or 33 are available in the thirties. Guess there are plenty of forties available, if you want," Plumber said.

Three-Three, I supposed that would do. Hornet Three-Three sounded good to me. Asked Dennis if that meant he passed me? He didn't answer, said he was going to discuss some things with Leon Richards, you know about my being a crazy and impulsive Son of a Bitch, but he guessed I was going to be the Hornet's Son of a Bitch called Hornet 33 if Leon wanted to do a check ride and I passed it okay after Plumber told him about my poor judgment about that ridge-top landing.

Back at Chu Lai, Leon Richards climbed in, plugged his helmet into the radio outlet and said, "Okay, Three-Three, let's do this thing. Plumber said you gave him some cheap thrills, but we need another AC, and you might do in a pinch."

We did the check ride on the main runway at Chu Lai. It didn't take very long, considering I'd been building up to that very moment a long time. Back at the hooch, I dug around in the tape reels and found the Steppenwolf collection I wanted and threaded it on our reel-to-reel tape player. Turned on the music and flopped on my bunk. Those old songs blasted one after another and filled up the room. How they carried me home. The song "A Girl I Knew" rolled over to "Take What You Need."

That song put me in the arms of my wife. But now, 45 years later, this present-day now, Steppenwolf's "Born to Be Wild" still flashes me right back to teetering on the edge of that tiny LZ, heart racing, breathing stopped, and waiting with dread for Plumber's simulated engine failure.

16

SAPPERS AT KHAM DUC

My first day flying as a Wasp aircraft commander was with our whole platoon hauling Ass-n-Trash out to Kham Duc and then back to the rear staging area at Firebase Hawk Hill: we had a flight of five ships ferrying troops out and swapping them for those rotating back from the field. It was 7:00 a.m. when we arrived at the jungle airstrip with our first load, and they directed our flight to land and shut down for a little while. They weren't ready yet with our return load.

Our flight leader asked the guy talking on the radio, "Roger that, ya'll have any coffee?"

"Oh, Roger that, Hornets, we've got plenty of coffee all right, and how about biscuits-n-gravy, scrambled eggs, not the powdered stuff, but real chicken-laid eggs, bacon and sausage and ham."

At the landing area, some infantry grunts directed us toward the mess tent, about a 100 yards that way, and they added, "But if you see any dead Bad Guys, don't mess with them, not yet. The demolition boys need to check 'em out. Sappers with satchel charges; they might be hot. There were probably about 20 of the little son of a bitches running around the whole damned place about three in the morning last night. Demolition boys need to check 'em out."

For the prospects of real actual breakfast, we'd step over dead bodies for bacon and eggs. You have dead bodies, no problem at all. On our trek to the mess tent, we did see one sapper, a little skinny guy with no clothes, wearing only a loincloth. Clothes got hung up in the barbwire, so the NVA just went without stinking clothes. This guy was on the ground on his knees with his legs folded up under him awkwardly. His big backpack was holding him up so that he was sitting at a 45-degree angle. He had taken a head shot in the forehead and six or eight rounds through the body. His mouth hung open, an ace of spades stuck out, and both of his ears were missing, cut off by the American grunts. We walked on by, didn't stop, but it was difficult to not look at the ventilated carcass. There were a few Americal guys snapping photos, laughing, and joking about the dead sapper. He didn't look so fierce knelt down on his knees. Getting breakfast was vastly more important to all of us hungry Hornets than gawking at some dead North Vietnamese guy.

Oh, man, golden brown biscuits, big, light, and chipped-beef gravy, real sliced tomatoes, good Lord, orange juice, and home-fried potatoes. We filled our metal plates. Some of our guys even had two plates, and I saw a door gunner go back for thirds and fourths. It seemed like months since we'd had anything but C-Rations for breakfast. Everyone ate until we were all stuffed to overflowing.

As we were walking back to our ships, we watched over at the edge of the cleared area as a front-end loader was digging a deep hole, his big scoop heaping dirt high. There was a tangled pile of dead North Vietnamese sappers waiting there at the edge of the new mass grave. On the edge of the runway a medevac helicopter was being loaded with eight black rubber body bags that contained newly dead American grunts finished with their war, going home early. So, it appeared that some of the sappers had indeed made it to their destinations and set off their bombs. This battle for Kham Duc would be competing piles of dead bodies just like these, and North Vietnam was prepared to have their men piled up and put in mass graves for another 10 years, 20 years or 50 years, as long as it took. And that was certainly longer than the U.S. was willing to load body bags of dead American young men into medevac helicopters.

Next to the medevac ship on the airstrip there was a silver-colored Air America helicopter; the CIA was out early doing their business. They had three little scrawny NVAs in loincloths who were being loaded and hand-cuffed to the floor deck. I pitied them for what those three guys had in store: probably very rough interrogation for weeks, then a reeducation camp to wipe out any remaining communist indoctrination that lingered in their little pointed heads, or equally likely they would just disappear into some other mass grave.

17

THE JEEP AND LARRY HOOD'S
FIRST DAY AS AC

On Larry Hood's first day as aircraft commander the air force had dropped a 5,000-pound bomb called a Daisy Cutter, designed to blow a really big hole in the triple canopy jungle and making a new landing zone. This one was on a mountain ridge a couple of ridges west of Kham Duc, by the Laotian Border. I was sure the world ended somewhere out there, and you just fell off the edge of the earth into a bottomless pit of jungle, like an unstoppable nightmare, nothing but jungle unending. I guess the Americal Division was wanting to establish a series of early-warning listening posts to take the first impact if the NVA sent an attack force against Kham Duc. The sounds of Americans being overrun would let the airfield base camp know that trouble was quickly headed their way.

We'd have to land one ship at a time. It was a very vulnerable time for everyone because it took a while to accumulate very many troops in the LZ, but we safely got two complete lifts in, nearly 100 men. On our third trip, about midmorning, things had gone fine so far. Everything looked like this was going to turn out to be an uneventful day of flying in the war. Coming over the mountains, we could see yellow smoke popped in the LZ, like the grunts thought we might not remember where we'd put them, like we couldn't see the brown scar that Daisy Cutter bomb had made in the mountain jungle from a couple of miles away. We could see everything just fine from up above, thank you.

If there were any enemy on the ground, down in the valleys, or just somewhere lower down the mountains looking up through the trees they could see exactly where the hell this new LZ was by the yellow smoke. Okay, thank you, thank you. Smoke: that was a good reliable LZ marker for Charlie.

As we approached the Landing Zone, our flight strung out, loitered over the valley, and each ship made its run into the LZ to drop off their troops, first ship, second ship, then I made a run. I was in clean and out clean. Then the forth ship made his run. Larry Hood, our brand-new Hornet 32, flew the next-to-last helicopter in line in the fifth spot.

Larry never got his call out fully: "Three-Two taking fire…" Bang, Smash, Clang, BOOM filled my earphones, the sound of a ship going into the trees! It was bloodcurdling to hear the loud crushing and crunching of that crash broadcast over our radios. My fear for the well-being of Larry and his crew rocketed to the max. Larry Hood was damned shot down! Well, hell! His first day as an AC and he was shot down.

Leon Richards, commanding the trail ship, flew over the crash site on his approach to the LZ and radioed out his news flash: "No explosions, and they're not on fire. Say again, no fire, yet."

He disembarked his troops and quickly took off, circled back over Larry's crash site, and sure enough, Richards began taking fire. He radioed, "I see men crawling out. I see Hood walking around."

Richards directed the gunships and pointed out where the two machine guns were and where the AK-47s were firing from. We listened on the radio as the Stingers worked hard to get their rockets through the trees. Everyone in the flight wanted to be the one to go back and pick up Hood and his crew, but the air mission commander ordered the flight to return to the staging area at Hawk Hill and get another load of troops. He'd do the extraction when Hood's bunch got together in the LZ.

Leon Richards's last radio call was, "The crew looks okay, all four, but a few grunts are down."

When we came back to the LZ, seeing Hood's busted up and crashed helicopter was a sobering sight. It was sad, a smashed Hornet bird lying there dead on the steep slope of the mountain. It was amazing to see the big trees Larry's chopper had broken into kindling wood and the helicopter's rotor blades bent in half and broken, the transmission thrown all the way forward into the cockpit, the counterweights in the ceiling, and the tail boom busted off with its broken tail rotor tangled with vines, bushes, and little trees. I couldn't see why someone hadn't been killed. After his day's extremely bad luck, the new Hornet 32, WO1 Hood, was a very lucky man to still be alive.

At the end of the flying day most of the Wasp pilots hitchhiked up to the 91st Evac Hospital, to the Officers' club. A big celebration was in order. Hangovers were assured for tomorrow. To hell with being at operations that particular night. I could do scheduling later, even if I was under the weather just a little bit. My good friend was a new aircraft commander, and he had walked away from a shoot-down, all in one day. So Larry could tell us all about it, blow by blow, what it was like, and how he pulled off that miracle, and someday he could tell stories to his grandchildren, "Grandpa was a hand-

The remains of his helicopter after it was shot down on Larry Hood's first day of flying as a brand-new Aircraft Commander, call sign Hornet 32. It was only the first time Larry was shot down. Altogether, Larry was shot down a total of 13 separate times in his year of flying in the War, earning him the loving nickname of "Magnet-Ass."

some and dashing and fearless helicopter pilot in that danged nasty ole Vietnam War, a Hornet, by golly, a mighty, mighty Hornet."

But there was a third reason for a celebration: our new platoon leader, a shiny new captain of our own, Richard "Dick" Salmond, brand-new in-country, a brand-new Hornet, and by God, was he a good-looking boy! He would be a hell of a good-looking man someday, but at the time he looked about 16 years old at most, and no one could figure out how such a young-looking kid got to be a captain in the U.S. Army or got a set of silver wings pinned on his chest. But we would salute the bars, honor the wings, and make him ours. It would have been good if 1st Lt. Sparks had still been around to take him under his wing and mold him, teach him. But instead, teaching the New Guy, that was Leon Richards's latest little pet project.

I was feeling good that night for the first time in months. I was literally thrilled that we'd had a ship shot down *without* anyone's being killed, and I had no connection to it whatsoever. It was sick and twisted reasoning, but I was so goddamned glad that I had no connection to it. There were no new dead aviators to haunt my dreams, like McDonald or Jack Smith, resulting from Hood's misfortune, and I felt like the jinx that hung over me had passed by with no catastrophic results for once.

At the club we dined on some actual food, and we had pushed a couple of tables together and were busy about partying loudly. We thanked the heavens above there were real, live round-eyed women there: Nurses, pretty women who spoke English, clean women, and some of them would even dance to the jukebox songs and laugh with us, talk to us, party with us.

By eight o'clock we had a howling good time going, howling until we got thrown out of the place because the movie was starting. Thrown out—at least out on the deck. Man, they had this deck sticking out over a cliff above the South China Sea, with surf breaking on rocks about 100 feet below. What a sweet setup they had; the view was out over the ocean and the moon coming up, waves rolling in. The night still hot and muggy with a breeze blowing in from the ocean, warm and wet. I closed my eyes and touched my wife's face in my imagination, traced my fingers along her cheekbone, followed the curve of her jaw and lifted her face for her kiss. Eyes closed, I guess I must have said her name softly to myself, *Jane.*

"Your wife?" a young nurse asked.

My eyes popped open in surprise and I said, "Pardon me, I didn't know anyone was there."

"Didn't mean to intrude. Your wife?"

"Wife? Yeah. My wife. Thinking about home. It's just that this deck makes me think about a bar in Destin, Florida. They had this roof-top deck, the ocean below, the warm breeze, the same. My wife and I went there a few times when I was in flight school."

She turned, leaned on her elbows on the railing, looked over the water and said, "Yeah, this spot always makes me lonesome for home, too, back in the world. Don't know why. I never went to the ocean or was ever on a spot like this one before."

Asked her, "May I get you a drink, Captain?"

"If you don't think your wife, Jane, would mind."

Suggested the same as mine. "Scotch and water?"

She answered, "Chivas Regal, on the rocks, no water."

I made a fast trip to the bar and returned.

She wanted to know what our special occasion was, and I told her about Larry Hood's big day and getting our new platoon leader, reasons to party. We leaned on the rail and talked about the war, what it was like flying helicopters, having that freedom of going through the air, going anywhere. The movie was on inside, but outside music was playing over the speakers. There must have been a tape playing that someone had made: Roy Orbison songs played, one after another. Just slow songs, love songs, lonesome songs. One started, and she asked to dance. Took her in my arms, a slow waltz, and she laid her head on my shoulder, and sang along softly. It was a Christmas song, "Pretty Papers." As she sang, I could hear that she'd begun to cry, quietly, gently, and she started holding me tighter.

I asked her if she was okay.

We returned to the rail before the song ended, and she wiped her eyes, saying, "I'm just feeling bad tonight, more than usual. This year, Christmas, I know it's July, but this Christmas is going to be the third Christmas I've spent in Chu Lai, here at this same ole Hospital, and I've had too much to drink tonight. I just needed to talk to someone tonight, I guess."

Then she turned and walked quickly away.

She had never told me her name. But the poor girl, facing a third Christmas in Vietnam would make any woman want to cry. The movie had ended inside and everyone was drifting back in to the bar. We partied on, drinking hard, toasts aplenty, until we were the only ones left. Our captain hit his glass hard on the table like a gavel and yelled out, "Alright, boys, let these hardworking people close up."

Outside, we were faced with hitchhiking back to our Company Area, but our Boy-Captain Platoon Leader strutted up and down a row of the doctors' Jeeps until he spotted the particular Jeep he was looking for, one with the keys in it, and he jumped in and fired it right up.

"Let's go home, Wasps, in OUR OWN Jeep!" he shouted.

We hurriedly packed that Jeep like a sardine can, then we all purred off into the night in our purloined ride laughing our asses off. Nine of us jumped out at our platoon area, and Captain Salmond started an inspection tour of his newly appropriated Jeep, kicked the tires, lifted the hood and checked the oil, and generally admired his nice new acquisition.

"Okay, fellas, we've got OUR OWN Jeep now, our own Wasp Platoon Jeep."

So our baby-face captain borrowed a Jeep up at the hospital; some doctor would probably miss it by morning. I figured we'd take it back and drop it somewhere around the corner, then walk to the PX and hitch a ride back to the Hornets' Nest. But even before we went flying the next morning, Captain Salmond already had the damn Jeep down at the Hornets' maintenance hangar getting a new paint job on it and new identification numbers stenciled all over it and a name put on it: "I Get Around!" Hell, he was planning on keeping it! We all laughed because Mr. 16-Year-Old might have had a baby face, but he had a big set of brass balls and you had to give him a ton of credit for that.

In a single stroke and for the price of just one little ole Jeep, Captain Dick Salmond had bought total acceptance into the Wasps, set himself as the leader of our pack on the ground, at least. In the air, our warrant officer ACs still had to make a combat pilot out of him. But for then, he was already the commander of one U.S. Army Jeep, the new Wasp Platoon Jeep.

Young Captain Salmond might have looked 16 years old, but he wasn't. Actually he was 24, the same age as me at the time. He was married and had two little kids. He went to OCS when he was 18, so he must have been a smart guy to pass the Officer's Candidate School Entrance Exam. He hailed from Colorado, and his wife and kids were still there. Besides having a talent for stealing Jeeps, we'd already discovered you couldn't push him, not at the poker table, no, not at poker. When he had cards, he'd clean your clock: five-card stud or Texas Hold 'Em. It didn't bother him to take poor ole warrant officers to the cleaners.

When we came back that evening after flying, his Jeep was freshly repainted and ready to go, all done in merely one day. Now that was impressive: no one got anything done in the army in only one day. The color was a darker shade of green, and the seats had even been changed. He'd swapped his Jeep's seats with the maintenance guys for a set of seats from their Jeep, old tattered seats for his nice new ones. They even stenciled the numbers from a maintenance Jeep on Cpt. Salmond's Wasp Jeep so if anyone checked it was totally Hornet registered. We just needed to keep the two Jeeps separated. We didn't want any Inspector General seeing doubled-up numbers when they were around.

To really prove that Cpt. Salmond had big brass balls, the Wasp ACs piled into his nice new Jeep and went to the Americal Division Officers' club. We had grilled ham and cheese sandwiches and a few drinks until we figured the movie was over at the hospital Officers' club, then we went rolling in up there. Cpt. Baby-Face boldly pulled into the same empty parking space we'd gotten the Jeep from the night before. At the bar, Cpt. Dick announced a round of drinks for the house, said he'd heard that very day that "Daddy's got a brand new Baby Girl!" Fawning nurses all crowded around, congratulating the new poppa. (Of course, he had not heard any such news about any baby girl—his new baby had four tires and a new paint job.)

After the crush, the rush of orders, the bartender said, "Say, Captain, we had a Jeep stolen, about the time ya'll left last night, so by any chance, did you see anything out of the ordinary going on?"

"Stolen Jeep, huh, when we left you say?" Captain Dick said.

The bartender answered, "Belonged to one of the hospital's bird-colonel doctors, a bigwig."

"Us, see anything? Well, we have our own Jeep, outside, named 'I Get Around.' Like I said, it's just outside if you wanna see it."

With that, Captain Dick turned around to one of the nurses and began a conversation. After a few minutes, I saw the bartender looking out the door and scratching his head. The WASPS Jeep was sitting right there, "I Get Around," big as life. I guessed that was the best way to establish that "I Get Around" was OUR Jeep. Bring it back to the hospital where we got it, show it around and let anyone who wondered know that it was *OUR regulation U.S. Army–issued Jeep.*

Cpt. Dick was doing this as a show. It had nothing to do with the Jeep. He was showing our aircraft commanders that his mindset was exactly like theirs: the best defense was a strong offense. Charge in, head on, guns blazing. In his place, he had to do something dramatic, show he was bold and snatch leadership from the vacuum, position himself clearly out front. We had to give him praise; in short order he'd checked off all the boxes. I could see that all the ACs were comfortable with this performance art, were accepting of him, taking him in.

Captain Dick called for another round for all. "A toast to nurses and doctors everywhere who brought my Baby into the world today."

Hooting and hollering, everyone drank to that. I studied the room, looking for a particular nurse, the one from the previous night, *Miss Pretty Papers.* She was way over in the far corner sitting with two other nurses, not joining in with the frivolities at the bar. I sipped my Chivas Regal and water and watched her daintily sipping a glass of white wine.

Someone's Creedence Clearwater tape played war protest songs. I guessed people at a hospital were probably philosophically opposed to the war: "Bad Moon Rising" rolled into "Run Through the Jungle." Couldn't understand what the singer was saying. Back in the States, we had that album at Fort Wolters and played it over and over but never understood the lyrics. Heard plainly enough, "Devil's on the loose," yeah, everyone here at the hospital knew that was damned true, and then "Hey Tonight," started blasting over the speakers.

Miss Pretty Papers' two friends got up and left, leaving her sitting there alone. I wanted to buy her a Chivas Regal and immediately rush over, but I figured there must be a steady stream of fools always trying to jump her bones.

I bought a pair of drinks, walked over, sat hers down, and said, "Just wanted to thank you for the dance last night," then turned around and went out on the deck.

Longing to be back home, I looked out over the water and ached all over from being alone in the pretty moonlight. Creedence sang "Fortunate Son," and I remembered the staff sergeant from the enlisted mens' club back in Cu

Chi when the Stinger ship was shot down. The man was feeling bad. A crew chief he'd scheduled was killed, but anyone he'd picked everything would've been the same.

Miss Pretty Papers came outside and handed her drink to me. "Thanks, but I have the early rotation in the OR tomorrow." As she turned to go, she quietly said, "Maybe some other time."

As she reached the door, she stopped. I was just finishing draining my drink. She turned around and came back over to me at the rail.

She said, "That might not have sounded right, some other time for a drink, that's all."

"That's all I thought you meant."

She said, "We had a dance last night, and now you're back tonight buying me a drink. Just in case you're wondering about me, getting any funny ideas, I'm not wanting a man. You seemed okay, so I talked with you a little while and we had a dance, but I wasn't coming on to you or anything like that."

I said, "Never thought you were, Captain."

"I'm engaged to a wonderful man in Cincinnati, and I wouldn't betray his trust."

"Yes, Captain, you've made everything clear."

She took her drink back, had a pull on it, and said, "Will you stop with the captain crap? My name is Bobbi Sue Wolters, not captain. I'm just a nurse who happens to be in the army, that's all."

"Okay, then, it is Bobbi Sue, if you prefer. I'm Ed Denny," I replied, "and I wouldn't betray anyone either."

"Yes, I remember, Jane, your wife. Then that's settled: you're married, and I'm engaged and sure the hell not looking for a man."

But I was probably lying about the no betrayal bit, because if I had thought she was willing, she would have been a big temptation. She was a fine-looking woman, a beautiful woman with a beautiful figure. No one would ever have to know anything about her and me.

"I do have the early rotation in the morning, Mister Ed Denny, so I'll say goodnight, and maybe some other time for that drink," she said.

I laughed, said, "Okay, Captain Bobbi Sue, have a good and peaceful night."

I turned back to look at the water. No one would ever have to know. A beautiful woman, a beautiful body. It was a moral test that I had failed before, but she had made it perfectly clear I'd never face any kind of test with her—but still, in Vietnam, *"Devil's on the loose,"* just like in Texas. I drained her drink and went inside. She was still there, over at the door, laughing with a circle of other nurses. When I was at the bar ordering a drink, she waved for me to come over. She took me by the arm, went out the door, and stood in front of "I Get Around," our newly procured Jeep.

She was laughing and pointing at "I Get Around."

"Ya'll named it that? You're the ones who took the colonel's Jeep, aren't you? How funny! Everyone dislikes him so much he thought someone here at the hospital did something to his Jeep. You crazy pilots really are crazy! How on earth did you get it painted?"

She took my Scotch, toasted the Jeep, "To 'I Get Around,' be a worthy ride," and took a sip, then handed me the drink back.

DEATH, DON'T COME KNOCKING:
SERNA AND LARRAGA

It was the same old stuff, just a different damned day, another day of flying combat assault into an isolated mountaintop single-ship landing zone out west of Kham Duc for the Yellow Jackets Platoon. Then, in a flash of time, the uneventful day exploded and all hell broke loose. The Hornets had one of our Slicks all shot up! Some people were killed! One of our Hornets' door-gunners was dead, plus three Americal infantry grunts were killed and three others gravely wounded. They were shot up in an enemy outburst while approaching an LZ on short final.

Even though I was flying a general support mission, and it was a Yellow Jacket Platoon door-gunner who had been killed in the combat assault, I heard everything over my radios as it happened. *Any* Hornet being killed struck way too close to home, threw my equilibrium way off kilter. My initial reaction to the event was like a guillotine slicing down: Death, don't come knocking; leave me alone. My damn door was closed for a reason. So evil-hearted Death, don't come knocking.

Since our relocation to Chu Lai, nearly two months had passed with no one's being killed or even wounded. We'd been lucky a long time, but hell, once again we had another Hornet Slick all shot up and a crewman killed. Back at Cu Chi, after Fox and McDonald and Chasin and Smith were all killed in a ten-day stretch, I'd slammed my emotional door shut and wanted to know nothing else about Death. I'd built a wall as high as I could and as thick as possible with a stout door that was well barred. I didn't need to hear details of Hornets who had been killed or have dreadful images stuck in my mind, roaming through my nightmares. For too many nights, I already had gut-wrenching nightmares as it was, dreams that usually produced drenching cold sweats.

Regardless of what I wanted and despite my refusal to acknowledge it, Death went about its business just the same. Occasionally grunts were shot and killed in our Helicopter's passenger compartments or grunts we inserted into LZs jumped off our choppers and before they took one step, Viet Cong AK-47 rifles opened up and blew holes through them. Ignoring Death never changed anything, and too frequently there was another unwanted supply of bloodshed visited on the Hornets.

Not very long after Chasin and Smith were killed, there was a Stinger gunship shot down near Cambodia that I completely blocked out of my thoughts as thoroughly as possible. They were running on a target, rockets flying, with enemy return fire pouring out. It was an Old West–style shootout, but the Bad Guys won that time. The wounded aircraft commander crash landed as carefully as possible, as well as a dying man could. On impact, the helicopter instantly burst into flames, but the pilot and crew all got out safely. However, the AC was already dead in his seat—another Stinger killed. The gunship burned up, and the AC's remains were later sifted from the ashes. I didn't know the guy who died, and I tried my best to avoid even thinking about the tragedy.

The army hated to give any credit to the Bad Guys, and they would rather say, "Since the pilot's body was burned beyond being of any use to our pathologist, there is no evidence that enemy fire killed anyone, so let's list this as 'Pilot Error.'" The damned gunship being shot up and burned was not good enough hearsay evidence for the army, no. The pilot's one and only Error was developing a sudden case of lead poisoning while flying in close combat.

He was a 1st lieutenant, in-country about ten months flying with the Stinger gunships. He was the same age as me and married like me. I always wondered if flying gunships gave him the feeling of having some control over the chaos roiling all around him. I didn't want to know even that much about him. I blocked thoughts of that man's death in every way I could. Box him up and send him home. Pin his wings on his chest. Tell his momma he did his best.

This most recent death grabbed me in a profound way. I soon learned that the dead Yellow Jacket door-gunner was Angelo Larraga, a guy I had become pretty good friends with, and my head started spinning with déjà vu of the most severe sort. This whole exact goddamned scenario had already happened to me before when we were still down in Cu Chi. A crew chief named Sonny Serna had been killed down there in the invasion of Cambodia, and some events leading up to Sonny's death and Angel's death were eerily the same.

Coincidentally, both Sonny and Angel were 20-year-old Hispanic crewmen who somehow had learned Austin Scarborough and I spoke a little Spanish—just border lingo we had acquired from growing up along the Rio Grande River in Texas—so they each became friendly with us. Austin was a big guy,

6'4" tall. Angel and Sonny were both more my size, 5'8". Coincidentally, both Angel and Sonny had received a pair of Levi blue jeans sent to them from home, but when they washed them the pants shrank and were too small for them, BOTH OF THEM. Then my friends each insisted that I take the brand-new blue jeans since they would obviously fit me perfectly. Once again coincidentally, each of them died three days later. When Angel was killed, that thrust all of the coincidences between Sonny and Angel into very sharp focus for me, and I tried to resist thinking about the entire subject.

Damned Death was back, haunting me again, taunting me again: something as trivial as two guys giving me blue jeans. When I got back to our hooch, I pulled Angel's pants out of my footlocker then hunted way down deep searching for the other pair of Sonny's jeans that I had: this crap was way too crazy. The damned blue jeans connection. I never saw that shit coming! Death was evil the way it kicked down my door and busted in on me. I knew Death didn't exist as an entity. Not some malevolent, manipulating Supernatural Being, it was merely an inert random event. However, oddball coincidences that should have been random seemed very connected, and I hated being the link between singularities that were separated by time but were so identical.

I stacked Sonny's older jeans on Angel's newer ones and took both pair outside to a trash can, got out my Zippo and set the abominable things on fire. I held the burning pants and let the fire grow until it was roaring. This was a totally screwed-up foul deal. It made me feel creepy all over. I was totally too connected to dead young aviators.

Oh, yeah, that was going to make for some bizarre nightmares: goddamned Death-jeans stalking after me like zombies wanting to take my life, probably nightmares narrated in Spanish by young matadors speaking from a bullring in Madrid or Barcelona or Juarez: Serna and Larraga dressed out as bullfighters basking in showers of roses tossed by all of their beautiful and young female aficionados. It was so crazy that having the two pairs of blue jeans totally freaked me out and seemed nearly as important to me as the death of the two young men. But nothing was required to make sense in Vietnam.

I had been in the war for only about one-third of my whole tour, and the body count for Hornets killed was already at nine, averaging a little over two a month. That was not a good statistic by any measure. Nine dead Hornets: five pilots and four crewmen. But things could have been worse, and I figured that the Hornets had probably been lucky to have only nine killed so far. Still, it was not good by any reasonable standard. I felt like I had some sort of direct connection to four of the pilots and two of the crewmen, but then, anyone who even knew any of the nine dead Hornets probably felt there was a direct link in their own relationships.

One thing I was sure of: if any enlisted crewman came around our hooch again carrying a pair of blue jeans and wanting to give them to me, I would run the other way like my damned hair was on fire. If some third young enlisted guy ever showed up and wanted to give me anything at all, my head would explode right then and there. So, damned Death, don't come knocking round my place anymore, and stop sending 20-year-old Hispanic kids around who want to be friends with Austin Scarborough and me just because we knew what the term *casa-de-putas* described.

19

LEON RICHARDS, THE SNAKE-EATER, WAS GONE LIKE SMOKE

We came into our hooch at the end of another day. Everyone was going about business as usual, with one big difference: Leon Richards wasn't there. His bed had been stripped and the mattress folded up, and his foot-locker and bookshelves were empty. All traces of him were gone.

I held my breath a second in hesitation, then asked, "Has Richards gone home?" I didn't dare to ask the other: "Has something happened to Leon?"

Roger Walker, his best buddy, spoke up. "Gone to Cam Ranh Bay, then on to the World."

I breathed again. It was not the other, not news that he was dead. Just gone home instead.

"Well, good for him."

We all knew he was real short, but pilots were very superstitious about discussing that. When someone was getting short you never mentioned it or asked anything about it, because no one wanted to put a jinx on anyone by being too nosey. No one kept a calendar on the wall marking off their days, X, X, X. If a guy wanted to talk about it, he would, but you didn't bring it up, and Richards never made a peep. I guessed that he and Roger Walker had talked about those sorts of things, maybe.

I said, "But I saw him this morning out on the flight line doing a preflight inspection."

"He had a couple of last-minute check rides," Roger said. "Taking care of business, same as he always was, a pro to the very end."

Gary Newton spoke up, said, "My last day, I'll be out at the flight line, too, but with my bags all packed, waiting on the first C-130 to come along and carry me away. I sure as hell won't be flying any on my last day."

Everyone hooted their strong agreement with that idea. So Leon Richards was there with us in the morning, then, poof, like a cloud of smoke, he was suddenly blown away by a breeze. Poof, and not just gone but actually gone back to the World. I didn't know anything beyond that, didn't know what his next assignment was going to be after his post–Vietnam leave. It was logical that he'd be an instructor pilot, go to one of the flight schools, teach knucklehead beginners who were starting at zero at Fort Wolters, or he'd be at Fort Rucker, teaching Huey flying. Maybe he would go back to some sort of Green Beret assignment, but I didn't know if the Green Berets had any in-house aviators.

Then I realized that my last little conversation with him was really my last one, period. Knowing that he was short and that I had IP school coming soon, I asked him what I needed to know about that whole deal. What good advice could he give me? But as was his usual, he just took my questions lightheartedly and answered in his easy going fashion, laid back, "Just take it as it comes, relax, and you'll do fine, no problem at all."

First, it was our old platoon leader, 1st Lt. Sparks, unexpectedly gone suddenly. Then Leon Richards gone! Who was going to provide us with the depth of their experience? Where would we turn when we didn't know what to do, how to fight? Sparks, and now Richards, gone: what big empty holes they left behind. I'd been doing our platoon pilot scheduling since we'd moved to Chu Lai, and Richards was always the one I turned to when I had questions of any sort. Now, since he was gone, it seemed there was no one left to help when questions came up, until I realized we still had all our senior aircraft commanders to turn to for leadership.

The look of Richards' bunk, and the empty footlocker: things were exactly the same in every detail as for someone who had been killed and all their personal stuff taken away by the brass. Either way, anyone dead or gone back home, the results for those left behind seemed just the same. The missing were long gone, be it Heaven or Hell or back to the real World. I'd never expected that I would feel so down and saddened that someone had gone home, but that was how I felt about Leon Richards vanishing from our group with zero warning that he was leaving us.

When it got to be my time to go back home, everyone would know that I was going, because it would be obvious from all the cartwheels I'd be doing for days in advance. I wouldn't just silently ride off into the sunset without saying any good-byes, not like a puff of smoke like Leon Richards had.

20

IP SCHOOL

Down at the 1st Aviation Brigade Headquarters at Long Binh, I unpacked my little travel bag on a bunk. Counting the one I was wearing, I had a total of four flight suits: two brand-new ones the Hornets supply officer had issued me to go to instructor pilot school with, along with my two older suits that still had Steve Chasin's name written in them. The laundry-pen ink had held up well after many washings. I couldn't help but think that Steve should have been the one to be at the IP school, certainly not me. Steve would have made a terrific instructor pilot teaching everyone about his "Zen of Helicopter Flying," but unfortunately he'd already been killed by the damned war.

A chief warrant officer 2 walked into our barracks with a flourish, took a fifth of Scotch and slammed it down on a table—*BOOM*—and said for everyone to gather around. There were about a dozen of us in my little instructor pilot school class, and we all formed up around the table.

"Listen up, men. This is your first lesson: twenty dollars, each, so get it out. Twenty dollars, that's what I'm betting you. Now pass it up here—that's right. I'm betting each of you right now I can chug this whole mother-humping bottle of Johnny Walker, every drop, the whole thing, in one long chug! Impossible you say, no way, you say. You know the story of the little train? I think I can, I think I can, I think I can. Well, I'm the little train who damned well knows he can. Anyone want out of the bet? No. You're all betting against me 'cause ya'll are full of doubts about yourself, so you project those sorry doubts onto me. You're thinking, IP school, I don't really know if I can cut it or not. You see, you're wondering and having doubts. Let me show you. Difficult is hard to do. Impossible just takes more determination. Now I'll show you: mother-humping determination wins every time."

He opened the bottle of whiskey and passed it in front of everyone to see, then turned it up and began drinking: half a bottle, three-quarters, drained it. He sucked on the bottle, then took a guy's hand and shook the empty bottle in his hand and said, "See, not a drop left, not one little ole drop."

There were mumbles, some applause.

"Ya'll thought, no way, Jose, no way in hell. But you all saw me do it: determination wins, so I highly recommend that you get you some of that shit. Leave the doubts behind, get determination and this instructor pilot school will be easy. But with no determination, you're totally screwed, totally."

He gathered up the $240 from the table, walked out the door, and instantly in came a flock of chief warrants and hard-bars. Hell, there was a chief warrant officer 4! I'd never even seen a CW4 before! The hard-bars were all captains. A major stepped up and began speaking first.

"Now that guy is a crazy son of a bitch, drink that bottle of booze like that. I would have doubted he could do it, even when he said he could, but the point he was making is suspend your doubts, doubts about yourself, doubts that we can teach you, or doubts about anything. Suspend all doubting. Transform 'I think I can' into 'I KNOW I can, I KNOW I will'! Do that, and at the end of this school, we'll be shaking all of your hands. Otherwise, he was completely right about you guys being totally screwed."

Then they called each of us and introduced us to our senior instructor. Outside the window of the barracks, I watched as the Scotch drinker was throwing up in the flower bed just out our door: alcohol bulimia, drink it down, throw it up, and pocket the $240. How naive we were. Marked it down: don't bet with these guys, not on anything, because you know they're always going to be three steps ahead of you—at least three steps ahead—on everything. This was definitely not any of their first rodeos, and I guessed they must all have been on at least their third Vietnam tours.

Looked around the Long Binh Army Base some and saw that the place was perched at the absolute top of the Military Industrial Complex pile and located just outside of Saigon. At the Officers' club restaurant, they had starched white tablecloths and china plates, real silverware, and linen napkins. Filet mignon with lobster tails were listed on the menu together for $7.00, I believe I recall, or maybe it was $8.00. Whatever the tiny price, it sure beat the hell out of eating nothing but C-Rations morning, noon, and night! And, oh, sweet heaven, they had hot water for showers, honest-to-goodness real hot water. At Chu Lai, we had an elevated steel barrel filled by a garden hose, and the water was solar heated, IF the sun shined; IF NOT, then everyone had cold, cold showers. And the Long Binh barracks we were staying in actually had an indoor latrine with sinks and running water, and flush toilets, not stinking outhouses. They had all of the normal basics that we totally lacked at Chu Lai. I was sure there was an Olympic-sized swimming pool somewhere, and a volley ball court.

At the 1st Aviation Brigade Headquarters, the facilities were just as nice as any Stateside base. A year of war spent here wouldn't be tough. At the mess hall at breakfast, eggs were cooked to your order. How you like your hash browns? Toast—wheat or white or biscuits instead? Gravy: pork, beef, milk, or red-eye ham? In two weeks at Long Binh, I gained back a few of the 20 pounds I'd lost so far in Vietnam.

The flying schedule was very civilized, too: four hours in the air in the morning and four following lunch when we were learning exactly what the 1st Aviation Brigade expected in the way of a check ride. It was not intended to be a test, not something you passed or failed. A check ride was intended to be an opportunity for pilots to practice their emergency procedure maneuvers. And if there was anything they were doing wrong, the check ride was their chance to correct whatever problems might be detected. So we practiced the maneuvers over and over for hours on end, autorotations one after another. My instructor said that if God taught Jesus how to land the perfect autorotation, he'd do it at the instructor pilot school at Long Binh. That's what they wanted: pure perfection. At the graduation ceremony, I received my instructor pilot certificate and a handshake from a bird colonel with a nicely framed personal photo of that moment.

Probably the most interesting thing I learned in my two weeks at IP school was how to set up and operate a prostitution ring offering premium personal services for pilots to consume. You needed the cash on hand (Military Payment Certificates) to pay the girls weekly. Everything ran on a revolving credit plan, and the customers then paid you monthly with a check drawn on their U.S. bank. You just mailed all the checks to your bank back home, and the circle was completed. It was the easiest way to get American money out of Vietnam. The only thing you needed to get that sort of business started was to get yourself appointed as the manager of the Hooch Maid ladies. Very interesting indeed, a warrant officer pimp, and the damnedest part of it was, the pimp was from an aviation support company based at Cu Chi, the Hornets' old home. He got real vague, real quick when I asked if his company had taken over our former Hornets Nest Company Area.

For me, when IP school was done, it was a matter of going back to Chu Lai, back to the steady diet of cold C-Rations, enduring freezing cold showers, and certainly not having pleasure-women available on credit whenever you wanted. That afternoon, I caught a ride into Saigon and checked into the Continental Hotel on Tu Do Street, an old, French-built hotel. The room was superb, with a totally wonderful-looking bed and a basket of fresh fruit sitting on the table, top-class stuff all the way. I was amazed that they actually had apples and oranges in Vietnam. Where the hell did those come from?

That night as I dined alone in the fancy restaurant, the maître d' came over with a beautiful young woman and asked if I would enjoy a dinner companion. Or she could accompany me for the rest of the evening after dinner if that was also what I would like. She could speak English or French, should I care for dinner conversation.

Twenty-four-year-old Hornet 33 receiving his Instructor Pilot School Diploma from the Commander of the School at the First Aviation Brigade Headquarters at Long Binh, South Vietnam, near Saigon.

I looked at her, an obvious Euro-Asian. She lacked the jet-black hair and black eyes of the Vietnamese people. Her hair was dark but brown and her eyes were a golden brown, her complexion very fair. I guessed her to be a legacy of the French colonial period gone by, and she seemed to have all the best attributes of both people, tall for a Vietnamese woman, maybe 5'9", and a photo model's stunningly beautiful face. The traditional Vietnamese outfit she wore looked perfect, expensive—white embroidery on white silk, floor length but split up the sides and trousers under the gown. She seemed serene, considering that she was so blatantly being merchandised in this room full of people watching her.

I said, "I suppose some conversation would be nice, but what's the price? That matters."

The maître d' whispered to me, "Yes, sir, there is no price—this is a service of the hotel. But after your dinner, if you are pleased to leave the lady a gratuity we will see that she receives it."

I said, "I guess that'll be okay, so go ahead and seat her."

I was surprised when she ordered an inexpensive bowl of soup and iced tea, and I was really surprised when she spoke. Her English was fluent and perfectly spoken, with just the lightest touch of a French accent. She sounded very exotic, obviously educated and bright and apparently conversant with the topics of the day. She claimed her day job was as a translator for an American government agency. She had been raised in a Catholic convent and educated by French nuns. A few evenings a week she worked as a dinner companion at the hotel as her second job, which she claimed was interesting work. She said she'd met a broad variety of people, news correspondents, businessmen, bureaucrats, and occasional military officers, usually men older than I was—somber older men.

When dinner was finished, I called for the check. Chatting had been the setup; now it was time for her closing sales pitch and she didn't miss a beat at all.

"Would you enjoy going dancing a while? Or perhaps go to your room, we could make love?"

I laughed, told her, "My rank is low and my pay grade matches it. I'm sure I couldn't afford a woman of your quality and beauty."

When I paid for dinner, maybe, I'd have no more than thirty bucks left on me, and I doubted that would buy holding hands, so I said, "Anyway, I'm married, and I'm faithful to my wife."

"You need not be unfaithful. Let's go to your room. I'll bathe you, put you to bed, and massage your back, nothing unfaithful, just $200."

I laughed again. "I don't have $200 on me." I paid the dinner bill and gave her $10 and said, "For the pleasant dinner conversation."

She picked up the $10, leaned close. "For massage, you pay only what you can, only what you think is fair. Good deal, yes?"

I opened my wallet and showed her my cash, what little there was, and in my wildest fantasies of the moment, the devil side of me imagined her saying, "Darling, you are in much worse shape than I, so let's make this an evening of us sharing honest primordial sex, impassioned strangers controlled totally by lust, and we'll think nothing about money unless you need me to give you some so you won't be so incredibly pitifully poor." But she didn't say anything like that. She simply looked up at me, gave me her most beautiful Grace Kelly look, and slowly offered her hand to be kissed. That was the extent of what I could have for free. I guessed that the $28 I did have didn't measure up to her minimum for a back rub. Then she discretely got up from the table with a polite little bow and was gone without another word.

As I watched her walk away, I thought that if the war lasted another two or three years that living doll was going to never have to work another day in her life. Instead, she would spend her nights sipping ice-cold champagne in Paris or London or New York, and she would be the one receiving all the back rubs or anything else she wanted.

21

FIRST CHECK RIDES

After being at the 1st Aviation Brigade Headquarters, when I returned to the Hornets Company up in I Corps the latest news that had everyone buzzing out in the operations bunker was that, while I was gone, Hornet 32, Larry Hood, had been shot down *twice* in less than two weeks. He had his engine shot out once, and then a few days later his helicopter got hit by a rocket-propelled grenade that nearly took off the whole tail boom and screwed up his tail rotor and he spun in and crashed in the trees next to an LZ. That totaled three times Hood had been shot down in barely more than a month—three times when everyone miraculously walked away, and that was three times where Larry was flying one helicopter out of a formation of six helicopters. It certainly looked like bad luck was stalking him personally, but apparently good luck also came to his aid each time. I was glad that I'd been gone and missed those particular missions and missed seeing Larry's mangled up helicopters crashed out in the boondocks. As it was, I saw their wrecked remains back behind the Hornets maintenance hangar, and that was plenty enough for me. They were torn up, wadded into crumpled balls, and it was a fluke that no one had been killed in those hard crashes.

The rest of the news: the Hornets had a new commanding officer. The old CO had been relieved of duty because of some things that had occurred months before back at Cu Chi. It seemed like our maintenance guys had pulled a fast one and got their butts caught after our last inspector general's visit. After the IG had time to check all the paperwork and run all the numbers, they found that Hornets maintenance had a stolen helicopter stashed out in back of their hangar, an old Crusader ship that had been listed by the Crusaders as destroyed in battle, and the Crusaders had a similar one of ours. Obviously, the two sister companies had worked an under-the-table deal to swap helicopters. The choppers were two old, worn-out craft that had long been unairworthy, and they were being cannibalized for their spare parts. The IG people didn't see any good side to that whole arrangement, even if it was about creating a source of parts to have available when you couldn't get a part from regular supply channels. But the IG wanted all the paperwork correct, and they had viewed each of the misappropriated helicopters as simply being a case of stealing one of Uncle Sam's $600,000 assets, and they didn't like that situation at all.

Someone's head had to roll, so the current CO was jerked up and out of the Hornets that same day, even though he hadn't been with the Hornets when the helicopter swap had happened. That was my third CO in less than five months: it was like the Hornets had a revolving door: one day our CO was there and the next day they were gone. By the time I got back to Chu Lai, our newest New-Guy company commander was chomping at the bit to get started with his war. He wanted an orientation ride and a check ride in order to get his flight status confirmed and approved and get on to the war.

Wonderful. Everyone in operations was laughing at me. My first assignment as an instructor pilot was to fly with someone I didn't know, had never even met, someone who probably hadn't even flown a helicopter lately. He didn't want some ass-and-trash mission to get started with either. He wanted to jump into the deep end of the pool first thing so he was insisting on flying on a combat assault mission for his first flight. He wanted the real deal, to get right into the heart of this war.

So this guy was the very first check ride I had to give: our new commanding officer, a major who saw the Hornets as being his personal ticket on the train headed to becoming a lieutenant colonel, and he was impatient to get going. At the beginning of our combat assault mission, the major was hyperactive, like he was all wound up on speed or something, and he couldn't be still five seconds. He was talking nonstop, with questions gushing out of him like machine-gun fire.

We got through the first half of the day okay, and our platoon hit a series of typical mountaintop pinnacle LZs, each a little higher up than the previous one. Surprisingly, the major's flight skills didn't seem too rusty, not as bad as I had expected, and he made the approaches and landings in a couple of LZs with no problems at all. But his third attempted landing was jinxed. It was an LZ on a mountaintop pinnacle at about a 5,000-foot elevation, the very same LZ where Larry Hood had been hit by the rocket-propelled grenade a few days before. Our flight leader chose to take no chances on this return visit to the place, so he ordered the flight to perform a high-overhead approach to the landing zone. A high-overhead was where the flight passed right over the LZ at cruising altitude in a daisy-chain formation, and each helicopter in turn entered a steep spiraling dive toward their touch-down spot, descending as fast as possible. When our turn came, the major began his dive, and everything seemed fine initially. Our descent was fast, as normal, but then suddenly the bottom seemed to fall out from under us. We had gotten caught in a severe downburst column of wind and were suddenly falling double fast toward the ground.

The major looked at me with eyes big as saucers, and it was obvious that he wanted me to take the flight controls, because he thought that we were going to crash in a couple of seconds and hit the mountain at a high rate of speed, and all ten of us on board our helicopter were going to die right there, right then, on that remote damned mountaintop. I figured those were his first thoughts because they were my first thoughts: *Holy cow, we're all going to die right here and now!*

The turbulence of the downburst tossed our helicopter like a child's toy, but at the very last second we were able to pull out from the wind shaft and narrowly slipped away from the face of the mountain by only a few inches just before we hit the trees doing about 100 knots, which also happened to be about the rate of my heartbeat right then. We escaped the downburst not because of anything I did. We got out of it because of arbitrary luck, nothing more than that, and I knew that. We could've just as easily crashed in the LZ in a fireball. I realized we'd just escaped our deaths by the blink of an eye. My mouth was dry as a desert, and my heartbeat pounded hard in my temples.

Clearly that had been the instructor pilot's gods telling me, "Mister IP, do you really think you're such hot stuff now that you've finished IP school? You don't know everything. We can snuff you out anytime we want, and you'll probably never even see anything coming until it's too late, Joker!"

Everyone in our helicopter probably heard some personalized version of a message of doom screaming in their brain during that high-overhead approach and the deadly downburst we had randomly flown into, some haunting message they would never forget, something that would always serve as the basis of gore-filled nightmares for the rest of their lives. But the whole deal was just normal Vietnam combat flying: hours and hours of routine stuff punctuated by a few seconds of a near-death experience and its attached terror.

Whatever was ripping through the CO's thoughts, our chatterbox major was suddenly stunned into silence, and he basically went still for the rest of that day. I went silent too, wondering whatever in hell had brought me to this place. Me, *the instructor pilot;* who would have ever thought anything like that would come to pass? I was feeling like a total joke right then. Leon Richards had been a Green Beret before becoming a helicopter pilot and eventually an IP. How could I ever measure up to that mark? I wasn't a career man. I only wanted to live through this Vietnam War mess. I only wanted to get out of the army when my minimum time was done. When I took the flight-hours clerk job, innocent as that seemed at the time, my lot in the war had been set when I decided to try to take some control of my situation. Somehow I had fallen into a chain of timing-controlled events that carried

me along to being the Hornets' company instructor pilot and scheduling officer in addition to being the flight-hours clerk. I had never intended to be so
absorbed into the structure and mechanics of the daily nuts-and-bolts operations of the Hornets. Yes, I went silent that day, silenced by my doubts that
I could actually do the jobs I'd agreed to undertake. At least I'd never get
scrubbed off another mission because I was over the flight-hours limit.
There'd be no more bunker line duty officer or officer of the day crap for me
where someone could possibly die in my place. That bullshit wouldn't happen
anymore.

The next morning it was a dawn takeoff, both Hornet Slick platoons on
some special combat assault mission. No ass-n-trash for the Hornets that
day. The American Division wanted a two-platoon flight that could land
enough infantry troops at one time for maximum impact. They wanted to
put at least 100 troopers in some LZ with the first lift, and then 100 more
ASAP. They were going to put four companies of infantry, nearly 800 men,
around the base of a hill out west of Tam Ky, capital city of Quang Tin Province, which was located a few miles north of Chu Lai. A South Vietnamese
Army firebase with an artillery attachment and a company of ARVN infantrymen sitting on top of that hill. There was a nasty problem with that particular
ARVN firebase. An elite A-team of ten U.S. Green Berets had been stationed
there as U.S. military advisers. The previous day, the firebase had radioed in
and claimed that during the night some NVA sappers had infiltrated through
the outer perimeter wire, undetected by anyone, and killed all ten of the
Green Berets; and then the sappers had escaped back out through the wire,
still undetected. The ARVN wanted some instructions. They also wanted
someone to come out and get the dead bodies. They didn't like having stinking
dead GIs piled up around their camp.

When American had the little hill completely surrounded, the Hornets
were supposed to land on top and deposit a flight of U.S. infantry troops,
then everyone would find out what had happened to the Green Berets. Ten
Green Berets didn't get their throats cut during the night without anyone
hearing anything; there was no way that was happening. If there had been a
bunch of NVA sappers, the ARVN should have preferred dying fighting them
rather than facing the heat American was going to bring. Heads were going
to roll, figuratively or literally, and American didn't care which way things
went.

Yo-yos had two choices. One was to give themselves up and everyone
go off to be thoroughly interrogated (and probably tortured) in some South
Vietnamese prison until the ARVN top brass and the Americans were satisfied
with their story. As for those who were responsible for allowing this mess,
they would be tortured even more and then probably executed. Or they had
the choice that American really wanted: the ARVN could attempt to resist

and choose to fight the Americans instead. That was what Americal wanted so they could just kill them outright, kill every damned one of them, like cockroaches. At least, those were the rumors flying around the operations shack the previous night and were still around the flight line at dawn.

Americal wasn't saying anything; they claimed this was only a *training mission*, and they just happened to need a two-platoon flight for training purposes. Right. The Hornets didn't need to know more than that. We just flew them from point A to point B and asked no questions. We never heard a single word about that day or what happened on that firebase. That day never officially happened, but we put 800 grunts out in the field around that hill and then followed that with two lifts of troopers (with some obviously angry Green Berets) on top of the hill for *training purposes*. Then we went back to Chu Lai and hoped that a big ARVN versus Americal Division gunfight didn't happen.

That day, I was flying with Gary Newton, one of our senior aircraft commanders, doing my second-ever check ride, and I felt really self-conscious. I'd flown with Gary when I was a green New Guy. I demonstrated an autorotation and managed it okay. Then Gary flew around the traffic pattern and did his autorotation, and I never even felt when the helicopter's skids touched the runway! His touchdown was softer than a feather landing on a baby. I clearly saw my place, so I leaned back and let Gary do his thing, and he flew perfectly through all of his check-ride maneuvers. Any inflated ego I'd developed about my flying abilities at IP school quickly readjusted to the reality of my own limitations.

22

DEATH COMES
TO THE HORNETS AGAIN:
KOCH

We were working a single-ship mission out at Firebase Mary Ann, which was located southeast of Kham Duc. I had sprayed "Herbicide Orange" at Mary Ann a couple of weeks earlier, and it was amazing how fast that Orange worked (the Hornets had been spraying that lethal stuff 3 or 4 times a week for about a month at that time). The jungle we'd sprayed outside the perimeter wire on the downslope sides of the mountain below the firebase was already naked, only the remains of bare trees left standing and they were obviously deader than hell, just waiting to fall over in a pile with the first good windstorm. It was pleasing to see how the available open ground for a firing zone had been greatly expanded and the security of the firebase correspondingly improved.

The Infantry forces at Mary Ann had a platoon-sized patrol out trudging through the jungle, sweeping the territory along one side of a river valley. They had been out three weeks and seriously needed supplies and a rotation of people. The infantry grunts finally had made it to an old landing zone where a helicopter could get into them for the first time in too many days. They had wounded who needed to come out and a dead platoon leader they'd been carrying in a body bag for a few days. A sniper (or team of snipers) had been stalking them and taking shots for over a week. So we were bringing them a new 2nd lieutenant and a few other guys, plus water, food, and ammo.

We got to the LZ, which was located a third of the way up the side of a tall mountain, but it was a tiny little hole in the jungle over 200 feet deep. It was only a few feet bigger than our rotor-blade span, maybe no more than ten feet extra on each side. We came to a stop above the place and hovered all the way down into it as carefully as possible, totally white knuckle the whole time. It was like flying our Huey down a water well.

When we got to the bottom of the hole, the ground level was sloping enough that our rotor blade was nearly hitting the dirt on the up-slope side and the thing was full of shattered old tree trunks, so you couldn't possibly land anywhere. We held the most stable hover possible while the grunts got supplies and people off and then started loading us back up: eight wounded, four on stretchers and four walking but badly wounded. Plus, there was the days-old body bag that stank to high heaven.

A sergeant standing on my skid hollered in my window and said they had one more guy ready to go for his scheduled R&R. Could we manage to haul him? Our load was looking pretty maxed out, and I was concerned about the weight. A review of the engine gauges and the takeoff-power chart showed that we would be right at the limit but still on the green side of things, if only barely. I gave the sergeant a nod, and a very happy R&R-bound guy climbed aboard. Everyone backed away, and we started our vertical ascent straight up the tight hole. As we left the helicopter's ground effects, our rate of climb started to slow markedly. The poor old helicopter was laboring, giving all it had.

The helicopter rose up ever-increasingly slowly until we were nearly out of our confines, our rotor blade nearly clear of the trees. But our slow climb finally became a shuddering stop. We were hanging there in midair, totally stuck and no more power to be had. The engine and rotor RPMs were starting to drop slightly, ever so slightly, but enough that we would soon start to settle back into the hole and out of that 200-foot hover. A crash in that particular LZ wouldn't be pretty, and there was no telling how many guys on the ground would be hurt by our thrown helicopter parts and pieces.

In complete desperation and not knowing what else to do, I pushed the right tail-rotor pedal and brought the nose around to the right to transfer some power from the tail rotor to the main rotor and we lifted just a bit but not enough. With nothing left to do, I pushed the cyclic forward slightly, and we began moving slowly. The main rotor blade went into the treetops, chopping away. The noise of the rotor blade smashing into the trees was thundering. The body of the helicopter entered the trees, dragging through the top of the goddamned jungle. But it was working, we were cutting our way out, and as soon as we had some forward airspeed, we were flying, and the bird jumped up and out of the jungle; but vibrations were horrible, enough to shake the fillings out of your teeth. I'd beaten the holy shit out of the main rotors, and they were so totally screwed up I thought we might have one of the blades come apart or just be totally thrown off. That would have been the worst nightmare.

You can imagine how I was called on the carpet for that little deal. But everything I had done down in that LZ before attempting a takeoff was correct. The maintenance guys told me the problem was that the takeoff-power chart and the engine-power rating were both wrong by a little bit and the helicopter wouldn't pull what the charts said, but that little bit mattered a great deal. That little bit of information helped to pull my ass out of the red-tape fire.

The rotor blades were beat to hell, with many huge, deep gashes, so the chopper couldn't fly because it might sling apart at any time. So, had to get it slung back from Mary Ann to Chu Lai by a Chinook. I was glad we'd made it all the way back to Mary Ann instead of crashing in the jungle. What really saved my ass was the infantry commanding officer at Mary Ann proposed us for medals for getting his wounded out. He said his guys in the LZ who had witnessed things suggested a DFC, a Distinguished Flying Cross. The really nice part was that the infantry commander never mentioned anything about the R&R guy. That would've cooked my goose good, bad charts or not.

But the real screwed-up situation was the infantry grunts out in the field who were enduring tough times. Ten or twelve guys who looked like they were in charge became sniper targets. The dead lieutenant we had retrieved was the second platoon leader killed that week. Most of the top sergeants had been wounded or killed also. That was why the patrol had left the river valley and taken to the mountain with its dense jungle. They wanted to make the sniper have to get close enough to be seen and finally eliminated with goddamned extreme prejudice, and they had their own snipers in the thickets looking for whoever had been tearing them up so much. Cat and mouse.

Three days later, another Hornet ship was going back into the little LZ I'd been in. It was a new day, but it was the same deal: New Guys put in and the wounded and dead taken out. The 2nd lieutenant platoon leader I'd dropped off was already dead, plus two sergeants dead and four wounded badly. It was really a screwed-up situation, number 10. The difference was that the sniper or snipers had moved in and taken up positions covering the sorry little LZ. The grunts' snipers had not been able to spot anyone and hadn't eliminated the fire they were taking steadily. As our Hornet helicopter got near the ground and the swaps were being made, as soon as the new platoon leader hit the ground a shot rang out and he fell dead from a head shot. Three more on the ground fell dead in rapid succession. The next shot took the helicopter crew chief. Kenny Koch was killed, and there was nothing our Hornet guys could do about it. They had to keep hovering there as more wounded were loaded. It was a fish-in-a-barrel sort of deal, an undetected sniper real close in, taking one quick shot after another.

As soon as they could, our helicopter got the hell out of that firing-range trap. Kenny was dead, along with two infantry sergeants who never made it off the helicopter. The only possible reason I could figure why the sniper didn't kill our pilots was that he didn't want the helicopter to crash and close down the LZ. He must have wanted more choppers to attempt to land down in that hole so he could work them over, too—*Bang, Bang, Bang*. That would've been ideal for the sniper.

The next day, the Hornets were put on a company stand down. An Americal chaplain did a basic memorial service for Kenny Koch. It seemed strange at the time, but medals were passed out when the chaplain was finished. They gave me an undeserved one for that LZ, and then the AC, pilot, and door-gunner from Kenny's crew received medals. There was even a posthumous Purple Heart for Kenny. We had a new awards and decorations captain, and it seemed unlikely for anyone to get a medal one day after an event happened. I knew Americal liked to give out medals, but that whole decorations ceremony felt totally odd and seemed to be very out of kilter.

23

R&R Was Coming Soon, Concussion Grenade

Everywhere in our area of I Corps around Chu Lai it hadn't stopped raining for three days and three nights; it never let up with the steady rain for even one little minute. Rain, rain, rain: so this was Vietnam's notorious monsoon weather. There were only two conditions available: damp or wet. Everything was either and even our hooch roof was leaking into our little home from a dozen places. We had pans and pails setting around everywhere, and at night the sound of drip, drip, drip was what sang everyone to sleep. The plywood floor was slick with moisture, and my damned bed was dank when I slithered into it late at night.

Flying was totally beyond miserable, with ominous gray clouds hanging low, solid overcast, and the omnipresent steady rain. When it came to flying, there was no breaking out through the clouds. If you wanted to fly somewhere, it had to be low-level—under the overcast or not go at all. Those were your only two choices. But the war didn't slow down any: everything was still business as usual, with the normal 24 hours a day, seven days a week war schedule with the same sorts of missions to fly every day. And everyone was saying this stuff normally lasted for months! Steady rain for months! Maybe three months or maybe a little more!

My ticket out of the rainy weather was the fact that my R&R was coming soon, but it never could have been soon enough. Six days with my wife, Jane, in Hawaii, with all the fringe benefits like hot showers and a comfortable king-size bed, a DRY one. No more staying out in the Hornets' operations shack till all hours of the night and getting only four hours of sleep per night. Hell, in Hawaii we could sleep as late as we wanted, till noon or later, if that pleased us. Six days with no hint of C-Rations permitted at all, nothing but real actual food. I could see it coming: candle-lit dinners in nice fancy restaurants with a three-piece piano band playing softly or bacon and scrambled eggs for breakfast and hamburgers with hot French fries and cold chocolate milk shakes at lunch.

There would be a rental car to drive and all of Hawaii to roam around and see the sights, relax. I would have six days of not sitting on my ass and projecting my best ever *Just Take It* in some goddamned hot LZ: no accepting that NVA or VC were trying their damnedest to kill you, or at least kill your U.S. Army Huey helicopter.

It would be six days with no impromptu funerals with a rifle stuck in the ground by its bayonet, a young aviator's flight helmet perched on top and a Purple Heart hanging there, lifeless, in the wind. One more Hornet's death wasn't going to change the tiniest thing about that damned war or its outcome. The government wanted to tell everyone that we won all the battles, but that was not exactly true, no, no. There were plenty of little fights where we got clobbered pretty hard, but the government didn't count those as *battles,* just little set-backs, tiny unless you happened to be one of the *"Acceptable U.S. Losses"* on the military's score card of Body Count. Then you might have taken being dead personally.

R&R was what I was focusing on. I tried to think about Jane and a big bed with crisp sheets. I'd long ago given up wanting my lover to come to me in sweet dreams, come in the night, release me from this crazy place I was in, even if just for a little while. Those dreams came so infrequently that I'd given up on them after a while. Too often my dreams tended to be the exact opposite of sweet dreams: instead, they would involve trying to get to some hospital as quickly as possible with a damned chopper full of dying young men or some other ugly crap like that. Sadly, Jane had become only a letter on my bunk at the end of the day or a letter I would write telling her that everything with the Hornets was going perfectly okay and 1 Corps was a really interesting place to fly with all of its beautiful mountains. Reading her letters was the only time I had to even think about her for a few fleeting moments. It seemed that I'd been alone so long without my female partner that even the possibilities of having sex no longer occurred to me. Not even the nurses at the hospital had made me dwell on the issue for very long, except maybe one—Captain Bobbi Sue—and she was not available. She'd made that perfectly clear.

One night right after the monsoon rains had begun, at about three o'clock in the morning, while the Hornet's Company Area was totally sound asleep, there was a tremendously loud explosion right outside of our hooch that thoroughly shook our little plywood structure. Austin Scarborough had NOT hit the floor first. He was hard asleep, but he sat up right away. Incoming must have hit really close by. We'd been lucky about incoming at Chu Lai so far, and none had ever hit around our area since we'd been there. That was a welcome change from Cu Chi where we had incoming at least once or twice a month during my time down there. We all stumbled out of bed, bunker bound. When we got outside there was smoke floating all around the maintenance senior sergeant's hooch that sat right next to ours. Lights started coming on, and people quickly started appearing. Men in their underwear from the sergeant's hooch staggered into the black night holding their ears, coming through the drifting gray smoke like ghosts. That explosion wasn't incoming. All of our hooches looked basically okay, and the big bang had sounded like it went off right next to where I'd been sleeping. There was nothing blown up, just some smoke. Then it quickly became clear what had happened: a grenade, a damned concussion grenade had gone off under the sergeant's place.

Someone had just sent a message, a very explicit warning meant for someone in that hooch, maybe for all of them. Who could know? Whatever was going on, it was serious business. There was obviously something very wrong in the maintenance platoon for this to happen. The only good thing was that no one had been killed or seriously hurt, except for maybe their hearing. At least it hadn't been some damned incoming Viet Cong rocket or mortar.

There was the expected standing around and talking that went on for a quarter of an hour, but nothing was really done about the incident. No one had seen or heard anything or anyone. Hell, everyone had been asleep. There was no way to tell who might've done it. The only thing for sure: it must have been some pissed-off, disgruntled, enlisted guy who set off the grenade—and how big was that group? At any rate, it wasn't our platoon's problem. Maintenance would have to sort out their own business about the concussion grenade. We weren't involved, so it was back to bed for most of us.

I really didn't know anything about the maintenance platoon, their work conditions or the workload they had or their work schedule. I just knew that our helicopters were on the flight line come early morning. Every night the maintenance captain had fits putting enough ships on the board for missions. Occasionally he'd have to call Division and tell them he couldn't have as many choppers as they were wanting because we had too many of our ships shot up or he hadn't been able to get some replacement part he was needing and it was back-ordered. He was all the time scavenging parts from some helicopter that was in maintenance for a few days of work to use on flying ships: a constant juggling act, rob Peter, pay Paul. And I guessed they were short of qualified mechanics like our flight platoons were always needing aircraft commanders and crew chiefs. And I guessed maintenance worked long hours, however long it took to get everything done, every day, and every damned night.

As pilots, we knew that if maintenance put a helicopter out on the flight line, everything was right with it. And we all knew that a Hornet chopper would fly you around all day long and then bring you home that night and be ready to fly again tomorrow, if you didn't get it all shot up. It was rare a bird that ever got a red *X* put in the log book when it had its morning preflight inspection.

If someone thought that tossing a grenade would make the workload magically ease up or make demanding sergeants quit riding everyone's asses, dream on, friend. That stupid threat wasn't going to fix the impossible. Speaking of stupid, no one could fix that either, so whoever had sent that bang-bang-grenade threat followed it up a few nights later with an actual frag grenade that was intended to kill or seriously wound as many people as possible in the sergeant's hooch. You could not fix stupid.

FLYING GRAVES REGISTRATION

The general support mission our crew was assigned to was "Graves Registration." None of the other Wasp aircraft commanders wanted it. Everyone I asked about it earnestly begged off. Some of them had done it once down in Cu Chi and a couple of guys had done it at Chu Lai, and no one wanted it a damned second time, no way in hell. It seemed it was my turn, though not willingly, but I could no longer avoid scheduling myself for it. What it amounted to was flying dead bodies in from the field to a morgue out on the far end of a peninsula at Chu Lai, a little finger of land jutting out into the South China Sea, discretely separated from the rest of Chu Lai as far as physically possible.

The reason nobody wanted to do it was simple: the ACs all told me the stench was really bad, so wear your oldest flight suit so you could toss it in the trash, because the smell would never come out. And don't take your regular helicopter, get some old dog that maintenance can park for a few days and don't come around the hooch until you've had about three showers, minimum. They said the best advice they could give me was to put Vicks VapoRub on my upper lip and up inside my nose and then put a bandana that was totally soaked in Old Spice cologne wrapped around my face, and even all of that wouldn't be enough to block out the smell.

Forewarned, we flew over to the morgue and got a list of Americal firebases to visit that day for corpse pickup. It included just about every little dot on the map for the northern part of Americal's area of operations, and it would take all morning to fly out to all those places. We made our first stop at Tam Ky, a town north of Chu Lai and situated along Highway 1. We landed at a soccer field next to an ambulance that was waiting for us, and everything looked totally routine. Maybe the guys I had talked to had exaggerated this whole deal, but we all got out of the helicopter while they loaded two body bags on board. When the ambulance was opened up, even from a distance the smell instantly told us there was no exaggeration at all. Oh, the stench was so much more than just nasty. The crew and I all applied our odor countermeasures and tried to keep in mind the solemn, necessary aspects of our mission. Flying with those dead bodies in our helicopter was going to be horrible business, but someone had to do it.

We boarded our ship and ran her up ready for takeoff as quickly as we could, but the crew guys still said from the backseat, "Hey boss, let's get some air moving back here as soon as we can."

Yeah, I heard that, and we took off, slipping sideways, trying to get as much air as possible flowing through the helicopter. My eyes were watering, and only my sunglasses and the Old Spice bandana kept anyone from seeing the tears rolling down my face. The only polite way to put it, that smell would instantly gag a maggot. We flew out of trim and sideways all the way to our next stop, Firebase Hawk Hill, where we picked up two more body bags and were given field coordinates for two stops in the boondocks where infantry patrols had bodies. Then it was over to Firebases Center and West, and four or five stops out in the field. After that, our cargo compartment was piled high with body bags, stacked like a cord of blackened firewood or maybe black trash bags thrown into the rear of a sanitation department trash truck.

Having them piled up so randomly really bothered me. Things looked like someone had just thrown them on our helicopter haphazardly. It felt like we were violating some basic rule of human dignity, but things really felt wrong when four shirtless young grunts put in a bag at Firebase Siberia, then draped an American flag over the body bag and the big growing pile. With that, we headed straight back to Chu Lai to deposit our load at Graves Registration.

The body bags were placed on the landing pad all in a straight row, side by side. I didn't count them because I didn't want to know the number, but there must have been nearly twenty bags. Seeing them all lined up reminded me of the dead Viet Cong Lt. Sparks had killed in their bunkers along the canal banks down south, when I was still a New Guy. The smell of rotting bodies was just the same for these dead American boys as it had been for those dead Viet Cong. That scene at the canal all flashed back to me in vivid detail like it had happened just yesterday. It was that deeply seared into my memory and still felt that fresh. I saw it all: The ARVN general with the massive burn scars, eyebrow gone and mouth half melted away, his damned laughing, his .45 pistol firing away, and the stinking goop and maggots flying.

At Chu Lai, the body bags at least prevented us from having to look at those Americans' faces, concealed their death grimaces, and hid away any maggots and the bloated state of their bodies and their wounds. As we stood there and looked at the long row of bags, I just had to get away. As soon as our chopper was empty, we went to refuel and got out of our helicopter, took a break, had a cigarette, and breathed some fresh air. Before we went back out to finish our mission we needed to find a water hose to rinse out the floor of our helicopter to get out the liquid that had seeped from some of the bags.

At the refueling depot, our crew chief found the American flag from Firebase Siberia pushed under my seat where it had been put aside when the morgue guys at Graves Registration had unloaded us. I guessed they had forgotten to take it. The pilot, crew chief, door-gunner, and I stretched out the flag from the corners, and, in silence, we did our own little folding ceremony: tucked it into a proper, tight, orderly triangle. There was no one there to play taps, just helicopter sounds of rotors slapping the wind from the other birds landing to also refuel.

Back over at Graves Registration, I found the guy in charge out at the helipad where we had left off the body bags and asked him to put the flag with the corpse we had just brought in from Siberia. His buddies had sent it apparently to accompany his remains, so it was important. It must have flown over the firebase, and it was the actual flag he had died for, so hell yes, it was very important.

The rest of the day, we didn't let anyone pile up the bodies, and when the floor was covered with body bags we ended that run and returned to Graves Registration. I guess it took longer, but I felt somewhat better, if it was possible to feel any less bad. We watched the registration guys lining them up all in neat rows, soldiers in formation one more time, their very last time, at attention. Then they were taken into the morgue, identities confirmed, paperwork rounded up and boxed up, readied to be shipped to Mamma. See any heroes? *If I die in the combat zone, put a Purple Heart on my chest, box me up send me home, tell my Momma I did my best.* See any heroes? In that letter don't tell Momma there ain't no heroes, say instead, *He was a true hero. America can be proud.*

Even as that day was happening, I was trying to forget about it, blot out what we were doing, blot out the rotten smells of that day, and for 45 years now, I have avoided recalling Graves Registration. That was nothing I ever wanted to remember. I do remember the rain had stopped a while for the first time in days, and flying weather was minimally okay for a change. We could even see little patches of the sky for four or five hours. But by afternoon the solid clouds were back, and the damned rain started all over again.

To this day, nothing makes me sick at my stomach quicker than the smell of Vicks VapoRub or Old Spice cologne, and the two smells together would probably make my head explode like a hand grenade had gone off in my skull. I was doing the scheduling for our platoon, so I promised myself that I'd never assign that mission to myself again. I'd done it once, and I would sure never do it again.

25

ATTEMPTED MURDER:
THE FRAGGING

About 10:00 p.m. some guys in the Hornets Nest were already turning in for the night when there was a thunderous *KABOOM!*—a big explosion that very strongly rattled our hooch and knocked pictures off the walls and books off of shelves. With the senior sergeant's hooch in everyone's thoughts, we went running outside but everything looked okay over there. Still, there was smoke in the air and yelling cut through the rainy night. People were shouting somewhere, and it seemed like it was coming from our WASP pilot's hooch, which was right next door to our own hooch and adjacent to the senior sergeant's place. We went rushing in. The whole far end of the hooch was filled with smoke, and a ten-foot wide, goddamned smoldering hole was where a door used to be. There were three guys down on the floor, and others were already gathered around, stooping down to render first aid to the injured. There had been a poker game going on with six young officers crowded around a folding card table when the whole ass end of the hooch right next to them was totally blown out and turned into flying splinters of wooden shrapnel.

First, the senior sergeants, and now it was our Wasp pilots. Why would anyone in our Hornets Company be attacking our pilots? Obviously, this was not some damned concussion grenade again. It was a damned fragmentation grenade, and things were not an implied warning this time. Someone in the Hornets wanted people dead and nothing less. Who the hell would do that? Why? We gathered round and asked what could we do?

Bob Skyles was on the floor, one of our newest aircraft commanders, badly hurt, and his hands covered his eyes, blood gushing red between his fingers. He cried out pitifully, "I can't see, damn it."

Captain Salmond was trying to help him, said, "Get medics, an ambulance for the hospital."

Another two guys were trying to get up off their backs, with nasty-looking deep cuts all over their faces, torsos, and arms. There was lots of blood everywhere, pooling in the floor and splattered on the table, on the cards, the chips, and even the wall beyond. Towels, pillow cases, tee shirts, anything to use as bandages. People tried to wrap the injuries, stop people's damned bleeding.

I asked the captain what on earth had happened. He said they heard hollering, someone outside shouting out names, and he guessed they were maintenance sergeants' names, and the person hollered that this was from the guys in the damned maintenance platoon. Next, he heard something hit the wooden sidewalk, then, *KABOOM!* I looked outside and saw that an electric power wire ran from a pole to the hooch corner and hung right over the doorway, so a grenade must have hit the wire and fallen down by the back door of the hooch, just outside from where the Wasps were playing poker.

Captain Salmond pulled Bob Skyles' hands away from his eyes so his face could be wrapped up. Bob's right eye was totally pulverized, bleeding profusely, and his other eye was not much better. He was covered in blood, and Salmond the same, his hands soaked bloody red to his elbows.

Bob was crying out that he couldn't see: "Nothing, just black, am I gonna be blind? Tell me."

An ambulance arrived with a driver and two medics. They took over and rushed the three guys out and attended to two other less-injured guys. Then the siren raced off into the rainy night. A dispatch of MPs was on the way. The siren sounds faded away.

Captain Salmond buckled on his gun belt, wiped bloody hands on his pants legs, then checked his .38 pistol: spun the cylinder to insure it was fully loaded. He looked at us, said, "I'm going over there. Anyone coming with me to one of the goddamned maintenance enlisted men's hooches?"

When we got there, our platoon leader captain never broke stride, kicked the door wide open, and stomped in with his pistol drawn, and yelled, "Everyone on your sorry-assed knees right now."

He instantly punctuated his statement with a kick—*Smash!*—that shattered the screen of their old TV set. People looked shocked, and some started dropping but a few froze. *Crash!* Their studio-size refrigerator went over and spilled out its contents, just in case he didn't have everyone's attention.

He walked to a guy who was still standing and crammed his gun into his mouth. "On your knees, now, you son of a bitch, or else you'll die right now." The guy slowly lowered himself and others followed.

Ten of us were standing there, our guns drawn and aimed, where everyone was covered.

Captain Salmond jerked his gun out of the guy's mouth and wiped his hand across the guy's face, wiped blood on him and said, "Now listen up, you dumb-shit assholes, we are the Wasps. Someone in here threw a hand grenade tonight that blew up outside one of our hooches and badly wounded three of my best men, and you can probably tell that we're not the least bit happy about that stupid shit. In fact, you could say, we're pretty damned pissed off. Now, I could demand that you give me the son of a bitch who threw the grenade, but I won't do that because I don't give a shit which one of you assholes did it, because I blame every swinging dick in here, understand? And I expect each one of you damned fools to correct whatever problems you have here. So, are you men going to fix things? That's an easy question, and I don't hear a damned answer!"

Pow! He loudly stomped the floor and screamed, "So, are you going to fix things, or not?"

The maintenance guys mumbled, "Yes, sir."

"Good, now get down and give me 25!"

They acted like they didn't understand what he was saying.

"You're in the army now, you dumb shits, and I'm ordering pushups, 25 pushups!"

They slowly got into pushup mode and started.

Click. Dick cocked his pistol close to the guy's ear and nodded to the Wasps to do the same. We went among them, held pistols on each and cocked the pistols. Pushups finished, the men were on the floor.

"That pistol you heard cocking is what it will sound like before you take a goddamned bullet in your head if we ever come back, understand?"

"Yes, Sir!" they all shouted.

"One more grenade, anywhere, any reason, we'll come back and blow you ALL away. We'll kill each and every one of you. A bullet in the brain, if there is just one more grenade of any kind, one more and you ALL die. And don't think this is a parlor game. Don't think I am kidding around with you."

Then the captain knelt down to the guy and asked him, "You think I'm kidding around, buddy?"

"No, Sir, I sure don't," was the reply, the guy shaking, his voice quivering.

"You guys gonna fix your problems here?"

"Sir, yes, sir," his voice breaking a little bit more.

Cpt. Dick wiped more blood on the guy, smeared it all over his trembling face and in almost a whisper said, "If I ever come back with blood on my hands again, I'll fix your damned problems for you, buddy, without blinking. One more grenade, you all die, I promise you, one more and you all die."

Cpt. Dick Salmond, our baby face, stood up, holstered his pistol, turned and left. The rest of us walked out behind him. Four MPs were standing there talking to our captain, whispering, looking very serious. The captain was nodding, agreeing with something. I didn't know for a moment if we were all going to be arrested on the spot until the MP saluted the captain. A smile spread across the MP's face, and he turned and went into the maintenance hooch.

The Wasps returned to our area, to our hooches. I hoped those maintenance guys believed Captain Salmond. Lt. Sparks was smiling for us from somewhere. The next morning, all the sergeant supervisors from the maintenance hooch were gone, transferred out of the Hornets, and by evening, all new ones were already arriving to take their old jobs. But those new senior sergeants looked like they could easily whip their weight in wildcats, and they wouldn't be taking any shit from their enlisted men.

26

R&R HAWAII:
HOT SUN OUTSIDE,
FREEZING INSIDE

Going on R&R—finally, the day had arrived. The Wasp Platoon was going to be in something of a bind for flight personnel for a little while. Bob Skyles, one of our aircraft commanders, was gone. His eyes—we didn't know much about his condition for sure, but when Cpt. Salmond went to the hospital the next day after the fragging, Bob was gone. The doctors tried to stabilize him, then rushed him off that same night on an emergency flight to specialized surgery at a hospital in Japan. But the nurses Salmond talked to said Bob's eyes didn't look salvageable to them. Damn, that was too bad. Bob was such a good-looking, clean-cut, poster-boy warrant officer, a great pilot and a generally great guy. The news made all the Wasps absolutely sick at heart and very angry about the whole stupid fragging deal.

At that same time, Roger Walker, another aircraft commander, and Bill Shobel, a pilot, were both recovering from leg wounds they had received in a gunfight with a sole Viet Cong they had run across out west of Tam Ky. Twin M-60 door-guns against one individual AK-47 rifle. It was a classic case of you had to be careful what you wished for. If you were going to go Dink hunting and shot at Charlie, it was probably best to kill the little son of a bitch, because that time Charlie blasted off the straightest shots and totally tattooed Roger's helicopter and the door-guns did nothing but kick up dirt all around the damned guy. Oops. There was a steep price to be paid for missing your target.

With two other pilots still recovering from the fragging, and my being gone on R&R, the Wasps were going to be short by three ACs and three pilots. Things were certainly going to be a balancing act, but I would just have to put that out of my mind, think of Hawaii, a warm sun, and my wife and I strolling on some perfect beach. The idea was get away, forget Vietnam, even if just for a few good days, rest and try to relax. I felt like I was in a dream when I got on that C-130, headed to Saigon to catch that jet airliner, the one that would carry me so far away. Could barely wait, and time passed so slowly.

Saigon's Tan Son Nhut Airfield felt like an actual civilian airport, with its commercial airlines ticket counters, boarding gates, and taxicabs parked out front waiting for fares. Downtown please, the Continental Hotel. Oh, the bed, and the hot shower with the steamy water. Stood in the shower half an hour. It felt like the first time I'd had the clammy dampness off of me in months: scrubbed my body so long and washed my hair with real shampoo. Amazing. First flush toilet I'd used since IP school, which was also the last time I stayed at the Continental Hotel.

I read my R&R orders after showering. I had always thought I'd be in Hawaii six days, but looking at the actual dates, when you took out for the travel time, it was not six days at all, only five days. How had I ever made such a miscalculation? Felt ripped off, totally cheated, and that stinking son of a bitch of a war had cheated me again.

Then, finally, at long last, I was on the jet airliner, but I was so tired that I slept nearly the whole trip. It seemed like we stopped somewhere to refuel, maybe Guam, maybe Midway, but I slept through it. However, my sleeping was anything but peaceful. Every time I fell asleep nightmares came. There was the familiar dream of Steve Chasin: his bunk, his unopened mail from home, the little package, the cassette tape recording of his twin sons, Jimmy and Stevie Junior, singing, "Happy Birthday, Daddy." Woke up, told myself he had no kids, so stop dreaming that crap! Never happened! It's war, people get killed, and if I'd been flying with him, I would've died, too. But I wasn't with him, Jack Smith was. But that was just a random thing, and if I could've changed things that already happened I would have, and no one would have died that day. So why did the past haunt me? Stop that crap, too. But the bad dreams just rolled on. Woke up from one nightmare, then went back to sleep and another one came: the back of my helicopter filled to capacity with wounded guys crying out to stop their deaths. Or flying through a tight valley below mountains, running a gauntlet of machine guns up above us. Get past two guns, the next pair takes over, the firing ripping us to pieces. The firing goes on and on with no end. The blood flowing across the floor gets deeper, clouds of blood in the air, coating everything. The crying and screaming slows, stops. My body keeps getting hit, taking rounds, over and over. The helicopter is soon burning, a ball of fire shooting through the valley, fire burning my flesh away... Wake up, fight sleep, then fall asleep again.

Dreamed I had to pee and woke up and stumbled to a stand. Saw across the aisle three guys also asleep, heads bobbing down limply. Lights low, nighttime, most everyone asleep. Horrified, my heart nearly stopped right there. The three guys weren't asleep, they were corpses: *McDonald, Smith,* and

Smitty from Tay Ninh. Sitting behind them, dead *Serna* and *Larraga*, dressed in their blue jeans. One more corpse next to them, name tag *Denny*, a warrant officer wearing silver wings. Why were those damned dead guys there? Why on my damned plane? They didn't need R&R!

I rubbed my eyes, woke up more, and looked again. None of those guys were corpses, and they were no one I knew. See, just dreaming. The jeans weren't blue jeans at all but blue airline blankets covering their laps. And that name tag didn't say *Denny*, because when I looked again it read *Penny* with a mother-humping *P*, goddamn it. But he was a warrant officer and had pilot wings. I wondered what his dreams were like. I didn't want to think that I'd been hallucinating, because that was what happened only to actual crazy people.

Why wasn't I dreaming of moonlit strolls hand in hand along some beautiful beach? Or rolling in my sweet wife's arms? Or Jane doing a seductive little hula dance? Or simply having a nice meal? Why always that Death crap, that Vietnam crap? At any rate, it was a long flight, and my stupid nightmares made it pretty miserable most of the way.

Eventually we were there, and everyone got off the plane. I had been cold the whole flight, because the air-conditioning blasted away the whole time. Outside, the sun felt hot, but I was freezing inside, still cold from the plane.

Then there she was, on the other side of the last gate, standing there with the other wives, and she was waving to me. She was wearing a new dress she'd sent a photo of, all tropical looking, a floral print, bright yellow with red and orange flowers, and a short skirt that showed off her pretty legs well. It was her, all right, with a big smile on her face, a giant smile. She took off her sunglasses so I could see her full face. When I reached her at the gate, her arms went around my neck, and there was a welcome kiss. But the only thing I could think of was, *I'm freezing inside, still cold from the plane.*

After months, I was seeing her, holding her, kissing her, but cold was the only sensation I had: physically cold, the shivering hard sort of cold. But emotionally I just felt like an empty jug, nothing inside, no feelings, not of any kind, no joy, no happiness, just empty and drained, dog tired to exhaustion. Everything about the situation felt so wrong of me. I'd been waiting for this for so long, but it seemed my wires were all crossed, with things inside me shorting out, all power gone. There was nothing there but emptiness, a cold black void. I should've been overflowing with excitement, like a Texas oil well gushing delight skyward. But there I was, an empty jug, nothing inside.

We caught a taxicab to the hotel, a *Denny's* Hotel. Jane had such a sense of humor. Honolulu had a Denny's Hotel in 1970. The next day we would fly over to Kauai, a less-populated island without all the hustle and bustle of

Honolulu. That first day all we needed was a Denny's Hotel king-sized bed. Sleep came and took me away much too soon. Sleep, like a hydraulic press crushing me deep into a dreamless state, with all brain activity absolutely flat-lined, thank God. A big brass band in the hotel room with us would not have awakened me from that sleep. Didn't move a muscle until morning arrived, with Jane sitting on the edge of the bed, offering a hot cup of coffee and a newspaper. A room-service breakfast was there, everything anyone could think of: over-easy eggs, French toast, ham and bacon, biscuits-n-gravy, oatmeal, tomato and orange juice.

I ate a little of everything but didn't make much of a dent in it. I couldn't eat much. I guessed my system was shrunk from eating so little on a daily basis for so long. I hadn't looked at myself in a mirror in a long time, and I was pretty damned skinny. I felt better than the previous day; jet lag and the big time-zone change had affected me a great deal, I guessed, and the night-mares that had robbed the rest from my sleep on the airplane hadn't helped any.

The time at the Denny's Hotel that morning was minimal, just a quick shower and then rushing to the airport for a short hop over to Kauai. We got our rental car and went to the new hotel, some Hawaiian named place, the Hyatt Kapa King Resort or something like that. Jane had an itinerary that was packed with places to go and things to see nonstop. We were busy driving here and there all over the island: first, it was black-sand beaches, then a 1,000-foot-high water fall. It was one restaurant here for lunch, one there for dinner. It was rapid-fire days, and in the blink of an eye our time was used up.

We had talked endlessly, small talk about things at home in El Paso, cir-cularly about Vietnam—she wanted to know about it, but what she wanted to know was whether things were really okay there, was I safe? All the bad news items she saw on TV weren't really as bad as TV made them out to be, were they? She had created this whole self-protective story she'd been telling herself for a long time. She thought the very worst part of Vietnam was that it had us separated and was wasting a year of our lives, but it would be over in just a few more months. Then we'd be back together, and we could move on like nothing had really changed. But I knew nothing could have been fur-ther from the truth.

I couldn't tell her the college guy she'd known was gone forever and I didn't know what I'd be, but every core thing about me from before had been turned upside down or just killed off altogether. Sure couldn't tell her I had no clue who I was anymore. We were total strangers because I was one to myself, a stranger I knew nothing about because I was just doing my job and trying not to think about anything that was going on around me. Couldn't tell her about Steve Chasin or Jack Smith or any of the other Hornets who had been killed or that it had been only random chance that saved me from being one of the dead, a coin toss or officer of the day or probably other times I didn't even know about or that I had somehow accepted that I was living like a dead man.

I certainly couldn't tell her that everyone I saw on Hawaii looked like they were living pointless lives, robots with stupid existences, doing stupid jobs: a waiter filling my already mostly full water glass or a hotel maid making our bed that we would immediately get back into, such waste of time. How could I ever be some motel clerk again or some student listening to a history professor rant about the evils of war, like he knew anything about it? Couldn't tell her I wanted more than anything to get on the plane bound for the States with her and leave the army behind, leave Vietnam for the Americal colonels to decide the level of *Acceptable Losses* for purposeless missions to take objectives they wanted to keep only until the weather turned bad. Couldn't tell her I wanted to go home. In Vietnam I was only raw material, a resource that could be used up in a war that had been over for a long time by then but had not stopped yet. Hell, the war had been over since President Johnson had chosen not to run for a second term. Johnson knew it was over. Pointless lives, stupid existences, and if you were getting shot at? *Just Take It. Take It.* Things never got more insane than that, Mr. Warrant Officer Robot. So why do it? You'd been put there, probably by volunteering. Your buddies were in the same pile of crap as you, and they needed you to do your job, cover their asses like they were covering yours. That was the one and only sane reason: your fellow robot buddies. If they could just take it, so could you. Everything else about Vietnam was totally screwed up and crazy.

So when our R&R was wrapping up, I'd really never told Jane anything about war or even what my life was like there. And I certainly didn't mention to her that I would probably have to go back to Vietnam again for a second tour after a year's duty spent back in the States. We'd talked about that plenty in the past, before I ever went to Vietnam for my current tour. We both knew all about that, so there was no reason to bring it up again. Hell, at the end of a second tour, sometime in 1973, I'd probably be the last fool left there to turn out the goddamned lights when the stinking party was finally over, and I didn't want to be thinking about that ugly-assed scenario. That just sent chills up my spine.

I tried not to make Jane's trip to Hawaii only about providing me with sex. The whole time was about us being together on a more holistic level than just screwing. We'd walked the beach together, tried the water, but it had been too cold for me. We'd been lots of places and done lots of things. We ate in good restaurants, had tropical cocktails under the stars while watching the surf at the beach at our hotel a couple of nights, went to a movie (*MASH*) and drove the daylights out of our rental car.

The sex could have been more, but in any circumstances there could never be enough when you are 24 years old. But you couldn't store it up and keep score and have that matter, because the only screwing that mattered was always the next one. And you could always imagine that the next one would be the most fabulous experience of your whole life. Still, it could have been more, but I was still feeling emotionally cold, just felt like an empty jug, nothing inside, no feelings of any kind, no joy, no happiness, just empty and drained like I'd felt when I'd first arrived in Hawaii. Things hadn't changed much. I had no idea there was a name for that feeling, *depression,* but depression it was, and I came to know its name too well after that, years later in the VA shrinks' offices.

From the beginning of our time together, it had made me sad to think I'd be leaving again so soon, but that time had come. The last few minutes before I was to board that jet airliner, the one to carry me far away, back to Vietnam, I tried to tell Jane the important things I hadn't adequately said yet, like how I felt about her and how important she was to me, those sorts of things. I tried not to make it sound like some final message of the heart from a condemned man. I just wanted it to hold her over till I was finally able to come back home. Oh yes, back home, where we could pick up our lives and start living again, together again, back in El Paso, where I used to feel right and life made sense.

At that moment, the scariest thought I'd ever had in my life occurred to me: coming into some hot LZ with door-guns blazing might be the only place I'd ever feel truly "right" again, ever. Everything on the line, life and death, all balanced. All things around you, every idea, all pointless in the face of your imminent possible death. Could you ever feel more alive than that? The act of making yourself do that repeatedly by force of will, that was the meaning: finding the depth of your will, your true limits.

Standing there holding Jane, kissing her, saying good-bye, I didn't need such trash in my head. I was wanting to capture that moment, store it, to bring back that experience in my lonesome nights in Chu Lai. That was what I wanted of that moment. I began to turn to walk to the plane. Jane popped a quick little salute, trooper sharp, and said, "I'll see you again in old El Paso, Warrant Officer Denny."

I stopped, kissed her again, said, "Yes, El Paso. Everything will be right in El Paso."

I walked to the plane. On the stair, I turned, waved, and took a last long look. I was still wishing the sex could have been more, but next time it would be in El Paso, at our home. On the plane, a young stewardess came by and I asked for two blankets. I explained that I had a really bad chill. The air-conditioning was already blowing cold and hard, and I didn't want to suffer all the way back to goddamned Saigon.

27

FLARES ALL NIGHT

Coming back to Vietnam from my R&R, and after I had adjusted to the nice smell of Hawaii, I was rudely hit with the stink of Vietnam once again, that nasty odor of burning human sewage and death and decay and who knew what else. Figured the stench of Vietnam smelled like Hell. And Hell couldn't have stunk worse or was too different. If you never knew anything about Vietnam other than the smell of the place, that was enough to make you hate it. Instead of spending the night in Saigon, I found the first C-130 I could catch that was going to Chu Lai and made it aboard just before takeoff. If I was going to readjust to the Vietnam stink, I figured that it might as well be Hornet latrine smells. After a quick flight, we landed on the Chu Lai runway just after the sun had set behind the mountains out in the west.

Back at our hooch, everything was as quiet as a tomb: no one was back from flying yet. In the gathering darkness, I stripped out of my tropical-worsted khaki uniform travel clothes and folded them all away. The next time I would unpack that uniform would be when I was going back home at the end of my tour of duty. It still looked the same as it had the first day I had arrived in Vietnam: just warrant officer's bars and some silver wings. But I had to smile when I saw that I'd picked up a decoration in Hawaii, a smear of lipstick on my shirt collar. That must have happened that morning at the airfield in Honolulu. I would leave that exactly like it was. Got back into a flight suit, and when I put the shirt on I glimpsed S. Chasin's name written there inside the collar, so things were exactly the same as they ever had been. When I strapped on my holster and checked my pistol I finally felt fully dressed and ready to be back in the saddle again. I was back in character again as *Hornet Three-Three*.

Needed to get out to operations to start catching up on paperwork: tally the flight-hour totals, review the check rides' logbook, and take a look at the scheduling situation. I was a full week behind on everything. Pushing myself back into routine things kept me from dwelling on wanting to be back home in El Paso with Jane. Midnight came and went, but no missions had been called in from the 23rd Division. One a.m. rolled around and still no regular missions, but we did get a call from Division headquarters. A little artillery fire support base (FSB) down south of us, between Chu Lai and Duc Pho, was being probed by the enemy. The guys at the FSB expected that a full-blown ground assault was surely eminent. They needed a helicopter flare-ship ASAP, and Division needed the Hornets to get a bird up, this was an emergency. Say again: EMERGENCY—that FSB needed help immediately!

The logistics of getting a crew out of bed and out to the flight line would take too long, so the operations officer asked me if I would go. A maintenance officer, a captain, who was working on aircraft scheduling spoke up and said he could go with me, he would get two more guys from the maintenance line to be our crew. That was obviously the fastest thing we could pull together right then.

We arrived on station orbiting over the FSB with our helicopter full of flares and called up the base command on the radio and asked what they wanted us to do. They had Bad Guys repeatedly testing the perimeter wire along their south and southwest sides, so they wanted flare-illumination out those directions. The night at that hour was absolutely dark, with thick overcast and no moon or stars, just total blackness. We were just lucky there was no rain right then and hoped it would hold off.

We took a position, and the backseat guys launched two parachute flares. When they lit up, the black night became like day, as if a big light switch had been turned on. The countryside burst into a harsh white glare. Any Viet Cong or NVA running around in the open were going to wish they could become invisible, because they were caught with no place to hide. The only thing left for them to do: immediately drop to the ground and start praying.

We set up a routine once we established exactly how long the flares burned, the best drop altitude, and where the flares drifted. Things very quickly stabilized, and the Bad Guys stayed back, although the little firebase kept steadily taking mortar and small-arms fire. But at least there were no overt mass ground assaults of screaming suicidal wild Vietnamese devils.

We were there nearly two hours until we ran out of flares and were getting very low on fuel, and we had to make a very fast dash back to Chu Lai to resupply and refuel. By the time we returned on station over the FSB, we'd been gone a little less than thirty minutes. Naturally, the firebase was totally dark, and the Viet Cong attacks had increased a great deal, so the fighting was fully engaged as we began dropping more flares.

We listened on the radio to conversations between an air mission commander and a flight of Dolphin Company Slick helicopters trying to do a nighttime combat assault with a load of infantry reinforcements from Duc Pho. The AMC and the flight leader were arguing. The AMC wanted the flight to land at some rice paddies out in the countryside near the firebase, but the flight leader wanted to land at a big open space he knew about on Highway 1, about a quarter of a mile farther away. The flight leader knew that place was clear of any big dangerous obstructions and the flight could land there in the dark without worrying about hitting anything.

I got on the radio and broke into their conversation and asked if they needed some of our flares to light up the countryside for their formation's landing. The AMC flatly told me no. He basically sounded like I should mind my own business and keep the flares over the firebase area like I had been instructed to do.

The argument was stopped when the AMC said to land the goddamned helicopters where he had ordered, and he repeated some map coordinates and a landing heading. The radio went silent for a few minutes. Then all hell broke loose. Multiple radio calls were trying to broadcast on the same damned frequency at once, cancelling each other out. Finally, the flight leader got through: one of his flight's helicopters had flown into a damned tree, and that pilot was doing an emergency landing over at the highway where they should have gone in the first goddamned place. The flight leader had aborted the attempted landing that the AMC had ordered. Instead, he was putting the flight down with the infantry troops at the highway where there weren't a bunch of big-assed trees all around the area.

The AMC barked his original LZ orders back and started pulling rank on the flight leader. But immediately, and with just as much fervor, the flight leader yelled over the radio for the air mission commander to take his little-girly manhood and go screw himself with the pitiful thing. Holy shit! Did you hear that? The radio was super silent for a while. In our helicopter, even though the situation was as serious as a heart attack, it was still impossible to suppress our laughter. Things would be hot around Duc Pho come morning. Man, you could think all those sorts of things you wanted, but you could not say anything like that over the radio with the whole world listening. But Americal would fix that little spat their usual way: Medals all around for everyone! That would sooth all the ruffled feathers. While the temporarily blown-up combat assault was working itself out and some angry folks came to some agreement on where to land the infantry reinforcements, we were circling over the little firebase and we could see enemy troops moving on the ground out in the open, massing into positions, preparing to charge the firebase. Mortar fire had become increasingly frequent to the point that it was raining down nonstop, and things were looking increasingly like the Bad Guys would be coming in force at any moment.

I called the AMC and, as politely as I could, suggested the obvious: what was needed was a team of Dolphin Shark gunships. (I didn't say the other obvious thing: The Sharks should have been brought out earlier, instead of the infantry troops. The Sharks could stop this attack in its tracks with a mini-gun C-Model gunship or even just a few well-placed rockets.)

He replied that there was no way gunships would be allowed to fight in the dark because it was just too dangerous for the friendlies. There were way too many villagers in this area for that. Told him that with our flares for light anyone could see the Bad Guys plain as day. He said if that was so why didn't I just go down and get them with my door-guns and that way the Americal Division would know who to talk to if I killed a bunch of villagers? I told him we were only an unarmed Hornet maintenance ship sent out in an emergency but we'd drop flares for him to do that with his door-guns if he wanted.

During our conversation with the AMC, from back on the ground the firebase radioed they had four breaches in the perimeter wire, Bad Guys were inside the compound, and fighting had gotten to be close-quarter, man-to-man fighting. They needed the reinforcement guys to hurry the hell up. Things went on like that for some time, but the Americans in the firebase were holding their own and killing the Bad Guys as they got inside the wire. The night wore on into the wee hours without any reinforcements ever reaching the firebase. We deployed our last two flares and were low on fuel again. We had no choice but to race back to Chu Lai to resupply. We returned to the fire support base with another load of flares as fast as we could get our old Huey helicopter to fly.

We repeatedly radioed the firebase as we approached but got no reply from them. Their radio was silent, which was not a good sign, not good at all. As we got there, over toward Highway 1 where the Dolphins landed the infantry, a frenzy of muzzle flashes said the reinforcements were engaged in a hell of a big hot firefight of their own, so they were never going to reach the firebase that night.

We popped two flares off to the south side of the firebase, but everything was stone still, no muzzle flashes or mortar explosions going off. We circled above and saw nothing going on. We dropped down low-level to see things better. Where the red, white, and blue U.S. flag had been flying all through the night, a VC flag fluttered in ghostly flare light. That long night hadn't worked out right. The American flag was gone from its pole. Our flag was replaced with a red and blue flag that had a yellow star in the middle of it: a damned Viet Cong flag was flying over our destroyed little firebase.

I felt like throwing up, felt like screaming. We banked around hard and fast, made another low-level pass, and came to a hover over the smoking place. Yes. It was a VC flag, their sign that they had snuffed out every American. The VC had prevailed in that small battle. But no one back home would ever know about that fight. It wouldn't make it to the evening news. There was no movement, and everything was deadly still, only wafting smoke over the silent place. Numerous dead Bad Guys were scattered here and there where they'd been killed during their assault, some tangled in the barbwire and some piled in front of American fighting positions. A lot of dead Vietnamese paid the ultimate price it cost to raise their miserable flag. Guessed Americans made their last stand in bunkers; guessed that was where our dead lay, guns in hand, with death's ugly shroud settled over them.

The eastern horizon was becoming ever so slightly visible. Shark gunships would be hunting in the coming dawn light, looking for any Bad Guys left around there, looking for whoever had taken our flag. Looking at the drifting smoke, I felt totally sick at heart. I'd talked all night to some officer on the radio, and from the sound of his voice I could tell he was someone I would've liked. But his radio was deathly silent now when the sun was so damned close to coming up and ending that long night.

Gunships sat in their safe revetments all night, while Bad Guys ran free in the darkness by the hundreds, like ants eating our little firebase. But Americal refused to endanger villagers. The VC would disappear into the area villages, and this would stay hush-hush, swept away. Reinforcements had not come at the last minute with guns blazing, no, they were pinned down nearby, but still so far away. How many dead on both sides? More than I wanted to know. We had won the Body-Count War, three or four times over, but the VC had won their battle there that night. Even now, all these 45 years later, I block those memories of that night the American firebase died. Twenty-four hours earlier I'd been in Hawaii, and it seemed a world away. Thirty hours earlier I'd been in my wife's arms making love, and it seemed an eternity away. I should've slept over in Saigon that night instead of flying and dropping flares all night.

┌─────┐
│ **28** │
└─────┘

CUT ME, CUT ME,
GO AHEAD

After hovering there over the dead fire support base, with bodies every-where and the haunting sound of rotors slapping swirling smoke serving as our Taps for the dead Americans, every fiber in my being ached with pain from being tensed like a spring all night and from the lack of sleep for so long. The last bed I'd been in was all the way back in Hawaii. By the time we returned to Chu Lai, that bad night had left me only wanting my bunk and for sleep to blot out my thoughts.

My hooch was silent, with everyone gone flying. Still fully dressed, boots and all, I flopped on my bed and stretched out, but sleep was a long time coming to me because my mind refused to shut down. My bunk was right next to the hooch door and up against the outside wall. Sometime after I'd finally dropped off, there was a loud banging on the wall, right next to my head. *Bang, Bang, Bang.*

Something was hitting our hooch wall. I got up and looked outside to see what all the ruckus was about. There were two guys fighting, crashing into the side of the building. I hollered at them loudly, telling them to take their bullshit somewhere else, but they ignored me. I saw the one who was pushing the fight had a knife out, a switchblade knife with about a six-inch blade flashing in the light. The second guy was trying his best to hold off the knife. I hollered a stream of profanity at them again, and the attacker finally looked at me said something in Spanish. I guessed it was to keep out of what was happening, that this fight wasn't my business.

Horseshit if it wasn't my business: I was trying to sleep in my hooch right there, so all of their damned noise was certainly my business. Take this somewhere else, you idiots. I sure didn't want this sort of aggravation. I was way too tired for any of that. Get away from my hooch and cut out all the damned noise, you two fools.

The guy wielding the knife was wearing a wife-beater tee shirt, a little

145

sleeveless strapped tee shirt, and he had ugly tattoos all over him and a stupid-looking bandana of some kind wrapped around his head, like he was trying to look like some gang-member thug, a Pachuco Mafioso, and he obviously was totally out of control, in a violent, hot rage.

They continued and the tattooed guy with the knife soon overpowered the other guy, and the knife blade slowly but steadily sank in the guy's belly up to the hilt. All of that was certainly my business then. I couldn't very well stand there and watch one fool murder another fool up against the side of my hooch. I drew my pistol, went down the steps, and screamed at them to stop. The bloody knife came out, and the tattooed guy looked me in the eye, and then he rammed the knife back into the other guy for a second time, full force! That in itself was reason enough for me to shoot him right then.

The last thing on earth I wanted was to get into something like this, but I had to stop that crap, so I immediately went into my best El Paso tough-guy mode, and I pushed between them and pushed the tattooed guy back. They'd been jabbering Spanish rapid fire, and I didn't understand most of it, except the cussing. Oh, yeah, I understood the cussing, and understood: "Money, pay me my money, now, today, and marijuana, and heroin." I sure as hell knew all those words from my limited Rio Grande border vocabulary.

The guy with the knife was hollering more Spanish at the other one over my shoulder, trying to get to him and push by me like I was just a temporary minor inconvenience to him. I held up my pistol for him to see and tried to push him back, but he jumped up and placed his knife at my solar plexus like my pistol didn't impress him any. A standoff. That was fine: I was the one with the gun.

This kid was no Mexican. Mexicans weren't stupid: you showed them a gun when all they had was a knife, everyone suddenly tended to get a whole lot friendlier. Maybe he was a New Yorker: Harlem or the South Bronx. I guessed he thought he was really tough, some major bad-ass. It seemed that he thought he was gonna back me down or stab me. That was what was going through his little pea-brained mind. Back me down, then finish his little job, finish cutting up the other guy, stabbing him. In Texas, we called that a Mexican standoff. Who's gonna give up, be the asshole to blink? The tip of his blade was touching me. I held up my pistol, and slowly, deliberately cocked it, then jammed it up under his chin, leaned in to his face real close, and asked, "You brought a knife to a gunfight? Not a good idea, now put it down pendejo."

He tilted his head the cockiest amount as the pressure from his knife point increased noticeably.

"Is it gonna be like that, *puto cabrón*? Is that the way this is gonna go? Then cut me, cut me, go ahead, *chingada*. One drop of my blood, you'll be soooo dead." I answered with my pistol pushed up harder under his chin. We stood there like that a few seconds. "Come on, fool, cut me. I want you to— cut an officer."

By then I was feeling so much anger and rage at that rag-head idiot I would have shot him. But it was more than just anger at him, it was being in Vietnam in general, and last night watching all night what happened to men because of this war, and this scumbag piece of shit lived in the rear with the gear and the queers and he was perfectly safe and alive. I was feeling such hatred for this guy: I had such overwhelming rage in me that I actually wanted him to cut me, even minimally, so I could pull the trigger, shoot him, and it took all of my will power not to do it. As my finger tightened on the trigger, the pressure of his knife eased up some and then stopped. His hand pulled away from me, and the knife slipped away. Two guys jumped him, grabbed his arms. A little group had gathered around us, eight or ten people, and they swarmed him. Then his knife was on the ground, and he was driven down onto his knees with his arms penned behind him.

I let down the hammer of my pistol and turned to the other kid. He was bent over and holding his gut, but he was still standing. He had been close to being stabbed to death for drug money, right there against the wall of my hooch. He was lucky someone had been home trying to sleep that day. Mr. Rag Head-Latino was one lucky son of a bitch that I didn't notice there was a group of witnesses standing there watching our little deal go down. Just having his knife on me in a threatening fashion was enough for me to blow the top of his little brainless head into the wild blue yonder. And as pissed off as I was about things in general, my pistol trigger could've been a satisfying outlet.

I asked if those two knuckleheads were from the infantry outfit next door to our Hornets Nest Company Area. Someone from the crowd said no, they were from the Hornets Maintenance Platoon, so they were ours. That threw everything into a new light. I had just assumed that those two bozos had to be from some other unit that was housed around us. An MP Jeep and an ambulance pulled up, and everyone wanted to know what the big problem was.

Drugs, hard drugs, in our maintenance platoon? I had no idea, never even dreamed of that. In addition to the whole fight scene that had just happened, I told the MPs about the fragging we'd had recently and our man Pancho Villa the Rag-Head there was probably connected to that. Hell, he was probably the one who threw the grenade to show how tough he was, or at least was somehow involved.

My friend Bob Skyles was blinded by someone like him, and parts of me wished that I'd killed him for that. I'd never felt such an urge to kill someone, and I wanted to punish the kid for making me feel like that. All it would have taken was the slightest little cut or his knife blade fully into my heart, either way looked like a fair trade for me if I got to put a bullet in his brain. If it was the knife-through-the-heart route, then at least I could've stopped thinking every damned day and night about men being dead in my place, killed instead of me.

All I wanted right then was for all this commotion to go away so I could get back to bed.

So, the Hornet Company had some level of a drug problem. That was troubling news.

HOOD'S CHECK RIDE, SCREAMING WOMAN

The weather was actually sort of nice for a change, compared to the monsoon rain we had been having for a long time, at least a month or six weeks. It was only partly cloudy, with high scattered clouds and a pleasantly warm sun shining. Larry Hood—Hornet 32—and I flew a single-ship general support mission (hauling ass and trash) in the southern section of the Americal area of operation for Larry's periodic check ride. Larry was a fellow hooch mate of mine and one of my best friends. We were both in-country about the same amount of time, me having only two weeks on him, and I had selfishly scheduled that mission for us so we could get some lunch down at the Dolphins' Duc Pho mess hall as a little celebration for us both passing the six-month in-country milestone. We were half done with our time in that crazy place and were on the downhill side of our one-year tour.

Our lunch was also to celebrate Larry's being the luckiest man in Vietnam, if you ignored the part about him also being the unluckiest man in Vietnam. Larry's unlucky part first: in the approximately three months that he'd been an aircraft commander, Larry had been shot down and crashed six times already. The luckiest part: out of six crashes, two-thirds of them very hard crashes in mountaintop LZ areas, no Hornet crewman had been seriously injured, not one person. The odds were poor for someone to experience a combat crash and survive uninjured. But for six helicopters to all crash and no one be hurt got into the spooky end of all the strange things that happened in Vietnam. Larry's situation made you almost think about miracles, because things had already surpassed mere good luck a while ago.

Larry's nerves must have been totally ravaged, but he got up and went on flying every morning when he was scheduled, like everything was just business as usual. I asked what missions he wanted, but he had no special requests. He didn't know anything he could do differently. Every time he had been shot down, the circumstances had been different, his position in the combat assault formation different—the list of variables could go on endlessly. I agreed with him: everything that had happened to him was purely random, and there was nothing you could do about random shit, not one damned thing. But behind his back, others in our Platoon lovingly called him "Hornet Magnet-Ass 32."

During free time in the morning, between our mission errands, Larry flew all of his check ride maneuvers, and we finished up just in time to eat at the mess hall. We had a chance to talk with some Dolphin pilots who had been on the FUBAR nighttime airlift trying to reinforce the firebase where I'd flown dropping flares all night. What a sorry outcome that was. What was sorry was that Americal Division wouldn't fight at night and everyone knew it, most of all Charlie.

The Dolphins guys told us the real truth about that little fire support base. Highway 1 north out of Duc Pho ran near the firebase, and a separate side road ran right up to it, so anyone could drive an army truck from Duc Pho to the firebase in about 20 minutes, maybe 30 minutes at night. The reason a convoy wasn't sent out there when the place was being attacked that night was because the Viet Cong controlled the area. When it was dark and Americal wouldn't fight, it was because they were afraid of killing the wrong people. No collateral damage please. No convoys shooting up the whole countryside. No helicopter gunships blasting rockets all over. No mini-guns ripping up everything in sight. Not a thing, not in the darkness of night. Americal didn't even like infantry out walking in the dark and stomping around the weeds getting into a fight.

If you were at an Americal firebase and were attacked, you better be able to hold out at night, because Americal might not come to help. Not until dawn's first sun gave some light—just the way it was, wrong or right. Just the Vietnam War: "It don't mean nothing."

After lunch, the unit we were working for asked us to go to an outpost up north and take some officers into Chu Lai. It was that kind of day, "Hood's Taxi." So we were zipping along, enjoying the weather, when a radio call came in on Guard—the emergency radio channel for distress calls: "Any aircraft, any aircraft, we need Dust-Off." And they gave the name of a village that was only a mile from our then current location.

Larry immediately banked into a sharp turn and headed in their direction then called them to say he was on the way and would be there in less than a minute, just a few seconds, get ready for us. We would be approaching from due east. He asked for a situation run-down report: "Village having a holiday festival, a county fair sort of a day with big crowds of people, and a Viet Cong sapper blew up a satchel charge in the middle of the main event area. Many bad injuries and many dead. Secondary bombs going off around here. Viet Cong all over the place shooting village leaders and others at random.

South Vietnamese troops hunting after them. Be aware, gun battles going on everywhere. Popping smoke now at the place to land."

Larry radioed, "See yellow smoke, confirm."

"Roger the yellow. Come on in, Hornet 32."

We sat down in an elementary schoolyard: a carnival midway of little rides, game booths, food stands, and a scene of panicked chaos with people running every direction trying to escape. Women, children, running, screaming, crying. The only organization was a group of U.S. infantrymen performing triage on a crowd of wounded Vietnamese civilians, some visibly critically injured, limbs gone, torsos torn apart, organs spilling out, blood and gore covered all. As soon as our skids touched the dirt, troops started loading us up with wounded. I heard a radio call for any additional helicopter in the area to come, provide needed additional Dust-Off—situation dire, say again, situation dire.

It was then that I saw we might be taking some fire from a few crazed Viet Cong who had been running around shooting randomly. Now they had a new target: a nice juicy Huey sitting on the ground, our Huey, and they charged toward us furiously. ARVN were chasing after them, shooting them the best they could, but our door-guns were powerless in that situation because there were civilians by the dozens everywhere, and there was no place to shoot without civilians being hit. Larry told the crewmen in back to use only their M16s if they had to and be very careful with the aim.

Larry was watching the loading of the injured, and we had more room. We waited there longer as the ground guys helped more and more people get on board. Repeatedly there was the damned *ting, ting, ting, ting* of rifle rounds hitting us, but we still didn't budge. I watched Larry, and he was a totally calm and cool customer. There was no military purpose to this. The Viet Cong attacked, embracing their own probable death, for no other reason than to terrorize civilians, to teach them it was dangerous to participate in any sort of community function or activity. Just terror, a VC suicide terror mission, insane.

Squishy-Plop. A grunt dropped a woman down on the floor right between Larry and me, just behind us. The squishy-plop sound came from her worst injury. Everything from the hips down was completely blown away. The grunt had sat her down upright on her torso stub. Her arms were also gone, and only shreds of bloody meat hung from her shoulders. The whole front of her was burned to a charred black. Her clothing was melted into her incinerated flesh. But the worst part was the fact that she was still alive for the moment and screaming at the top of her voice. It was obvious from her condition that she had only moments more to live, and she was an unbearably horrible sight. Why the hell were they loading damned dead people on our helicopter? But she wasn't dead yet, on the contrary, she was wide awake and screaming full blast. I had never seen a living person who was so totally destroyed, but miraculously she wasn't dead yet. Her screams were the most bloodcurdling painful outcries anyone could ever imagine, and her screaming was like a white-hot machete chopping into me, taking chunks out of me.

Larry gave the guys on the ground a hand signal that we were all loaded and taking off, then we were airborne, headed to Chu Lai. I scanned the instruments, everything green, no flashing warning lights, and that was amazing.

Screaming, screaming, how was the little old woman still alive? Over the throaty sound of our engine, the howl of the wind, the chatter of the radios, and all the other hurt people, her screaming was louder than everything else. Screaming, screaming, over everything, screams. I turned in my seat to see her, looked into her terrified eyes and saw her utter disbelief and what had to be unimaginable pain.

Chaos ran wild; screams had infected everyone back in our cargo compartment. All of our injured passengers were then wailing, crying out, shrieking as a chorus for the screaming old woman. The intercom was blaring with the crewmen wanting instructions, how they could help them. The only thing we could do was fly and get to the hospital as soon as possible.

I looked at the woman, tried to calm her. My thoughts tried to tell her, *I know, only monsters, only the evil of hell itself could do this to you. For what? You did nothing to deserve this happening. It'll end soon, be over, finally done.*

Her eyes looked into mine and bored hard like she was trying to connect to me, that maybe a connection would mean she was alive. Screams became speech, words I couldn't remember or pronounce and would never understand. She was talking to me, but in Vietnamese, shouting to me between screams and over all the other noise. I couldn't fathom what she was saying or get my arms around the horror she must have been experiencing, to be so obviously a dead person but still alive momentarily—but hopelessly dead nonetheless. Awake, aware, and feeling everything while Death pulled her deeper into its inescapable dark clutches. The horror I saw in her, absolute terror. The horror I felt seeing a person dying such a totally horrible and protracted death was immeasurable. She started repeating one word to me, and I took it as PLEASE, her beseeching request. If it had been me, I would have been begging for that nightmare to end.

I watched her and listened to screams and that one word, repeated over and over. I pulled my pistol from its holster. If she'd had any arms left, any hands, I would have given her my pistol so she could have done it herself, made things stop for herself! Twenty-five years later, I told my VA shrink how I twisted around in my seat and flashed my pistol up fast. She said her one word again as she leaned toward the gun instead of turning away from it. Then I quickly turned back around, not looking anymore. I'd seen everything I ever wanted to see about that pitiful old Screaming Woman.

In the helicopter, silence instantly saturated everything. My pistol had brought silence. No more howling, no screams, only silence. I turned on the Saigon rock radio station, and "Sleepwalk" was playing. Turned it up to the loudest setting. The intercom was quiet, no one said anything. Not then, not ever. Not one word was ever mentioned to me by anyone about the woman the damned Viet Cong had blown up.

Rotor blades slapped the wind their hardest as Larry flew as fast as he could. The only screaming was the jet engine's roar. The only moaning was the Huey giving her limit. Larry flipped his switch to hear Saigon radio blaring. Then the crew's switches, also: "Sleepwalk" blasted.

The shrink wanted to know how I felt about the whole episode, the Screaming Woman. How I felt about that? I had to chuckle. How I felt? Well, let's see: I regretted the situation ever started, the Viet Cong blowing her all to hell, regretted we were the ones to get her, regretted they plopped her like a potato sack upright and just behind us where we heard all her horrified screaming, experienced all of her pain, regretted seeing how prolonged dying could be. If that was happening to her, the same thing could happen to me, such a bad ending. How I felt at the time? Numb and relieved. Relieved that it was done for her and she was quiet and I was released from experiencing what was happening. She was killed when the Viet Cong bomb went off. She just took a long time dying. Was she talking to me? I thought so! Asking for things to end? I sure the hell would have! Asking me to help her? But I could do nothing for her, nothing. The only thing I could do, make everything stop, because I couldn't take any more of it. I didn't do anything for her: it was for myself.

Maybe that day tested my weakness or my strength. Either way, I found my absolute final limits. But how I felt? Wished that never happened, that day never came, or the goddamned Screaming Woman, because what happened back then proved to me that every aspect of who I'd been before had been replaced by someone I didn't know. It was *Invasion of the Body Snatchers* and only Hornet 33 was left behind: Ed Denny was long gone to his personal hell, just smoke blown into the endless void of featureless black nothingness to spend the rest of eternity alone with his worst thoughts. But I never felt bad about that lady. I did that old woman no harm. It was myself I hurt. Because I killed any hope I had left that I would someday unwrap my experiences of being a pilot in Vietnam and let all of that fall away from me. What I was doing was not a series of experiences. It had become who I was.

It wasn't that I had become something overtly bad, no, not that, just something I wasn't expecting. It was that I was something different. My change was just a process I never knew would happen, had not considered, and even if unchosen, nonetheless unavoidable. There was no getting away from events, no escaping the path I'd put myself on. The only thing about me that was still as it had always been: I hadn't totally given in to living like I was a dead man or felt the hopelessness of *"Vietnam don't mean nothing"* ruled over me. I was still refusing to be a pawn of random chaos and still wanted some control of my own eventual fate.

We came in to the helipad at the Chu Lai Hospital, and medics were waiting for us with a train of gurneys all lined up, ready. Our cargo was quickly rushed into the hospital. Larry did a good job. They were all still alive, except the woman who never had a chance. When the orderlies saw her, they left her to be dealt with last. She could wait.

I looked at her: just a little tiny torso, with her legs gone, arms gone way above the elbows, all of her front burned, with her head hung limply, and her chin rested on her chest. No more screams: she was silent. I was still looking when the orderlies finally came to get her. They laid her over onto a stretcher, and a gush of blood rushed out from where she'd been sealed to the deck. The orderly looked at me and said, "Sorry." But by the way he looked at me, it was obvious he'd guessed everything about our trip to the hospital.

The enumerable ugly dreams that day spawned—with the Screaming Woman featured in the starring role—those dreams were far worse than anything that actually occurred! In nightmares, she would talk to me calmly in English, perfect English: "Before we fly, can we find my legs? I'll need to take them with me. The doctors will want them at the hospital. Arms, too, if that's not causing you too much trouble." Then she would gesture with her arm stubs, strings of loose meat flapping from her stumps. But most often, she was just the Screaming Woman. Screaming, screaming, and nothing could stop her, nothing. And the nightmare was that there was not a damned thing to do to help her, nothing. She joined a growing pantheon of dreams. Nightmares: cockpits engulfed in flames or Death's boney fingers tightly grabbing my arm and pulling me away from being killed, not at that time, not at that place—there is a better place for you and a better time to die or galleries of the faces of men I felt had died in my place or the worst nightmare of them all: my tour in Vietnam was extended indefinitely for the duration of the remainder of that war.

After that day it always bummed me out to see a bouncing bobble-head doll on the dash of a car. Talk about flashbacks every damned time. Or how about being on a long car trip with a two-year-old kid who starts screaming and won't stop: another flashback trigger big time.

30

AVIATION SAFETY OFFICER SCHOOL— CAPTAIN SALMOND

A s Halloween came and went and 1970 was slipping toward Thanksgiving, things for the Hornets had become generally peaceful and routine over the previous few weeks (if you didn't count all the times Hornet 32, Larry Hood, had been shot down, plus a couple of other notable exceptions involving a Stinger and a Yellow Jacket), and we had not suffered any major Hornet combat casualties or deaths. Even though no two days were the same, it still felt very much like a case of "same ole shit, just a different day," and if that was what peace and quiet felt like, we could use all of that we could get.

A call came in on a Friday, and someone from the 1st Aviation Brigade told our operations officer that we had to have an aviation safety officer. A school for that would start the following Monday, so have somebody there, preferably the company instructor pilot. Check-in for the school was in two days, Sunday. The school would be at Long Binh and would last from Monday till Friday, just one week. That was not much notice, and I was on a plane the next day, going back to Tan Son Nhut Airport in Saigon. When we landed, our military airplane parked right next to a group of civilian airliners, symbols that the Real World actually still existed somewhere, some distant faraway place.

As we walked from our plane to the terminal, I couldn't take my eyes off the airliners, their silver wings gleaming in the sunlight. Merle Haggard sang in my head, *"Silver Wings, roaring engines, headed somewhere in flight."* In my dreams, those wings were taking me away, leaving this behind, going back home, flying to Texas before I was totally out of my mind. I watched men boarding those planes, headed for R&R or home. For a second, I wanted to run over and cut in line, if I could have, but a stretch in the Fort Leavenworth Prison didn't seem like anything good on a resume. Yeah, right! Somewhere in flight but not that day.

So I grabbed a taxicab and headed to the Continental Hotel instead. Some real food, a nice hot shower, a real bed with clean sheets, and maybe that beautiful Eurasian woman I'd met before. I briefly wondered if she'd be around the hotel that night. After all, it was Saturday night, date night, so I deliberated: *"Bathe you, massage you, pay what you can."* I hadn't forgotten about that particular deal. Pay what you can, and I love you long time. Best to get that out of my mind. So I behaved myself in Saigon, then showed up for my class Monday morning, bright-eyed and well slept.

There we were, Aviation Safety Officer School. The first thing the instructor asked was this question: "In terms of their ranking in flight school from the top to the very bottom ranking, who do you think has the highest number of pilot error-caused crashes? If you say the bottom pilots you'd be exactly half right. Those in the bottom five percent are tied with, now get this, tied with the top five percent. That's right. Crash rates for those two groups are virtually the same, believe it or not! The bottom group because of inadequate skills. The top group crash from Superman Syndrome. The Superman Syndrome is when pilots think, *Yeah, I'm good, damn good, the very best. I can do things with this army helicopter nobody else can do except in dreams. I should have an S on my wings, a big S for Superman. That's me, Superman."* So began a five-day, total saturation level, fast-paced course of aviation safety instruction.

For housing, I had a very nice room, with an attached bathroom, at the Transient BOQ (Bachelor Officer's Quarters) near a mess hall and walking distance from a 1st Aviation Brigade Officers' club, where the wine was in crystal glasses and the food on fine china and you could have a two-inch thick steak—filet mignon—and a freshly steamed lobster with a giant Australian shrimp cocktail served by waiters in white dinner jackets. And the whole deal cost less than ten bucks. It was totally unbelievable how some people had things in a war zone. No sleeping and eating in the wet, muddy bush for them.

At the Transient BOQ, there were guys roaming around with no unit insignias of any sort, no rank, and no name tags. They introduced themselves as Mr. Smith or Mr. Jones and said they worked for Army Intelligence, hush, hush. And it seemed that beautiful Eurasian women hung around the BOQ area at all hours, day and night, and they sure didn't look like maids. So, I assumed they were bargain-priced perks provided for the 007 guys who quartered there. An interesting place, with everyone abused by all the cruelest hardships of war.

I had originally thought safety officer school would be terminally boring, but I was surprised. The whole thing was actually very fascinating, crash-site investigation being most interesting. The week passed quickly, and it was nice to have hot showers instead of hot LZs.

I arrived back in Chu Lai Sunday evening and the very first thing I went to the operations shack, and the next day's schedule board was posted earlier than usual, I was glad to see. That meant I didn't have to worry about that chore. One thing I saw made me into a joker. My big mouth totally overloaded my ass, and I made a stupid comment I shouldn't have. For combat assault air mission commander, a guy who everyone called Captain Elmer Fudd was on the board, scheduled with another captain assigned to fly as his pilot, a brand-new New Guy who was totally green. I asked who made that particular stupid pairing, putting two hard-bars together on a mission? Elmer Fudd and some New Guy with zero experience. Who was going to fly the helicopter if they had a problem and got into trouble? Would it be Elmer Fudd or Gomer Pyle? (Gomer Pyle was the nickname we gave the New Guy the first day he arrived, and we found that we had ourselves another West Point ring-thumping jerk in the Hornets. Naturally, our first West Pointer was Elmer Fudd.) But nobody laughed at my poorly constructed joke. I couldn't see that our most recent company commander had walked into operations and was standing there, right behind me, and he had heard everything I said. The major quietly told me to step outside.

He stepped right up into my face, his nose nearly touching mine, and he screamed, up one side then down the other. He shouted in my face a long time and peeled all the damned skin right off me. He made it goddamned clear that he didn't like my comments about hard-bars, about Captain West Point or Captain West Point Junior, the New Guy, or my saying negative things about their skills. Since I was the company instructor pilot, people paid attention if I said negative things about pilots. He peeled the skin off, first the front and then the back. He also made it clear he wasn't happy with my belittling superior officers! That was the most serious of my offenses! All I could do was take my dressing down and say "Yes, sir!"

He was totally right. But my dumb attempt at humor was only a poor cloak for the cold hard truth, at least as I saw it. Elmer Fudd was what he was, and you couldn't fix stupid, even West Point stupid. After the major left and I went back into Operations, everyone had a roaring laugh at my expense. I would never get off the major's shit list, not ever! "Elmer Fudd," "Gomer Pyle," and "Shit-List Denny," funniest thing they'd watched in a long time.

Through all the laughter, the operations captain said not to worry about anything, because the CO was just all stressed out: it was a bad time for the Hornets. A lot of things had happened while I was away down in Long Binh. There had been a bad crash with one of our guys killed. So my comments about captains' flying abilities had hit a raw nerve with the commander. The guy killed was a captain and, worst of all, it was a pilot error crash and had been something avoidable.

A Captain killed? Who the hell was it? The operations captain stammered around some and looked at the floor because he knew what a good friend of mine the dead man had been. Then he quietly said, "Your platoon leader, Captain Dick Salmond. They crashed at Tam Ky three days ago while you were gone."

I was stunned speechless from that news. Salmond killed? Are you kidding? This a joke? No, no joking. He was killed all right. A landing at Tam Ky that went totally wrong, resulted in a crash that became a fire. Salmond was killed trying to escape the fire. Oh, my God. I had to get over to our platoon area, get myself back home and find out exactly what had happened.

Dick Salmond killed: our baby-faced Jeep thief. It was impossible to get my head around that whole sickening concept—unbelievable. The operations guy conveyed his condolences. He knew how closely Dick and I worked together and what really tight good friends we always were. That was true; Dick and I had shared many nights out in operations doing schedules or flight-hours books for the platoon. Hearing that he was dead totally floored me. It was like a ton of bricks had just been dropped on me. It was like hearing the first news about a dead brother. Things had gotten to the point between us that I never thought of him as our platoon leader or a United States Army captain. He was just my very close friend and a sincerely good person. From out of the blue, that was the worst news I could have ever expected, and I felt like I'd just been run over by a mother-humping steamroller.

Our platoon Jeep, "I Get Around," was parked out in front of the operations shack. Nobody had wanted to drive it since Dick had been killed. Would I please take it and drive it back over to the Company Area. At least get it away from the operations shack. It bothered everyone to see it sitting there like it was waiting for Dick to get back from a mission and he would be wanting it.

The old Jeep fired right up like always. It did feel damned spooky sitting in it; the feel of the steering wheel and the gear shift, driving down the road, hearing the sound of the exhaust. I had taken many rides in Dick's Jeep. Oh, his poor wife and his two little kids in Colorado. That would be the worst possible nightmare for his family that they could have ever imagined: Dick killed. But everyone always knew what could happen. If you went off to the war and flew as a combat pilot, everyone knew that some of them died. The irony of spending a week studying crashes while my friend was dying in a crash was an overpowering heaviness on my brain.

A pilot error crash, what had they done? A crash at Tam Ky, that little provincial capital, not in some miserable hot LZ or some overly tight Jungle LZ? Larry Hood told me what he'd heard. Dick and Bill were flying with the Yellow Jackets for the day, Dick in the left seat as part of his aircraft commander transition. The flight was returning empty to Tam Ky and they came in real hot, practicing a fast approach as the Yellow Jackets liked to do sometimes. Dick and Bill were flying trail on the formation of eight helicopters, an extra big formation. It was Dick's third day flying left seat. They were landing in an open soccer field. The flight made real big flares to stop, and you know how it stacks up for helicopters back at the rear of the formation. Ultimately, it was more than Dick could manage. He threw a very radical flare, pulled power, way too much power, as much as 10 or 15 pounds over redline, which made him run out of left pedal. His helicopter started to rotate under the rotor. Just when all the rotor power he'd pulled kicked in, they popped up into the air maybe 40 to 50 feet or more and were starting to spin. Bill jumped on the controls. They both were on the controls, each fighting for control. Bill thought maybe they had hit the ground, maybe it was a tail-rotor strike causing the helicopter to start a spin. Anyway, he chopped the throttle when they were way up about 50 feet in the air. Whatever, they fell to the ground real hard. The hit broke off the left ground skid, and the tail boom broke from the body. The engine was still running full blast with the rotor still turning full speed, and they were lying on the ground with left side low. So the blade was nearly hitting the ground. Fire flashed up and they thought their helicopter could explode any second, and naturally everyone freaked out and ran. Bill, the crew chief, and the door-gunner all made it away just fine, no problems. But Dick ran out the lower left side, and before he was clear he got hit. The rotor blade struck him about waist high and sent him sailing through the air pretty far. He was alive and awake when people got to him, but they could see he was screwed up; internal organs completely filled his flight suit pants. They had ruptured out through his bottom end. It was just lucky that he wasn't actually cut fully in half. He was still awake as he was rushed to the Chu Lai Hospital, but from the amount of blood loss and the internal organs filling his pants, it was doubtful the doctors could do anything. Sure enough, he was soon pronounced dead. It was a totally ugly, freak accident.

A freak accident? No! It was an illustration of everything I'd heard the whole previous damned week. It was a sequence of wrong decisions that piled up and created an accident that was avoidable. I couldn't believe I was hearing of such a textbook case example. The biggest deal was, if I'd been scheduling, none of that bullshit would have happened, none. That's not to say that I could have prevented an accident, because I couldn't have. It was only that the sequence of events would have been different, and things would have turned out differently. Dick wouldn't have been at Tam Ky. Someone else might have been but not Dick. Before I went down to Long Binh we had an AC meeting and specifically discussed Dick. Everyone knew he was ready to transition, and he was chomping at the bit. I said he should wait until I returned, but when I left he overruled my wishes. He could do that. He was our platoon leader and he had the captain's bars.

I'd wanted to fly with him his first three or four days of flying left seat. That didn't happen, and that was his choice. Second thing, if I had done the scheduling Dick would have flown only with senior ACs in the order of their seniority, until he had a chance to accumulate some seat time. But I wasn't there to do the scheduling. Dick was the one who did the scheduling, and all the decisions that were made were made by him. He chose whom to fly with and in what order they came. Bill was the most junior AC we had in our platoon at the time, so he and Dick shouldn't have been paired up yet. Bill should have been the very last AC for Dick to fly with. Well, whatever happened, however it did, nothing changed anything. It was done and could never be undone. Captain Dick Salmond was dead.

Larry Hood took me over to formally meet our new platoon leader, a first lieutenant. He'd moved over from the First Platoon. I'd met him before and we'd run into each other a few times, so it wasn't like we were total strangers. But it was proper for him to formally meet me as a member of his platoon—size me up, let me know how things stacked up, and how he intended for things to run. As we approached the door to his room, I could tell the guy was gonna be okay. Loud Rolling Stones was blasting from inside. Mick Jagger was singing, "Honky Tonk Woman," about a divorcee he laid in New York City and how he had to put up a fight. We knocked on the door and the music stopped.

He let us in, and polite introductions were made. He'd always seemed like a nice guy in dealings I had with him before, and our meeting was pleasant enough, casual. He said he wanted me to continue doing scheduling until he got to know everyone in the platoon, if I was still willing to do that. I told him sure, since I was used to it. He was already an aircraft commander, so that was not an issue: good thing, since things had been sort of awkward for Dick to command the platoon without being an AC and was second fiddle in the cockpit.

He said that he'd been out at operations, in the background, and he'd heard what I'd said about hard-bars and overheard the dressing down I received outside. He bluntly asked me if I had something I resented about commissioned officer pilots?

I tried to answer. In flight school, you had two groups: "Warrant Officer Candidates" and the "Commissioned Officers." Flying, to the officers, was a career choice. Flight school was their 9-to-5 job. When the workday was done, they drove off in their Corvettes and met their townie girls. For warrant officer candidates, it was bust out of school, return to Ft. Polk as an E-1 and back to Infantry Tiger-Land. The level of focus was different. As for two captains flying together, the AMC I'd found to be arrogant, unwilling to take advice, and with brief AC experience, so a new pilot flying with him seemed questionable. I'd bet that our lieutenant shared my view of Captain West

Point, Mr. Ring-knocker, Elmer Fudd. But he pulled out his wallet and asked if I'd like to see a picture of his Corvette or his Mineral Wells wife first?

I breathed easier: the guy was a joker, and he pulled out a picture and showed me his Shelby GT-350 Mustang with a blonde standing beside it and said he ate Corvettes for lunch. We'd get along just fine.

31

MEDALS FOR ALL
THE WRONG REASONS

A Hornets captain ran the company Awards and Decorations program. He was perpetually manic, jittery, edgy, talky, and always jabbering nonstop. He'd taken his extra-duty job of A-and-D to be his personal crusade to get medals on a wholesale basis for Hornet aviators. Just a little while after the shocking crash death of Cpt. Dick Salmond, there was a hastily planned awards ceremony to get the sad mood broken, get everyone's mind on new things, instead of everyone dwelling on death and moping around in a blue mood. And I guess those intentions were mostly good. It was too bad the results flopped so badly.

Our wired-up awards guy buzzed around prepping the decorations recipients in advance of the coming ceremony, informing them about who was getting what, and just about everyone who had ever flown on a mission was getting something. When he got around to talking to me, I was flabbergasted. He said they were giving me ANOTHER medal that I no way in hell deserved. What the hell for? He couldn't remember the individual particulars because he had so many medals the army was awarding to all of us. There was some sort of mistake, a *BIG* mistake, because I sure knew I hadn't done anything to get the medal he told me about, nope, nothing at all. Hell, I was still pissed off about the FIRST one of those medals they gave me that I hadn't deserved after Angel Larraga was killed. What on earth was I supposed to do, go around the rest of my life and say, "See that Medal, I got that one because a friend of mine was killed in Vietnam"? And now they were going to hand out another batch of awards because of Dick Salmond. What was I supposed to say about that one? "And you see that Oak Leaf on my medal, that was the second presentation I got because I had another real good friend killed in Vietnam." Screw that sort of crap.

At the ceremony, when they read the citation that described the reason for the medal, I soon recognized that the overblown, flowery narrative

162

described something that had happened just a couple of weeks earlier, only a few days before I went off to attend safety officer school. Medals were not handed out that damn quickly. Things were totally wrong in that department, but what was even more wrong, the event they were talking about didn't justify the award of a medal to anyone, no way.

That whole ceremony was surreal and seriously warped and generally a big load of bullshit. The particular thing they described was this: our helicopter was flying general support out west near LZ Mary Ann and received a radio call from a medevac Dust-Off ship. They needed to extract two wounded men from a site where the Dust-Off couldn't land, so they needed to drop a jungle penetrator and then hoist the wounded out of the trees. Could we cover them while they did that? We flew over to their location, took station, and hovered there with them, sorta their personal guard. We didn't pack much firepower, just door-guns. The first wounded guy came out, no problem, and they dropped the penetrator back down and were getting the second wounded grunt loaded when both of our helicopters started getting shot at. It was just some small-arms fire. We returned fire, door-guns blasting away, ripping up the jungle. Wasn't much, but it was enough to make Charlie put his head down and stop shooting. Time seemed to crawl by while we hovered, and the hoist seemed to take forever pulling the wounded person up to the Dust-Off bird. When he was finally aboard, Dust-Off left. Nothing more involved than that, just normal stuff, business as usual, and we returned to our assigned mission and thought nothing further of it. So that was what this medal was about? That was just plain crazy; a totally screwed-up thing. Even crazier was that *I* was getting *any* medal. I hadn't done any heroic flying that day. In fact, I had done no flying, period, distinguished or not, zip, zero. That day we were doing a check ride, and I merely sat in my seat and watched the whole deal play out. I never touched the controls the whole time. Any medal, if deserved by anyone, sure the hell couldn't have been mine.

After the ceremony, I tried to talk with our A-and-D captain, but he was busy rubbing elbows with the American brass and kissing all the colonel ass he could get to. He didn't want to be bothered by me, so he didn't hear that the whole awards thing was seriously screwed up, a complete damned travesty when it came to my medal. But I couldn't get our twitter bug to be still long enough to listen to me about anything.

Goddamned it, I was so pissed off by the whole thing that I took my new medal and nailed it to the jamb over the door of our hooch in protest, but what really surprised me was that the other aircraft commanders who lived in our hooch were equally mad, each for his own reasons. They were all disgusted by the obvious attempt to sweep Dick Salmond's death out of people's minds, and each one of them had been given a medal of some sort, including a shit load of DFCs. What then shocked me, ALL of them nailed up their medals on the same doorjamb that I had. And it wasn't just our hooch, but every Wasp Platoon pilots' hooch had medals nailed over the doors.

It was a little spontaneous wildfire of protest. Nothing about that was preplanned or discussed. It was purely something that erupted organically. It was an overt rejection of the degradation of the seriousness and solemnness of army medals in the eyes of many Hornet pilots, and it all happened without anyone having to speak one single word about the demonstration openly. It was a completely silent protest, but all those medals nailed over everyone's doors screamed out our message loud and clear.

No one from the chain of command ever mentioned anything about the whole affair, but within a few days, maybe a week, the Hornet's A-and-D captain was transferred to another combat assault company that needed a captain to be their executive officer. It was a promotion for him, a new start, and a fresh, clean slate for the Hornets. He was gone from us—so long, twitter bug. About that time, all of the nailed-up medals disappeared. One day nearly everyone was out flying, and when we came home at day's end someone had taken down every nailed-up medal. We never had another medal ceremony, not for the rest of my tour.

It was enlightening back then to see how crusty old-timers were shaken in their cynicism that *"Vietnam don't mean nothing,"* because it did mean something. It meant some good people died while they were just trying to do their best, in spite of the situation. And it slapped you in the face that at anytime Death could reach out and get you. Our friend Captain Dick Salmond was a prime example that the boney fingers could grab your shoulder and take you away at any time of Death's choosing, no warning, and no advance notice. The phony bravado of "accept imminent death, the only way to live free of fear," took on more ominous tones when you saw just how actual Imminent Death could be in the sorry reality of that damned war.

Twenty years later, when I saw my military records for the first time, the medals that wacky A-and-D captain obtained for me were not listed on my discharge orders, nothing anywhere, so I guessed the guy never completed the paperwork or else he was passing out medals totally illegally on his own. I was relieved that there was no record that I'd been given medals I never deserved, and I was really glad that I'd never mentioned to a soul that I had ever been given that particular medal, much less TWO of them, and I just chalked the whole experience up as a wacky aspect of Vietnam War life.

Now that I look back on what happened, I see how profoundly disturbed everyone was by the death of Dick. He was not simply our platoon leader but a very good friend to all the Wasps who served with him. He might have looked like a kid you knew back in high school, about 17 years old, but he had quickly become our respected leader. And no one needed any stinking medals to remember him by, and certainly no stinking medal could make anyone forget about what had happened to him.

If Dick had survived the war and I ran into him somewhere, I would have asked him if he remembered a damned Jeep he procured for our platoon from some colonel back in Vietnam, and if he could tell me again the name of that damned old Jeep. I'm sure that would've made him smile real big.

32

GUNSHIP BODY COUNT:
LIKE A DEER TIED
TO THE FENDER

Body-count numbers were closely followed by most of the Stingers Gunship Platoon, and the tally of enemy kills were spoken of with pride by many pilots. A gunship pilot with 30 KIA impressed some, but saying "I've got over fifty confirmed and documented enemy killed in action" was seen as a major threshold only the very determined ever reached or crossed. The then King of the Stingers was a scrawny young kid from Chicago who hadn't celebrated his 21st birthday yet, still only 20 years old. However, when Viet Cong or NVA saw him, he was probably the last thing they ever saw: the vision of their very real *Imminent Death* arriving, imminent meaning only a couple of seconds at the most.

The kid's name was Arthur, the very same Arthur that I had once spent the day with practicing shooting rockets back during my early days when I'd been considering joining the Stingers Platoon if I was invited. He'd crossed the 50 KIA milestone long before and was then approaching 100 confirmed kills. His tour was also coming to an end in about three more weeks—maybe 12–15 flying days left—and he very much wanted that magic 100 number before he went back to the States.

Now for an ordinary Slick pilot like me, a day where every LZ was cold was marked up as a good day. For Gun Jockeys, it was a totally boring dud day. Stingers hoped to find Bad Guys running around out in wide open space in *every* LZ. We'd been in the Chu Lai Operation Area long enough that the enemy had gotten to know the Hornets, particularly the Stingers, and more and more the Bad Guys tried to steer clear of us and lie low. I appreciated that not every dingle-berry toting a rifle was still firing away at us, but that meant satisfying the Gun's blood lust, killing dinks, was getting tougher at our LZs, since ever fewer of the enemy were willing to engage the Hornets during combat assaults. The evolving situation made Slick pilots so glad, but also made the gunship pilots so sad.

Away from LZs, when the Stingers had some enemy troops caught and sent to hell, there were body-count conformation problems. The American Division wouldn't accept Stinger versions of KIA numbers without verification from one of their infantry field units. I guess American was so accustomed to being lied to by their own frontline troops that they didn't believe anyone about anything. Naturally it offended the Stingers that the American Division bean counters wouldn't take the Stingers' accounting of their Bad Guy kills.

At that time, I thought that Arthur's *official* KIA number was like 92 or 93. His *actual number*—there was no calculating that. He had probably killed more than 200 or maybe even as many as 300 of the enemy. Hell, there was one classified raid he went on into an NVA sanctuary in Cambodia a month before the U.S. invasion. A monster flight of thirty gunships went in on that mission. That raid was secret since it was illegal: Congress had a little rule that said the U.S. would keep the hell out of Cambodia.

When the gun pilots came back to the Hornets' Nest after that Mission, they were juiced-up out of their minds. They said it had been an absolute frigging slaughter. The guns had caught about 2,000, maybe 3,000, NVA regular troops totally by surprise, out in the open, figuratively with their pants down and their skinny asses out. The Cobras and C-Models mowed them down by the hundreds. *Howdy, so glad to meet you fellows. Boom, Boom. Here's a few gift rockets we brought and thought you might like to see firsthand. Boom, Boom. Now, here's what these mini-guns are all about—Burrrrp—amazing how they pour out pure streams of bullets and make an ordinary old day into the damned end of your stinking little world. So welcome to the war good little buddies.*

So, just that one raid who really knew how many Bad Guys Art had blown up? Maybe 30 or 40 or even 50 or 60. Whatever the number, it was a big bunch. However, none of that counted as body count. The Guns weren't even supposed to talk about it, because it never happened in anyone's official book: it was a secret deal. Hush, hush. Don't you tell anyone about that mission, or Uncle Sam will come visit you.

But body count that went on the books, dead people counted and verified (American called it "bona fide"), was something that would get into the records in some officer efficiency report of Arthur's time In Vietnam, a record that would follow him all through his future time in the military—so that number mattered very greatly to him. And he had a big argument going with American about his damned bona fide number, because Arthur was a kid who had decided to stay in the army and make it his lifetime career. It was hard to believe, but Arthur had become an army lifer—at least that was what the scuttlebutt said about him. And what he was fighting with American about was the difference between the numbers four or eight dead Bad Guys Arthur had rocketed.

Here was the deal: there was a flare-up after our Slicks had deposited some grunts out in an LZ, about 40 of them. As soon as the helicopters were gone, the infantry troops started taking fire. They were under attack and requested gunship help. Our Stingers came in to save the day and Arthur was flying as gun-team leader. When the Stingers came on station, the infantry troops were in full escape mode and running at full speed to get away from the enemy fire—like in the old Johnny Horton country song, they ran through the briars and through the brambles, through bushes where rabbits couldn't go, running so fast hound dogs couldn't catch 'em. They were being chased by about 12 or 14 ragtag Viet Cong looking to kill Americans. Arthur rolled in and cleaned up that deal. He and his wingman could spot only eight bodies when the rockets stopped, and the others were so blown up there was nothing big enough to find. So at the end of the day Arthur reported eight KIA, and that night there was a big party. Eight dead Viet Cong took Arthur over one damned hundred "officially dead" enemy before the wonder boy was even 21 years old. That would be his 21st birthday present. Hot damn! There was no doubt, Arthur was the main man!

But a couple of days later, Americal said, "No, it wasn't eight." And that was because the infantry after-battle reports had only FOUR dead Viet Cong listed as Stinger gunship kills. The other kills written up were a bunch of bullshit fiction the Americal guys just made up: "55 Infantry Unit Kills." Sorry, not eight—we'll put down four. Art was not over a hundred, and he screamed bullshit. Damned he was pissed off, SO PISSED OFF! *Fifty-five Infantry Kills* was a plain-out lie. There probably weren't a total of 55 damned Viet Cong within five miles of that place. How could that ever happen? Running so fast, the hounds couldn't catch 'em! How the hell did they claim any stinking KIA? They said a full battalion ambushed them? It was maybe 14 guys at the most! Fourteen, and Arthur killed them, every one. A damned Stinger killed them, not the infantry! Shot their asses with rockets and saved the lying infantry! So they could quit running and flop down on their sorry asses and take a break.

Damn, Arthur was pissed off at the Americal—those no-good, lying, chicken-shit sons of bitches. Okay, make it FOUR, which totals to goddamned 96. Art said he would take that, but the bullshit stopped right there! Right then! All bullshit stops and screw the Americal Division in their fat asses, the sorry lying sons of bitches! The BS stops!

The next day, Arthur passed the time between assaults hunting dinks out in the badlands, and when he ran across a lone NVA trooper he promptly killed him. Then he did something totally wild and crazy. He landed—put his heavy old C-Model on the damned ground out in the weeds. Then he got out of his gunship, went over to the guy—that extremely dead person who was blown all to hell—and dragged him back to his gunship. The corpse was shredded completely to pieces, like hamburger meat out of some meat grinder, and Art strapped him on the nose of his helicopter—tied him on real good. He was like a deer on a fender of an old Chevy pickup truck, with blood pouring out of the dead body: one very gory mess.

There couldn't have been a more gruesome sight, and the more graphic the vision of enemy Death, the better for Arthur's purpose. He flew back to Chu Lai to the American Division headquarters helicopter pad and landed his gunship right there with his freshly killed trophy. He got out and marched up to headquarters. He stomped into the lobby and shouted, "I've got body count I want to report!"

When the American receptionist sat there, still and stunned into silence, speechless, Arthur hollered, "If not here, if this ain't the place, where do I take our dead NVA friend?"

People were at all the windows, pressed up to the glass, looking out at Arthur's gunship: they had never seen the war up close. Not like this, not a dead person there on their helicopter pad.

Arthur hollered out his call sign and said, "Stinger 82. Give me credit for one goddamned dead NVA soldier, one KIA. Whichever one of you bean counters keeps the books on this shit, add it to my total, which makes *ninety-seven* now. And I'll be back with plenty more dead sons of bitches tomorrow."

The Division receptionist sat frozen, stunned, and mumbled, "Crazy Hornet fool."

Art marched back out to his chopper and cut his trophy guy loose and let him fall, *Splat!* An ugly pile of hamburger meat plopped there, blown all to hell, and Stinger 82 said he would be coming back tomorrow. Oh, damn! Damn, damn. Nobody wanted that Hornet mess at Division headquarters!

The phone wires over to the Hornets' commanding officer were totally on fire, blazing, wanting an answer, screaming. Americal brass were cussing, spitting fire. A damned dead Vietnamese was on their goddamned doorstep! What crazy son of a bitch would do that? Listen up, Hornets, don't dump damned dead men here. Not at our front door, understand—not ever! Yeah, Roger that, we got that particular message: no dead men at your doorstep. Not ever.

The problem was that none of this mattered to Arthur. He was still very pissed off at Americal. He was King of the Stingers, the absolute King. And he was ours, and the Hornets totally loved him. If he wanted to joke around a little bit once in a while the Hornets were perfectly willing to cut him a little slack, considering everything the kid had been through during his year of killing people all the time.

He could go over to Americal and ask, "Hey, which of you people running this outfit killed anybody today? Just one, killed just one, this week even? Or this month? How about ever? Killed one? Which of you assholes have been bathed in the blood? Been out there killing Charlie or the damned NVA every day? Since you guys are all busy back here in your offices every day, back here in the rear with the gear and the queers, I'll just bring some of the war to you until I get my total number to a hundred."

But Arthur didn't need on his career record that when he was flying gunships in Vietnam orderlies captured him with a big butterfly net because he had gone totally crazy, pure bonkers, and was dumping dead bodies here and there. That was sort of crazy by everyone's standard.

The reason I'm telling you about Arthur is that he was an archangel shooting lightning bolts and saving Hornet lives, time after time. Arthur's rocket skills saved many of our lives, and that was for sure. Probably many times no one was even aware of that. But there was one time I'll always remember about Arthur, and that was the day I was the witness to his 100th KIA from a damned front row seat, and I could stand up to anyone at Americal and say, "Hell, yes, that was a bona fide kill, if there ever was one in this whole war, and I'll swear to that to any bean counter who wants to know."

33

NVA MARCHING DOWN THE OPEN ROAD

It was called a "combat assault mission with a formation flight of five Wasp choppers," but that was a misnomer: what we were doing was much more mundane than the term "combat" implied. We were simply ferrying one company of fresh infantrymen from a Firebase Hawk Hill staging area out to the field to replace another company of guys who had been out in the boondocks for nearly a month, returning the worn out grunts back to Hawk Hill for a well-earned unit stand-down. It was a time for them to resupply and refit their company, and the men could get some good rest, get some sleep, have a real shower, put on clean clothes, and eat a hot meal in an actual mess hall. That night they'd sleep in a real bed, and be nearly human again. Nearly human, because the infantry were so used to being wild animals living out in an even wilder environment that they were sort of like a pack of feral dogs or hyenas or tigers or lions. It was best not to pet the animals, because they tended to have uneven dispositions and could get a little snarly.

It was nearly noon, and we were out at the LZ picking up our third lift of troops to go back to Hawk Hill, and Lord they were happy to be going to the rear for a few days. I sincerely hoped that having a shower was the number one item on their list of things to do, because, damn, they stank to high heaven. All those weeks with no change of clothes, no showers or even any deodorant, the infantry may have been the backbone of the army, the soul of it, but damn they stank horribly. They couldn't ambush anyone because you could smell them at least a hundred yards away. Enclosed in our helicopters, they smelled like a big pile of hog shit. You could put your nose up someone's ass crack, and it would've smelled a whole lot better than those poor grunts and probably been more hygienic.

As soon as we lifted into the air, they started partying, and damn boldly fired up marijuana joints right there in our helicopter, and evidently they didn't give a good goddamn who knew they were smoking pot: they weren't

171

dead, not that day, and what was the worst anyone would do to them? Send 'em to stinking Vietnam? Been there, done that, and that shit don't scare me any seemed to be their attitude. They were offering joints to our crewmen and hollering, "Stoned, baby, gonna get so stoned, flying higher than this helicopter, even higher than the whole blue sky itself! Gonna get drunk, screwed up, I mean SCREWED UP! Hell, yes, gonna be a big time FTA party tonight, yes, and everybody's invited. Gonna get so stoned and so drunk, man, gonna sleep for a week."

The radio crackled, Stingers calling us, and they were all excited. They had something going on, red hot stuff. There were NVA marching down an open road in broad daylight. "Oh, hell, yes, NVA alright, thirty or forty of them, a whole damned platoon out in the middle of the day, marching in formation, hut, two, three, four. All lined up, a sergeant calling cadence for them. We just flew over them, we saw them in their uniforms. NVA for sure."

Our flight leader asked what the Stingers expected us to do.

"Bring those infantry grunts, those troops you have on board. Divert from your flight path; come straight here. We would blow those Bad Guys to hell, but they ran into a damned little village. We need your grunts to get them, flush them out of there. There's going to be a great big firefight."

Flight lead replied, "Uhhh, yeah, Roger that, we'll tell them about it, but that won't be easy. These guys think they're going on stand-down."

I told our crew chief over the intercom and he relayed the information: "Hey, guys, listen up, we're gonna set you down, not where you're expecting, not Hawk Hill, not even close, but in the middle of a hot little village full of NVA soldiers, understand? Understand? We're not taking you guys home, not now, so stub out the party joints and lock and load and get set to go into a frigging hot fight."

They acted like they were deaf or we were speaking goddamned Martian or something, *No hablo inglés*. Hell, no, General Custer, I don't wanna go. There's a mean ole Indian out there, and he's just awaitin' to take my hair. So, hell no, I don't wanna go, no!

In the backseat of our helicopter, the crew was yelling to the grunts about what's up: "Going into a firefight. Listen, NVA there. No, not home. No, not home. Firefight! So throw out your joints, people, get ready, 'cause this is going down whether you're ready or not. Firefight! Understand?"

The gunships guided us to the village. Ready or not, we were there, on approach, and the Stingers were sure there was a whole damned platoon of NVA there, get ready. We flared for a fast touchdown, ready or not. As our helicopter skidded to a stop, before we could get anyone to disembark, a damned guy jumped up in the bushes. He was so totally screwed. We had just landed right where he had decided to hide. He was so screwed. A Huey full of infantry had just sat down only about 30 or 40 feet from him and he had no chance, but he jumped up anyway, and I immediately saw him. He glared at me. Our eyes were locked on each other. I could see his little round eye-glass spectacles and the light reflecting off the corner of his lenses. I guess it was a massive adrenaline rush that hit me, but time seemed to slow almost to a halt. It was like I was watching a movie, but I was seeing each picture frame one at a time, clicking by slowly, click, click, click. He raised his rifle, aimed at me. Everything played out in hyper slow motion—time a very slow tick-tock deal, spilling away. His face was that of a middle-age man or older, maybe 45 or 50 years old. The rifle looked like it was an old World War II weapon, some bolt-action antique his father maybe used to rout the French at Dien Bien Phu, or his grandfather carried during the Japanese War back in the 1940s. Fire and smoke burst out the gun barrel. The bullet spiraled in visible slow-motion flight and it looked like it was mine for sure. I was going to die right there at that moment. He had me. Shit, some old son of a bitch had me, and I was sure I saw the bullet coming and watched it as it arrived in a blink: the time for the sound of a heartbeat that pounded in my ears, one single miserable heartbeat. Maybe an inch; maybe more or maybe less, whatever it was, the damned bullet somehow missed. It seemed an eternity until I heard another heartbeat.

The bullet went sailing by my head. I wasn't dead. That took a second to register: he'd missed me. Even if by a quarter of an inch, I didn't care, and it didn't matter. It didn't matter, and I was totally stunned that he had missed at all. For the tiniest of a split second, I felt like giving the asshole my middle finger and sticking my tongue out at the old fart to make it clear to him that he had missed me.

In the passenger compartment, our crewmen were pushing grunts off the helicopter, out the door. Get out. We needed to go, needed to get the hell out of there right then. We couldn't wait.

After failing to hit me with his first damned shot, the old NVA man was working his bolt action, hurriedly chambering a round to take another shot at me.

Over the radio Stinger 89, Art's familiar voice, called to me, "Three-Three, don't move!"

What the hell did that mean? It didn't matter. We couldn't go yet anyway. Guys were still trying to stay on our chopper and were resisting being pushed off.

The NVA yo-yo adjusted his eyeglasses and was looking through his rifle sights, taking aim, when the pair of rockets hit after flying barely over the top of our helicopter. The damned NVA soldier had been no more than five feet outside the sweep of our main rotor blade, and Art had put two rockets on him right at his damned knees. Art had shot over the damned top of my helicopter. I couldn't believe what I had just seen. His rockets couldn't have missed our rotor more than mere inches. Where on earth did Art find the steely nerves to even try an outrageous shot like that? No one could have fired a pistol shot at that NVA old man any more accurately than Art's rockets were placed.

The soldier had been there aiming at me, then instantaneously he was gone and a billowing cloud of smoke replaced him. His remains were lying in some weeds a few feet away and I hovered over and looked out my door at him. He was blown up, with his bottom half gone, but his eyes were open and still moving some. He turned his head and looked at me. We hovered there a few seconds, and I watched him. He was still alive somehow, his chest heaving, so his lungs were still working, and I guessed his heart, too, but with his wounds, he would bleed-out in a very short time, only seconds. In the meantime, I could see in his eyes that he was fully aware of what had just happened, and he knew he was certainly dead. I was sure he hadn't expected that day to work out the way it had for him. And I certainly hadn't expected to have some NVA take a close-up shot at me that day.

I wanted to ask him if no one ever taught him to just squeeze the trigger steadily, and don't jerk the trigger or you'll mess up your aim, miss your shot. Lt. Sparks had told me back in the beginning that it wasn't the fastest shot but the straightest shot that always won. Once again Sparks was right. The dying man's legs were gone, and in that respect, he looked just like the old Screaming Woman that I'd had to watch as she slowly died sitting in our helicopter on the way to the Chu Lai evac hospital. That dying NVA soldier as revenge for her didn't seem to balance things out any. Would anything ever balance things out for her horrible death? If so, what would it take?

My crew chief kid said on the intercom, "Hornet rules: you shoot at a Hornet, you die."

Yep, that was how we preferred things.

Then the kid asked, "You want me to hop out and grab that nice old rifle for you, Mister Denny? It looks like maybe it's a collector's item."

The NVA's eyes stilled and his breathing stopped. He was gone, finished with his war. And just as I thought would happen, he went out easier than what the old Screaming Woman had endured.

No one would carry that old gun again. I said, "No, I sure don't want that damned thing."

"Can I have it myself then?" he asked.

"Don't have the time, we gotta get going."

The last stinking thing I needed was to have one of my crewmen running around on the ground with Bad Guys all around who knew where. I looked around, scanned the place and saw only chaos. People ran in every direction, trying to escape. How many men, women, and children would die, caught in the crossfire coming from soldiers chasing each other, and become this little battle's "collateral damage"? I guessed every battle had to have its "acceptable losses." Well, that was another example of death flourishing in a state of chaos and in last-minute, unexpected changes.

The pot smokers were going to need a fat joint after this deal, and I wondered if the ones who had already smoked very much marijuana on our helicopter were flying "higher than the whole blue sky itself" right then in that village. I heard rifle-fire exchanges starting up and rapidly increasing. I was sure that some of them must have been having a bad trip they hadn't been planning on that day.

As we flew away, I called Stinger 82 and told him, "Wyatt Earp or Doc Holliday couldn't have shot like that, and any questions about body count, we were in the front row seats for that KIA, and we'll sure verify he was a bona fide damned dead son of a bitch."

Art came back with, "Roger that shit. Hey, Three-Three, you think I ought to land back there and sign my name across his forehead in ink so those Americal dudes can't try to claim him as one of their kills?"

I said, "I doubt that would be a good idea, but does that one put you over 100?"

He answered, "With Americal, I've learned to not count my chickens till they're hatched. I saw him back there, and it was only half a man, so Americal may say my number is now all the way up to 99 and a half. But today is only half over. Maybe I can get another half this afternoon."

GOOD VIBRATIONS, SOUTH VIETNAMESE PILOT

One night I was out at operations working up the next day's schedule. Looking at the roster, it struck me how the makeup of our Platoon had changed: Warrant Officers Roger Walker and Dennis Plumber and 1st Lt. Guy Siegelman, leading aircraft commanders, were by then all gone. Of course there had been others before them: 1st Lt. Sparks, Leon Richards, and Steve Chasin, all people who had greatly influenced the current Wasps and me. And now with Dick Salmond killed, we were into the fourth platoon leader I'd known. It seemed odd, good ole Austin Scarborough was then our senior aircraft commander. Even stranger, Larry Hood and I would soon be the most senior guys in our platoon, when Austin went back home. Strange, it hadn't occurred to me that we were rapidly becoming the platoon's old-timers. Hell, we were gonna have to grow handlebar mustaches and start sitting around the hooch in our underwear in honor of our old buddy Dennis Plumber.

After the names were posted, I went over to the platoon area to tell the pilots who would be flying in the morning, woke up the ones who were in bed and told them they were up, and the AC they were assigned to fly with so they could wake the ACs in the morning.

It was one a.m. when I finally made it to my hooch bunk, but a young officer of the day waited there. He told me our schedule needed changing. The Wasps ACs would be flying with a group of *South Vietnamese* as our pilots on the day's combat assault mission.

The hell you say? South Vietnamese pilots, really? You joking? I had no idea that the South Vietnamese even had any helicopter pilots. I'd believe that deal when I saw it. There was no need stirring everyone up then, in the damned middle of the night—let everyone sleep. But, sure enough, when I got out to the flight line the next morning, there was a bunch of Vietnamese guys waiting.

Oh, my, didn't they look so very fashionable: brand new form-fitting flight suits, impressive gold-colored silk scarves around their necks, glistening chrome .45 caliber pistols, and everyone with matching watches, very fancy—wanna be on time, and they probably synchronized them. They had new chicken-plates (breast armor), plus their very own emergency rescue radios and hunting knifes in tooled-leather scabbards that would have been Jim Bowie's envy. I hoped they brought their lunch, rice and fish heads, because they didn't look like the C-Ration types.

There were about 15 of them, and we had spots for only six in our Slicks formation. The Stingers said "no thanks"—and how could you make those guys do anything they didn't want? The command-and-control bird said two could ride in the backseat and observe the mission. The rest would have to fly another time.

Now, personally, when I first came to Vietnam, I had no opinion about Vietnamese people, one way or another, none. But after dropping ARVN infantry troops in LZs and they shot at us too often as we left and having a new 35mm camera of mine stolen from my helicopter by departing ARVN, same deal for a flight jacket, and even little things like Zippo lighters, I certainly formed an initial opinion. Then seeing ARVN trying combat, they were total clowns. Once, we put ARVN grunts into rice paddies on one side of an abandoned irrigation canal, then another group of the unit on the opposite canal bank, and right away each group thought the other group must be the Bad Guys, and naturally they started to fire at each other. Their style of fighting was to plop face down in mud, poke their M-16s up in the air above your head and start firing, blasting away at no particular target. Each side shot at the other for a solid 30 minutes before anyone could stop the fiasco, and there were no casualties on either side. They shot for that long, and no one hit a damned thing. So you could say that, over time, I had formed a final firm opinion about the Vietnamese people I'd been exposed to, and I didn't think very highly of the Army of the Republic of Vietnam.

I wasn't too thrilled when I was introduced to Ho Chi Minh, Junior, my Vietnamese pilot for the day. Actually, that wasn't his name, it was just what I imagined his name could have been, but I couldn't very well call him that. That wouldn't have been politically correct. He told me his name, something like One Hung Low Jo, but he said his American nickname was just Joe, so I called him that but in my mind I thought of him as Ho-Joe and told him to call me Three-Three, but all day he called me Tree-Tree.

The previous night, out in operations, when the maintenance captain was assigning ships to fly, he said there was one old helicopter that was so worn out that he didn't think it could last all day without busting something, at least a danged radio sputtering out, or something. The old bird was named "Good Vibrations," which was a good name for it, accurate, because it shook like an old out-of-balance washing machine. Flying through the sky, the old girl would shake your damned liver out. We had a long, big laugh about that. I told him I'd fly her, old "Good Vibrations."

Ho-Joe and I set out that morning in the old helicopter, flying the formation trail ship. I asked him what his spiffy-looking crew was doing flying combat assault with us. He said they were training to take over for our sister company, the Black Cats up North at Marble Mountain, on the edge of Da Nang. They would be a VIP helicopter company like the Black Cats—did I know them? Oh, yes, our lucky sister company from another Mother, from the privileged side of our Family, where everything was new, everything sparkled. Yes, I'd been to their place before, visited them for a few days. Ho-Joe's superiors thought they needed to see and experience the fighting side of the aviation war, and not just the VIP world, so it was decided that they should fly with the Hornets to gain some actual combat flying experience, and as he understood things they would fly with us for one week.

And what about you, Joe, what's your story? He said he was born in Dalat and educated at boarding school, first in Saigon and then prep school in Switzerland; then he went to a university in Paris, you know, France. Helicopter school, Fort Wolters, and then Fort Rucker, USA. Yeah, same as me, except maybe the boarding school part and the Paris University part. So, Joe, you come from a rich family? Father only a university professor at Dalat, not rich, they say middle class in USA. Yeah, boarding school screamed "middle class" loud and clear all right.

We loaded up with troops and headed off to the war: working mountain LZs southwest of Kham Duc, tall damned mountains, and landed single-ship on the same pinnacles as always. There was nothing but triple-canopy jungle out there, tuff, just jungle everywhere you looked, miles and miles of it. Going out I let Ho-Joe fly some straight-and-level legs of our journey. The morning wore away, back and forth, one load after another, everything just fine, and everything totally cold. Ho-Joe got to fly enough, plenty of straight-and-level. I did all the landings and takeoffs, and old "Good Vibrations" was doing fine, too. Some shake-rattle-and-roll, as warned about, but I wouldn't have called her a washing machine—that was just plain rude to the elderly lady. The engine was strong, and it pulled a big load well. But her service hours were all used up, and the old girl was going back to Corpus Christi for a total refitting soon, a bones-up remanufacture with all new parts, and then she would come back to Vietnam good as a spring chicken.

The last load before lunch, I asked Ho-Joe if he was ready for a pinnacle landing. He did the approach and touchdown okay, no problems at all. The troops offloaded and we left. His takeoff was just the same as mine, full power with a steep climb-out and a sharp-banking left turn. I announced over the radio to our Command and Control, "Everyone out clean."

The ill-fated helicopter named "Good Vibrations" the morning of the day the helicopter later crashed with Hornet 33 and his Vietnamese pilot. Miraculously, it turned out to be a good crash-landing in the jungle on a mountainside—everyone walked away.

Just as I finished on the radio—*KABOOM!*—an enormous explosion sounded, and our helicopter violently rolled on its left side and spun sharply under the main rotor, the engine racing; the RPM tachometer needle blasted past redline. My initial reaction was that we had taken some sort of damned *BIG HIT!* I'd been riding loosely on the controls while Ho-Joe flew, and I immediately grabbed them into my control and levelled us up and straightened us out while rolling the throttle back, calming the screaming engine.

I yelled on the radio, "Three-Three going down!" But the air mission commander was talking to the Stingers and my call couldn't break in. It just made static for everyone's radios. "Three-Three going down, going down." Static.

The engine was running, so that wasn't the problem. The engine and rotor tachometer needles were split, the rotor RPM falling slightly, and when I twisted the throttle to rev the engine, it wasn't turning the rotor! *Screw me, that wasn't right—that was the shits!*

"Three-Three going down! Mayday, goddamn it, Mayday!" Static!

I desperately scanned the countryside—jungle, jungle, and more jungle everywhere and a steep mountain to the right with extra-heavy jungle in the valley floor. But out our windshield, way damned far away, I could see a lighter-green patch on a mountainside, and that was the sign of a grassy place possibly. Lord, we sure needed that, but it was too damn far off in the distance. Everything was clear—*we were going down*—period. No changing that, *so, screw me*, we were going to crash.

The only option: try to get close to the light-green spot, the grassy spot. It was the only place anyone might land to pick us up, so we might as well crash as close to there as possible. I rolled the throttle off and cut the engine all the way off. I decided to stretch out our glide path as far as possible, keep our airspeed up. I was grateful for every inch of altitude that we had, almost 5,000 feet. We would use it all, and need more.

"Damn. Three-Three going down, going down."

"Say again, Three-Three?" AMC finally called!

"Said we are crashing, been hit, going down."

A Stinger cut in. "We see them."

I shut off the electric fuel pumps and the batteries: we sure as hell didn't need fuel pressure when we went in, and I didn't want a goddamned fuel-fed fire. I'd been keeping all the lift I could in our rotor blades from the start, stealing RPM to maintain lift, but rotor RPM was steadily falling off, and if I took it too damned low we would stall and fall like a big-assed heavy rock.

Things never got to the point where I prayed, *Jesus, you take the stick*, but I hoped if there was any help available at all we'd sure take whatever there was. Studied our glide path, the damned distance to go. We had no choice but to keep stealing more and more rotor RPM, and we traded airspeed for distance by pulling the nose up higher and higher, because if we were going to fall out of the sky airspeed would hurt us anyway—wanted zero airspeed when we splattered, better off to fall in going straight down and take the god-damned Gs vertically. *Just Take It!*

I never expected to make the grass. It was just too far, too damn far. I was going to steal too much RPM, and the rotor would lose too much speed. We were going to stall, fall and crash: just wanted it to get as close to the light-green spot; get close and then bend over, head on your knees, and take It. Do your stinking job, and *Just Take It!*

We were gonna crash in the jungle—shit. But 200 hundred yards out I could see we might make it, coming in flat and shallow, if we didn't lose our lift and fall. I flared bigger, stretching out for the grass. I had the collective up under my damned armpit and held my breath. Our forward motion slowed to zero. We were smack over the mother-humping grass, about six inches above it, and still in the air. This was nothing short of a miracle, and this landing was going to be softer than a baby's ass! The collective had no more to give. It was pulled up to the absolute stop. The rotor was turning so slowly you could count the damned rotations, one Mississippi, two Mississippi, three Miss…

Go ahead, fall in, six inches, fall in. See if I care. We did exactly that, but it wasn't six inches, it was more! The light-green spot was crazy damned elephant grass, and it was about twelve feet tall. *Ker-splat!* We were on the ground, harder than I'd thought we would land just a fraction of a second earlier, but our helicopter was intact and we weren't on fire or anything, and kiss my ass, if we weren't still alive! The rotor blade came around one more time and eased into the slope of the mountain and buried itself there with a big jolt and came to a final stop without doing the least bit of damage because it had been going so slow!

The help I'd hoped for? It must have come. Something came. I sat there stunned and finally tried to breathe again. It was like I was needing to feel my heart start beating again. In the backseats, the crewmen were bouncing in their seats, whooping and hollering, shouting with joy. Ho-Joe had his hands clasped, in prayers of appreciation, I supposed.

The only thing I knew for sure was that I could have tried to duplicate that landing a 1,000 times and it would never work out like it had, not even once more. Everything had to be just right at the exact moment, the exact weight of our helicopter right then, the amount of fuel we had used up, the particular altitude we were at when things started, the ground distance we had to travel, our beginning airspeed, the correct amount of headwind instead of a tailwind, even the temperature and humidity that affected our lift just the perfect amount, the rotor RPM not getting so low that we would stall out but being so slow at just the right point in time that the rotor could hit the mountain and just stop. Innumerable variables all had to come together perfectly in complete harmony for that outcome to happen.

We had just crashed in the damned mountains. I had been so fearful of that happening for so long, ever since we moved to I Corps, and then it had happened. The actual experience of it was worse than I had ever feared it would be. From the moment of the big explosion and then finding that our engine wasn't turning the rotor, I immediately thought we all were surely going to die, the four of us on the helicopter. We were going to die in there when our helicopter crashed. I knew we were already dead—it was just being a drawn-out event that would eventually end in one final climax. But then there we were, sitting on a ledge on the side of a mountain, completely surrounded and encased by damned tall grass.

Stinger gunships roared over a few feet above. I had the batteries off and turned them back on. The radios were popping with rapid-fire chatter. I thought about everything a few short seconds. I wasn't a religious man by any means, but the four of us had just experienced a pure miracle that came from somewhere. Everything I'd just done was against the book. I'd never heard of doing those things. It was all purely intuitive and instantaneous. And for us to end up right there—what were the odds? Millions, billions to one? Who knew? Could so many things come together so exactly or did we just experience a miracle? Only thing I knew for sure, it wasn't my flying that did it—no. That was a matter of minimum skill bathed in tons of pure luck, which was its own miracle.

I sat there stunned, tried to breathe. Hornet 32, Larry Hood, arrived overhead and hovered there. Meanwhile, across the valley, the Stingers were working out on some Bad Guys who saw us go down and were shooting toward us. We stripped out the radios and machine guns, then climbed on top of "Good Vibrations" to leave. It was good to see Larry. It was good to be seeing anything.

When Larry got us back to Chu Lai, the guys in the operations shack told me the CO ordered me to go back out with the extraction team to rig my helicopter and to personally help sling it back in. Yeah, why not? I had nothing else fun to do for the rest of the afternoon, so why not? I loved the idea of stomping around out in the damned bush country. You do know there are Bad Guys out there, right?

I guess that since I didn't get shot by some yo-yo that whole extraction exercise was interesting, really seeing the spot where we had actually landed, what a little narrow ledge on the mountainside it really was, only about 20 feet wide before it fell away into a steep slope, and the upslope was much steeper than I had realized before. A helicopter could fall into that spot only from straight above, and if it was rotating the rotor had to align with the axis of the ledge or else hit the mountain. We hooked the Huey up to the Chinook, and it was interesting watching "Good Vibrations" carried on a sling like some little kid's toy helicopter. When I got back to Chu Lai again, the poor old helicopter was out at maintenance. The company commander was strutting around, inspecting the damaged old chopper from top to bottom, and the skids were spread apart like an ole fat woman's legs, pretty damned ugly, plus there was a big glob of mud and grass on one end of the rotor. I could see that the CO was pissed off, steam blowing out his ears, and him stomping around, pointing.

When I walked up and he saw me he made a beeline, jumped in my face and started cussing me out a blue streak. I just stood there, silent, and said absolutely nothing. I had obviously moved up another notch on that man's shit list, and I was starting to really dislike the stupid little asshole. He was getting up to about a nine point zero on my shit-o-meter, just like I already was on his.

He was right up in my face and hollering, "I thought you were supposed to be an instructor pilot, some fancy hot-dog pilot, and you can't even do an autorotation? The dumbest lame brain in flight school can do an autorotation or they shit-can the dumb turd! Now, look what you've done to my helicopter. They said you claimed you were shot down. Well, there's not one bullet hole in that helicopter anywhere, not one single hole. I don't know what you did, but you didn't get shot down."

The new Wasp platoon leader walked up in time to hear what was going on. He'd been flying air mission commander on our mission and was on the scene and saw the whole thing from his position overhead. It was a first lieutenant versus a major, a very fired-up major who disliked me, but evidently our lieutenant was a genius.

He stepped up and said, "Major, sir, I need to speak with you privately, now, sir."

They stepped away to the side, out of earshot of everyone, and started talking. The lieutenant was very animated, doing the talking. The maintenance captain came up laughing and said, "Hope I didn't jinx you last night telling you 'Good Vibrations' wouldn't last out the day, but I didn't think the old girl would crash on you or I wouldn't have put her up. Honest, I wouldn't have."

He asked me to describe what happened. I told him about the sound of the explosion, rolling over and spinning, then the engine not turning the rotor blades. He grunted and said they would tear it down, find out what had happened to the thing, but any case, the war was done for "Good Vibrations" and that helicopter would be going home. Then she would come back, reborn a fixed-up Lady. He was glad nobody got hurt and the helicopter wasn't hurt worse than it was. He said nobody could even see the real damage; with the engine as over-revved as much as I said, it was surely totally cooked inside and ruined for good.

I couldn't believe what happened next, but the major came over and apologized to me for what he had said earlier, especially the way he'd said it, blah, blah, blah. *Yes, sir, yeah, right, you stinker,* was my imagined reply to him, but I took his extended hand.

Back at my hooch at my bunk, I was so tired, needed food and sleep, felt so weak, I just fell back against my pillow. The way it went, wasn't that a miracle? Angels lifted our helicopter, then put it down there. The only place within miles, nowhere else, only there. The first and second and third man went instead of you before, and they all died. It could have been you who died just as easily as any of those three. Coincidence—tell me, you believe that? Miracle? Was it also a miracle that those men died instead of you? Or was all of that somehow the work of an entity that controlled Death, some entity that could grab you in its grasp, only to then release you. It had you out in the mountains. You were dead. You knew you were dead a long time.

Death could take you anytime or let you live, just to inform you in case you hadn't really learned that yet. Any time. Regardless of the circumstances. That day I had a sample of what experiencing your own death felt like.

Shit. I just wanted my brain to stop. I told myself that it was Vietnam, and *It Don't Mean Nothing.*

OUT AT HAWK HILL,
AFTER MIDNIGHT

Overnight standby duty at Hawk Hill Firebase was supposed to be a mission where you could get some rest. It was the type of mission the Hornets didn't catch very often: just spend the night in a bunker and sleep there at the firebase, or at least that was what I thought before I took the mission for a night. For us, it didn't turn out that way, and the first sign we had that there would be little sleeping that particular night was that shortly after midnight an artillery cannon unexpectedly fired a shell right over our bunker. That was enough to wake up the deafest person.

A couple of minutes later, a command-post runner busted into our little bunker and shouted, "Crank up the helicopter! Crank it up, crank it up!"

A cannon that sounded like it was no more than 10 feet away from our bunker fired another shell. The explosion was so damned loud my whole head was ringing and my ears were screaming. Then another booming cannon shot blasted out, and quickly another. I sure didn't want that. Outgoing shots roared, one after another. The runner leaned to my ear and shouted, "Crank up the helicopter!"

I yelled back, "We can't fly in this totally screwed-up weather."

The Vietnamese monsoon was back with its full force, and it had been raining all day and night. The runner pulled me by the arm out into the pitch-black night, into the wind-whipped pouring rain, and led me to the base command bunker. He had us running, splashing through the deep mud, soaked to the bone, and ice cold. We got there and the runner presented me to a major. At least then I could hear a little better since we were away from the damned firing cannons.

The runner shouted, "Sir, the pilot says they can't fly in this rain." The major nodded and yelled to me, "What's your name, son?"

I answered. He told me his name. Then he said, "We have a night-ambush site not far from here that's been hit, and they're surrounded. Two platoons, over 60 men, surrounded. They've been fighting well over an hour, and they say at their current rate of usage, they're going to run out of every-thing before too much longer. They need an ammo resupply—now, not in the morning, but now. Not when the rain stops, but now. When their ammo is totally gone, they'll be overrun and all of them killed. They'll all be dead before morning if we can't get some supplies to them real soon. They already have wounded right now who'll die if I can't get them picked up and flown out of the field tonight, rain or not. They need help. That means they need your help. There's no one but you. Understand, son?"

"I understand what you have, sir, but there's no way to fly in these con-ditions," I replied.

"That's exactly what Charlie is counting on, that's why they are attacking now, because they think we can't help."

"Sir, the conditions are zero-zero; how could I even find anyone in this storm, in absolute darkness? You can't see three feet at ground level. It would just be worse in the air. Isn't there something else to do?"

"No. No, there's only your helicopter with you flying it. That's my only hope tonight, son. My hope—and every man out there. I know I can't force you to go, the last call on flying is yours, but if you were out there tonight, wouldn't you hope that someone would bring what you needed?"

That major, that night, that rain. He thought helicopters were miracles, purely, and pilots were miracle workers, absolutely. Hawk Hill was an artillery firebase. Its cannons fired miles all around, so it dominated a large district, and NVA enemy units big enough to take on 60 American grunts weren't supposed to be so close. From safety officer school examples, I knew full well this exact situation made helicopter pilots try too much, feel obligated to try the impossible and kill themselves and their crews. Driving rain, pitch black, zero-zero. The major stood there in silence as the cannons roared, one after another, screaming, filling the silence, filling my head. I was hating the dark nights of Vietnam like never before. It appeared that the major was trying to out wait me, and it worked.

"Can you show me on a map where they are?" I asked.

The major replied, "We're loading your helicopter right now." Then he turned to a map. He drew a little red circle with a bigger circle around it, then said, "They're totally surrounded, no clear way to fly in without passing over the enemy troops. You understand that?"

I didn't bother asking embarrassing questions like "Why are they out there and don't have enough ammo with them, enough to fight through the whole night? That seemed like Infantry Education 101 to me. Who screwed the pooch on that little detail?" Someone would ask that question, some gen-eral back in Chu Lai or down in Saigon.

When I told the pilot, crew chief, and door-gunner what was happening,

I said they didn't have to go out into that crappy night with me: I could take infantry guys instead. This was their mess, not ours. They could handle the ammo cargo. Without hesitation, my crew said no way. If anyone went, Hornets would do it.

The pilot said, "I go where you go." The crew chief said, "I go with my bird." The door-gunner nodded his agreement. They understood the deal, and there was no hesitation on their part.

At the helipad, starting the helicopter, I closed my eyes and it was Steve Chasin saying with a grin, "It's the Zen of helicopter flying, just fly in your mind, man, in your mind, that's so cool, right? Just visualize what you want, man, and don't think about moving the controls. Forget the cyclic, forget the collective. Muscle memory, you already know how; like a kid catching a baseball, just reach out and catch it. The helicopter will fly itself if you turn it over to your muscle memory, then it will just follow your mind, your mind, man, like automatic. You want to go over there, just think about it, the chopper will go there."

I hadn't promised the major anything other than we would give things a try. In those conditions, no one would have normally gone flying, but since it was a life-or-death situation, we would at least try.

Our crank-up checklist items were all done, so we wound the throttle up to full speed and looked around to survey our situation: the wind was whipping around and the rain was coming down in sheets, so our windshield was a mirror. We didn't use windshield wipers because the windshields were made of Plexiglas and the wipers scratched the hell out of them. When I tried to see out, all I saw was my own reflection and that of the pilot and nothing outside but absolute darkness. Hawk Hill was on total blackout, no lights of any kind anywhere. Conditions were zeros across the board: no sky, no horizon, no stars or moon, no anything, just black night.

Lifted the aircraft weight light on the skids and visualized us lifting off slowly, held my breath, eased up the collective, and heard the rotors slapping the rain. We were at a low hover, hanging there. I scanned the instruments, blocked out everything outside, and pictured backing up a semi truck. We slipped away from the landing pad, flying backwards, into a totally featureless void. Using the same flight path as when we'd landed earlier that afternoon, we backed away what seemed damned forever, until I thought for sure we were clear. Locked on the instruments, wind buffeting us, a pedal turn onto our heading of 310 degrees. Nosed the ship over a little and started a gradual climb until the needle of the airspeed indicator began to flicker ever so slightly.

Outside, pure blackness, and the damned windshield was still only a mirror. Altitude steady at 50 feet, speed creeping along at about 5 knots. Didn't want more forward speed or height; if we got shot down, our best chance was to flop-in, hitting vertically. The Huey was best in a belly flop. No one was liking any stinking part of that little trip. Held it straight, level, on heading. Flying a helicopter purely on instruments couldn't be done with Chasin's hippy Zen muscle-memory hocus-pocus. There was no taking your consciousness out of flying the damned helicopter using instruments—consciousness was the absolute center of it. Everything flowed into your focused attention.

We soon tried turning on our landing light once, but the rain just completely diffused it, sucked it into the black-night void, and that proved to be a bad idea anyway. We instantly started taking small-arms ground fire. No one on the ground could see us at all; there was only the sound of us passing by somewhere overhead in the dark, and they were shooting wildly and randomly into the opaque night, but we were still hit at least five times that I counted. So we quickly turned the landing light out; it didn't help anyway, none. It was about three miles to where the embattled infantry were surrounded, and with us moving at hardly more than a walking pace, it took almost half an hour to get out there. Thirty minutes was a damned long time to have your heart in your throat. When we were getting near, the grunts beamed a single flashlight around the sky till they found us in the black, but the light immediately brought ground fire on us. They hurriedly switched to a red lens. We took up a high hover, finally. We were right over them.

On the radio, some grunt told us, "Dump our ammo, then go. Don't try medevac. Things are too damned hot down here. And thanks, buddy. You guys are pure aces to come out here like this."

It took nearly as long to return to Hawk Hill as it did going out to the Infantry grunts and the damned hits we had taken kept me glued to the engine gauges. I'd never been so scared for so long. We kept seeing muzzle flashes, but we took no more hits. The Bad Guys couldn't see us at all any more than we could see them, and as we got closer to Hawk Hill the radio voice guided us by our sound. Finally, we could see a lone flashlight on the landing pad welcoming us back at the end of our little journey into the black night. It had been an hour of torturous white-knuckle flying, totally terrifying flying, and it was 100 percent pure nightmare stuff.

When the aircraft finally settled to the ground, I lowered the collective all the way down with a huge sense of relief and chopped the throttle, then slumped back into my seat and shook like an old wet dog. I looked at the pilot, and he looked back, just as white as a ghost. Me too, no doubt.

"Let's never do that kind of stupid shit again, ever," I whispered.

He laughed, said, "Amen to that, brother. Amen to the shit part of it for sure."

I could feel any strength I had drain away and all of my energy flowed out. Pulled my Nomex flight gloves off, and my hands were trembling uncontrollably. For at least a full hour my fear had been at its farthest limit, maxed out. The helicopter's engine was at idle. The rotor blades turned slowly. Cold rain was blowing in my window, felt like ice pellets hitting me. I felt like screaming into the blackness, *If I die in the combat zone!*

The major, the man shining the flashlight that had just guided us in to land, stepped up to my window, and said, "Guess that wasn't as bad as you thought. You made it out there and back, and you said no one could do it."

I accepted the bottle of whiskey he offered, and took a long, long burning drink. Said, "Oh, it was much worse! I figured we'd crash in the first few minutes, and we'd be done with it! But it went on for an eternity."

At daylight, the first bit of dawn, I stood out at the helicopter looking around at where we were. The helipad was surrounded by obstacles like guard towers, radio antennas, and guy wires, none of which could be seen last night. I needed my damned day off after that peaceful night at Hawk Hill. Two Huey Dust-Off birds raced by flying low-level doing about 100 knots, from where we had been the previous night. It appeared that they were headed for the hospital at Chu Lai. Evidently some of the wounded infantrymen had made it through the night and were still hanging on. I wondered about the ones who might have died during the night. I guessed that whoever was flying Graves Registration that day would be coming around to collect any corpses that were out there. *Box me up, send me home.*

I guessed the firefight was over. The major walked up to the helipad, looking like a new penny, sharp, clean-shaven, showered, and sporting a freshly starched uniform. The rain was then just drizzle, but my flight suit was still wet from the soaking I'd had the night before.

The major lit a cigarette, and handed me one. He said, "More than 50 men are alive today, and 38 with no serious wounds at all. You know that could've been a different story this morning. There could have been many more killed in the night, maybe even all of them. Can I get the mess hall fellows to fix ya'll something special for breakfast?"

I said, "No, thank you, sir. We have to get our bird back to Chu Lai for repairs, and I guess the earlier the better, so we need to get going. I'm glad we helped some."

After we left Hawk Hill that morning, we circled out to the northwest before turning for home. We buzzed low and fast over the infantry we had visited the previous night. With our big white Hornet symbol painted on the nose of our helicopter, they recognized us as the ship that had been there during the night. They held up their M16 rifles and their M60 machine gun ammo belts and waved and jumped into the air! They were obviously very damned happy to be starting another day in the war.

There was already a little bulldozer there digging a big mass-grave hole, and there was a large pile of dead Viet Cong awaiting their final end, an anonymous unmarked grave site. I didn't know how many Americans had died in that firefight in the rain the previous night, but the dead Vietnamese had to greatly outnumber them. So Americal had scored a big body-count victory again, as usual. At least a damned Viet Cong flag wasn't flying over the place that morning like I had seen before, and I was grateful for that. Even though I hated the IFR flying we had to do in that scary darkness and never wanted to do anything like that again, I was glad that we had helped the infantry when they needed it, instead of feeling so helpless as I did the night we dropped flares all night and could do nothing more to help all those guys who were wiped out down by Duc Pho. It was a good-feeling relief that nothing like that happened again here at this place.

Back at Chu Lai, I crashed hard on my bunk. Overnight standby duty at Hawk Hill Firebase was supposed to be a mission where you could get some rest. So much for that bullshit myth. Flying on a rainy, pitch-black night was just a chance to scare the holy shit out of yourself. But 50 guys still alive that morning sounded like good news to me.

The hooch was empty and quiet with everyone off flying. Quick and easy sleep wouldn't come to me, and I forced my eyes closed, looked for a vision of my wife, Jane. R&R was not all that long ago, and I was with her for those few days. But no matter how hard I tried, her face wouldn't come to me. And it wasn't just Jane. The view of the mountains of El Paso wouldn't come to me. The taste of an iced Dr. Pepper with a hamburger and hot French fries wouldn't come to me. None of my memories of any former life I had ever known would come to me. It was like I had never existed before Vietnam. I just existed in the present moment. No past. No future. All things had been painted out, and there was nothing left in my memory but just the damned black, like flying in the swirling and driving rain last night. Just the damned black.

36

STEALING FOOD
OVER THE HOLIDAYS

Over the holidays, it would have been uncouth to have helicopters out looking for people to kill so Thanksgiving, and then again at Christmas in the spirit of peace on earth and goodwill to all, there were no combat assault missions assigned for the Hornets. We didn't get the day off for the holidays by any means; on the contrary, we flew all day, all ships flying general support, hauling canisters of hot food and cold beer out to the infantry troops who were in the field. In some cases, we even flew a few Donut Dollies to selected firebases. That was our holiday work: turkey-n-dressing, mashed potatoes and gravy, cranberry sauce and candied yams, green bean casserole and hot buttered rolls, along with sweet iced tea and plenty of Budweiser. We hauled load after load of insulated 5-gallon canisters of abundant food, freshly cooked and steaming hot, and not the Korean War–dated C-Rations the Hornets lived on day in, day out, meal after boring meal. It took a hell of a lot of A-1 or Heinz 57 sauce on a can of cold pork loaf to keep it from seeming like you were eating goddamned canned Alpo dog food. The only big differences between C-Rations and low-down dog food: the dog food probably cost more and it certainly wasn't likely to be over 20 years old.

Sometimes there was a crusty old first sergeant or a bright and shiny lieutenant colonel as an escort flying out to the field with the food to dine with the troops and theoretically cheer everyone up those festive days. Sometimes it was just the food canisters alone. That was what we liked to see, so then the Hornets could act like a pack of wild dogs. We had paper plates piled high, wonderful stuff, passed it around, the pilots taking turns flying or eating, then switching off and everyone got plenty. In most cases, it had been many days since we had eaten hot cooked food, and in some cases, it had been long, hungry weeks. For the first sergeants or lieutenant colonels it was probably one of the few times they ever got mud on their airborne boots or dirt on the seat of their pants from sitting on a fallen log and eating lunch.

A grinning Hornet 33 posing in front of his helicopter, and eating the pilot's priceless can of tuna fish sent from home back in the States, when 33 tricked the pilot into being the photographer after a day of flying Donut Dollies around to the local fire bases.

It was certainly the only time they ever shared beers with any privates first class.

And Donut Dollies, oh, man, they were a trip of their own. Some of them were actually very pretty, while some of them were more the Plain-Jane types. But they shared one very important thing in common: they were all sitting on a personal gold mine and were taking a one-way ride to becoming wealthy by 1970 standards. During my time flying in Vietnam, I probably hauled Donut Dollies around the Americal area of operations around five or six times. We got to talk with them, know them some. They were an interesting bunch, that was for sure. Usually, we carried 'em out to remote firebases where they would deliver the mail from home and organize games or lead singalongs, plain stuff.

One game they liked was called the dating game, where some grunt asked questions of three girls, and then he got to select one who would be his "date." The girls furnished a list of questions, and they all tended to be sexually suggestive: "Dolly, would you prefer a good back massage or having your feet rubbed and your toes sucked?" The grunt made his "date" choice based on which girl's answers he liked the best. The chosen "date" took the guy and they went to a bunker, where she gave him a thorough pipe cleaning for free. All three girls would set up shop, line up boys, Twenty dollars a go or get back in line three times and save money with our special: fifty bucks for a three-pack. The girls said that back at their place in Chu Lai they gave a full-service quickie for fifty bucks. An hour would cost two hundred and an all-nighter, figure a grand if you wanted to screw the whole time until morning—but maybe just five hundred if you got totally screwed out and slept after midnight.

37

THE KHE SANH SERIES:
QUANG TRI ROCKETS

Khe Sanh had already acquired a heroic status and was a fabled name by 1971, the time I flew there. Before I even started flight school, Khe Sanh was on every TV set in America nightly. A history-book classic battle: American Marines under siege on prime-time TV news, real hot Walter Cronkite stuff. That notorious siege happened back in 1968, and Khe Sanh had been abandoned since then, the same as Kam Duc had been abandoned in '68 but then was reoccupied in the summer of 1970. It looked like Khe Sanh was another step in some longer-term battle plan that the U.S. military was working out. They were trying to consolidate control of the largest area of South Vietnam they could before turning the fighting of the war over entirely to the South Vietnamese. The war had been over for a while then, and the Americans were just trying to get to a stopping point as soon as possible. And the U.S. would have to occupy Khe Sanh for appearance's sake in order to not look like we had been beaten by the NVA there. Everyone knew all of that, but that was nearly all we knew about what was happening around Khe Sanh right then; however, we would soon learn more.

In the middle of the day an emergency radio message went out to all Hornets and instructed them to return to Chu Lai ASAP. That included the combat assault formation—say again, ALL Hornets, no matter what mission they were flying on. At the Hornet's Company Area, hot rumors blazed: "We gotta pack up, hurry up, gotta go—we've been called, they want the Hornets for something at Khe Sanh, and they want us there tonight, in just a few hours."

That was something big. In my time with the Hornets we had worked in all IV Corps of South Vietnam, from all the way down in the Mekong Delta to Saigon over into Cambodia in the northwest and Phan Rang in the northeast, then into II Corps, and our latest station at Chu Lai. But we had never been up to the DMZ to do anything. I'd flown up to the far north a couple of times to Phu Bi and Camp Eagle and Dong Ha when I was being an errand boy for some Americal outfit or another, but the Hornets hadn't done any combat assault missions up there, and it was the last stop in our Asian paradise where the 116th AHC Hornets could ever be simple virgins again. If they wanted us for something at Khe Sanh, that must have meant that they were going to conduct a combat assault on the place to take control of it again. The Hornets would be up to that, very gladly. I recalled ole Roger Walker standing out on our skids shooting his movie camera when we assaulted Kham Duc, and I wished I could get a movie of Khe Sanh for him.

"Gotta hurry up, gotta go."

We flew out of Chu Lai as a big formation of three platoons headed off up north where the war was really going on. There was an electricity in the air, and everyone was totally wired up. Charging off into the unknown, ready for anything, we flew north and stopped to refuel at Marble Mountain, the home of the VIP Black Cats, and they weren't jumping to go anywhere. Life was generally easier for our blessed sister company from another mother, from the rich side of the tracks—so, no, they weren't called out to Khe Sanh. Evidently, Black Cats were not as expendable as the rough and tumble Hornets.

We were going farther north, up past Da Nang, all the way to Quang Tri. I'd always heard the name Quang Tri, but I'd never heard any good news about it. Quang Tri had a reputation for being in a dangerous area, and that was all I knew. We landed at a dusty airfield there, and they said we should loiter there until they called us the following morning. It was the army. Hurry up and wait: get somewhere as fast as possible, and don't be late; hurry the hell up and then sit around and wait while people got their stuff together. The airfield ground crew came out and guided us where to park our helicopters then showed us where our people were supposed to sleep: some dilapidated transient hooches that looked unused and abandoned.

As soon as we got on the ground, we learned that the 101st Airborne Division had already taken Khe Sanh, and the Screaming Eagles were working on opening Highway 9, which went to the old base and on from there all the way into Laos. So that left only two other possible reasons why the Hornets were told to get up there: we were going to launch a full blown invasion into Laos or else the inconceivable one, that the U.S. was actually going to make some sort of a damned strike into North Vietnam, and that sure made no sense at all.

The rundown old hooches we were sleeping in were bare naked, just plywood and wire screen, the basics, and were up next to the damned perimeter wire. The places looked like they had been totally deserted for a long time and were covered in layers of gray dust and cobwebs. At least we weren't sleeping under the stars. The first rockets hit in the middle of the night, a pair of them, very damned near us. We jumped off our bunks and ran outside, but there were no bunkers to be found. Our only protection was the depression of a drainage ditch. We laid there in the dirt and watched off to the west at the base of some mountains out there. We could see the flare of the rockets when they launched—one, two, a nasty pair—then in about 8 or 9 seconds we heard them passing overhead. They hit just beyond us and brought bloody screams. Soon there were howling sirens from ambulances and plenty of shouting. More rockets: another pair, and all we could do was wait for their arrival, tick-tock, tick-tock. The agony of waiting for them to hit seemed to last forever. Tick-tock, gotta *Just Take It*, tick-tock. Are these the ones—the goddamned ones that don't fly all the way over but fall squarely on top of us instead?

In my mind, there was a coin toss in the backseat of the Crusaders' helicopter and I won and Smitty went to his death in Tay Ninh. Now, in Quang Tri, we lay there in that ditch. *Twinkle, Twinkle,* two more damned rockets flying. Were they mine? Were they out to finally settle the score for Smitty? Were they still looking for me? Still searching? Then that pair went over us, and I could breathe again. Evidently they were not mine. But more screams came from somewhere; somebody was hurting, someone was blown up.

Welcome to Quang Tri—so glad ya'll came. It was at least an hour before everything totally calmed down, the rockets stopped, and the sirens faded to stillness. A brief final chance for some sleep returned, and maybe I would dream of home, maybe the desert around El Paso blossoming pretty. But ghosts-n-goblins came and went instead, rockets searching the late-night hour for me but finding other victims in my place. Death didn't care. Anyway, anyone participating in that war was a target for death.

The following day began with our latest brand-new CO and me flying off in the predawn. It seemed that our previous CO (the guy who disliked me so much) had been relieved of duty because the Stingers had failed to get prior permission before we put those American grunts down in that little village chasing the NVA platoon. The way the Stingers saw it everything turned out well that day. Americal got a big body count of dead NVA with only a small handful of civilian casualties, but the Stingers pulled the trigger without asking mother-may-I first. I guessed that Americal wasn't happy that the Stingers were using American infantry assets while they were so blatantly ignoring all of Americal's rules of engagement. But the last straw for that whole episode was when the Stingers answered the brass's complaints by saying they had radioed in to Division and were told that the general officer who could approve any engagement was busy taking a shit right then and to call back in ten minutes, but in ten minutes the whole deal was over with, which was the Stingers' attempt at humor. Americal didn't find that the least bit funny, and their general officer did take a big greasy stinking shit, all right, all over our CO at the time. Oops. Hence, we had another New Guy as CO.

Our new major and I were headed to Khe Sanh for a sunup briefing with the 101st Airborne Division, apparently the ones who were running whatever was going on around there. We flew along the route of Highway 9, a mostly dirt road, going generally west, and at that early hour combat engineers were already out working on the road with multiple bulldozers and graders and convoys of equipment hauled on big trucks.

The reason I went with the new CO was because I was one of the most senior guys left in the Hornets and was our senior flight leader at that time. I had only about six more weeks left in-country. Everyone else had gone home—Sparks, Richards, Walker, Plumber, Newton, and Scarborough, all gone—so that left Larry Hood and me as the old timers. And the new major and I would try to stand tall, be ready, and whatever the 101st had planned for us, we'd just take it, same as always.

In the air, the helicopter traffic was heavy, with everyone apparently going to the same place. Then we could see it on the horizon: Khe Sanh. The first obvious part was the big runway. As we approached, I saw many dozens of helicopters, maybe six or more companies total, already there, birds parked around everywhere. I could see the Dolphins and Sharks from Duc Pho, the only other assault company from around the Chu Lai area that I recognized.

This was going to be something big, much bigger than I first had imagined it would be. After we parked our Huey we were led to some deep trenches and walked through them, weaving back and forth, and it was so spooky. We were transported back through time to some ghastly World War I scene: Americans dead in sorry trenches like these 60 years before. More recently, three years ago, Marines had died there, and there we were, Americans, back in damned trenches again. We came to a bunker, a command center: maps on the walls, radio-telephones crackling, lots of aviators there, and bunches of higher officers clustered around. (See map on page xi.)

The briefing was just beginning. Yep, it was Laos. We were going to fly troops into Laos, to a new string of hilltop LZs, which would become future fire support bases. It would be only ARVN troops going on the ground and absolutely no American ground forces. The only U.S. job: fly South Vietnamese Special Forces and infantry units over the fence, put them down, then return to Khe Sanh, get more troops and then go again: simple, basic stuff. That stage of things should take only about three days to set up the initial firebases. We would be done long before the NVA could mount any sort of a meaningful response to us. The 101st Airborne colonel giving the briefing said it would take at least two weeks, minimum, before the NVA could maneuver major forces into place to respond to our offensive. They would have to bring their troops from North Vietnam, and that would make them targets for air strikes. Wouldn't our Air Force totally love that! The Screaming Eagles had opened the road leading into Khe Sanh no problem and then took Khe Sanh no problem. And we were there that morning: still no problems. Khe Sanh was fully occupied, Americans galore. There had been virtually no opposition so far, and things should remain that way for a while.

The ultimate objective of the Laotian operation was to cut off the Ho Chi Minh Trail at an NVA division basecamp that was headquartered at the Laotian town of Tchepone, which was about thirty minutes by helicopter west out of Khe Sanh and down Highway 9. If the ARVN could stop the flow of supplies that went to the NVA and Viet Cong forces in South Vietnam the ARVN could get the upper hand in the war for some time to come. If they failed in this mission they had named Lam Son 719, then everyone knew the war was over and the ARVN forces were the losers. Things were that simple. Laos was going to be the Battle Royal that would decide the whole war's outcome. Winner and loser would be decided clearly, and South Vietnam was throwing everything they could muster into the effort. The rumor mill said 30,000 troops, plus squadrons of armor (tanks) and tons of mobile artillery.

The briefers made everything sound utterly easy. As I recalled, Cambodia sounded easy at first, no problems whatsoever, EXCEPT for the ones we made for ourselves, like shooting our own U.S. Army troops with our own U.S. Army artillery, that sort of unexpected thing. FUBAR was what I recalled first and foremost about Cambodia. If the Americans could screw up like that, how could we expect any less from ARVN troops let loose in Laos?

"Whatever can go wrong, it most certainly will": Mr. Murphy's law. *Whatever can go wrong*: old man Murphy must have been thinking about the South Vietnamese Army when he first saw those words in his head. If there was any way to screw up things, the ARVN would find it ASAP. Cambodia sounded easy at first, but then we had two ships destroyed right away, with two crews killed in the blink of an eye. And both of those incidents had happened when the Hornets were working with ARVN infantry.

As soon as the rest of our company of helicopters got to Khe Sanh, the Hornets were ready! Want some tuff stuff done? That was us! But the Hornets going to Laos was so totally last minute and random, so unplanned, that I felt very apprehensive about the whole deal. I personally hated random or last-minute crap because bad things too often followed random—but no one asked my opinion about that. Okay, Screaming Eagles, you want some tuff stuff done? All right, we'd do this thing, kick ass!

We were flying two Slick platoons in our formation totaling sixteen helicopters, eight and eight, when we crossed the border going into Laos. We were carrying ARVN grunts, pale as ghosts, their eyes darting from sight to sight, headed for some hilltop LZ. The 101st Division's plan was to have a simultaneous assault on a bunch of LZs all at the same time in order to confuse as much as possible any enemy who were on the ground. That was why they had so many different assault helicopter companies at Khe Sanh at the same time. The idea was to fill the sky with Hueys so the NVA couldn't tell what the hell we were all up to.

Immediately, in the first couple of minutes, the radio was suddenly on fire with chatter: "Gunship shot down!"

People were shouting back and forth at each other, and on the radio there was a lot of static as everyone kept stepping on each other's attempted radio calls: "Do you see survivors?"

"Yes!"

"You can't help! Say again, stay out of there. Stay out!"

"Too late, Control. Shit, we're going down, too!"

"Damn it! Told you, stay out, until we can get some fast-movers on the site. Two C-Model gunships down. Stay the hell out! Heavy .51 caliber machine-gun fire. Stay the hell out!"

Excuse me, but that didn't sound like "no problems." That was happening only about a quarter of a mile away from the LZ we were going to. A big gun-fight was going on, and we weren't winning. And spread out over all the different helicopter companies, there were problems aplenty: lots of reports of taking fire were crackling over the radio. It looked like the NVA did indeed have some units on the ground in Laos, at least more than our earlier briefing had prepared us for.

And nobody hearing the radio liked the message: "Stay the hell out, you'll make things worse." This meant leave the aircraft crew alone and don't try to help. That was a pilot's worst nightmare: shot down and no one comes to help you, nobody! *Sorry, buddy, but you're on your own, sorry! Hope those Injuns don't get your pretty hair before you're able to hike out of there.*

"Hey, Mr. Custer, if that's your damned best deal, you mind if I be excused this afternoon? If that's the sorry deal, I don't wanna go. Please, General Custer, let's not go."

"Forward HO, you mother-humpers!"

We finally saw our LZ, and oh yeah, it looked just great. There were already damned burning helicopters crashed there. Apparently this was a slightly hot LZ. The Hornets were lined up as the third lift company to land on that hill, and there was a long daisy chain of helicopters coming behind us, Company after company. From the distance, you could see mortar shells hitting all around on the bare-dirt hilltop. Burning helicopters and mortar shells: Hell, that LZ had it all, *Rocket's Red Glare, Bombs Bursting in Air.*

Even ole General Custer would've asked, "Ya'll got some other real nice little hill nearby that would do as well as this one, but that doesn't have DAMNED MORTARS RAINING DOWN ON IT?"

It pegged the needle on my butt-pucker meter. So, was that what "no problems" looked like?

Okay, we're going in, now listen up, pay attention: "We're landing from a high-over-head dive but not how they expect; do something else. Zigzag and wander around the sky some. Everyone land in the LZ on different headings for each ship. Keep 'em guessing where we'll be."

Mortars were hitting the LZ in clusters, hitting fast with only brief pauses between volleys. Obviously, the NVA would time their mortars to hit just when the helicopters were on the ground. It seemed that the mortar shells must have been coming from a single location. Did the NVA already have this particular hilltop zeroed in with their mortars before we ever started out here? Was the element of surprise the 101st Airborne guys were counting on actually a matter of *no surprise at all?* Whatever the deal, "no problems" sure the hell didn't apply to that place. It wouldn't have surprised me any if two or three days before that assault started some helicopter hauling a TV news crew had landed and sat on that very hilltop while a reporter stood there and said into his microphone, "Look around, there are hills everywhere you look, but this one right here is going to be the first landing zone in the pending Laotian Invasion."

So the Hornets spiraled down the stovepipe in a swarm of Hueys, each helicopter on a different path, and 16 choppers went in from that many different directions and 16 came out with no damage. Naturally, no one spent any more time on the ground than necessary: everything was very much a fast touchdown and then get the hell out of Dodge. But that first landing was just the beginning, just the start of a very long day. We had to return to Khe Sanh and get more troops, then go back to the same LZ again, four or five more times into that place. When we were done with that rotten hill, the hilltop looked like a junkyard of smoldering and burning crashed Hueys. But to my great relief, none of them were 116th AHC Hornets. Amazingly, we were still untouched, and hadn't even taken one bullet hole.

Laos was gonna be a heavyweight fight, and by a count of the mayday radio calls I monitored we already had at least eight or more helicopters shot down in the first hour. "No problems," clearly didn't apply, and it was equally clear that there were plenty of NVA troops already all over the terrain. Plus, nobody was helping the gunship crews who had been shot down and had been seen still alive on the ground at the crash sites, and that was pure bullshit!

Peckerwood bean counters controlling that mess were probably saying, "We knew there'd be some acceptable losses, some crews we'd expect to lose. Everybody knew that all along." Personally, I categorized bean counters as assholes who viewed people as nothing but resources to be gambled with and some lost to eventually "win a victory." I just couldn't see how winning small victories would make any difference when the war was already lost. What the hell did it matter?

That day we probably did 15 to 18 assaults and about 75 percent were hot to some degree: lots of small-arms fire and machine guns to mortars. But very luckily the Hornets came through the day fine. The absolute worst part of it was that after going into an LZ as the first ship it seemed like time passed so slowly until the radio call finally came in that said our last ship was out of the LZ, clean and with no problems. It was only then that you could catch your breath and relax from your steel-spring tension for a couple of minutes.

That night we were back at Quang Tri, and it was more damned rockets all over again. At least we had hooches with our own ditch right out the door. Some guys said they were sleeping in their helicopters at the Quang Tri airstrip, laying on a full fuel cell for their bed. Quang Tri was Party Central that night. The place was packed with helicopters that had come from all over South Vietnam to be part of this Khe Sanh operation. That was a unique event: there had never been so many assault helicopter companies gathered together in one place before. So the NVA rocketeers worked overtime, and we were back in the ditches repeatedly.

By bunk time, I was a complete zombie, my brain numb from spinning in my skull at every hot LZ we went into. So the nighttime rockets seemed a fitting end to an all-around nerve-wracking day. For two sessions I watched the mountains out west and the flares as the rockets launched toward us. Would they get us? Land there in the ditch with us? Tick-tock—waiting for them to hit somewhere sucked. My tired ass just wanted things to stop so we could get some sleep.

Next day, sunrise, I was flying with the CO again, another lovely day in paradise. The second day in Laos was as shitty as the first. Three different landing zones and about 15 lifts, most of them hot, but we got away with it totally clean. No Hornets shot down, none killed, none hurt, but that was only because we'd been damn lucky.

After two days we were released from the initial invasion surge and told that we could go back to Chu Lai. That came as a shock to us. We didn't know what our intended role was in the overall attack plan, but we figured it would be more than just two days of setting up a string of fire support bases. But evidently that was all the 101st Division had planned for us. They didn't need us after the initial blitzkrieg, so it was back home and damn we were lucky. We couldn't have received better news, and everyone was glad to be away from Laos. In such a widely hostile battle environment, if you were flying a helicopter the odds were obviously stacked up against you. If almost every LZ was *HOT*, finally, statistically, the Bad Guys would get you, shoot your ass down.

We returned to the Hornets' Nest, but the Dolphins stayed up north, working with the 101st Airborne out at Khe Sanh. So the Hornets' primary area of operations was enlarged to include Duc Pho, which was where the Dolphins normally worked. We were thrilled: double the usual load of combat assaults, oh boy, but the Dolphins probably would've been more than happy to trade places with us.

The Hornets headed back south knowing that there were gunship crews still left out there on the ground trying to escape and evade for the second night in a row. On one hand, we felt like it was a purely chicken-shit judgment to say "leave them alone and stay the hell out of there," but the cold hard truth was that their old C-Model gunships had flown low and slow into an environment where low-flying helicopters were shredded up. Overlapping triangular .51 caliber machine-gun emplacements put three of those big guns on you right away, and then their neighboring .51s joined in, so they started hitting you from all sides. There was no way a helicopter could get in to the guys trapped on the ground without being shot down for the effort. The real truth was that little kids throwing rocks could bring down a helicopter if they hit the tail rotor or main rotor control links just right or beaned the pilot, like David and Goliath, or threw a rock into the engine air intake. Some situations required jet fighters with bombs to neutralize the antiaircraft fire— or napalm, which worked real damned good on little kids throwing rocks or just as well on damned NVA troops firing AK-47s and rocket-propelled grenades.

38

CO OFFICE, CW2 DENNY

Early one morning out at the operations shack, the operations captain said they had just received a call and I was supposed to report to the company commander's office. What sort of crap had I gotten myself into this time? I had tried to keep my mouth shut lately and keep my opinions to myself. That particular day, I was scheduled to give check rides all day, and going to the CO's office was eating into that.

At the orderly room the first sergeant said to wait, the CO would see me soon. I listened to a couple of spec-4 office clerks gossiping. It'd been a couple of weeks since we were at Quang Tri and Khe Sanh. The big topic at that moment was that the South Vietnamese Army forces had stalled out at a fire-base named A-Louie, not far inside Laos, only about halfway to their destination at the Ho Chi Minh Trail at Tchepone, the NVA division base camp. It came as no big shock to hear "the ARVN had stalled out." Where was the surprise in that? And they had screwed up with their nice new American tanks, so once again, one had to ask, where was the surprise in that? The spec-4s said the ARVN had about 30 tanks in a long column that went down Highway 9 into Laos and parked in a tight little circle out in a valley alongside the road and proceeded to sit there day after day for a whole week. It was long enough for the NVA to bring in their own tanks and then park them on the back side of hills where they couldn't be seen by the ARVN. From their secure locations, they then shelled the hell out of the ARVN tanks in a one-sided duel. *Bang, Bang.* It was like gunnery school target practice.

Naturally, the South Vietnamese jumped out of their targeted tanks, ran off, and just abandoned their damned ole tanks where they were parked. Then the North Vietnamese Army simply took the ARVN/American tanks, the ones that were still operating, and headed for the hills with them. So the U.S. Air Force had to go hunt them down, then bomb and destroy them. That was only about sixty million American bucks instantly pissed away for no good reason, just because the South Vietnamese never had used those tanks one time to engage any sort of North Vietnamese military forces. *Whatever can go wrong, it most certainly will.*

Then they said the Major was ready and for me to go on into his office. I was half expecting to be chewed out about something I'd done or something I hadn't done and should have, but who could guess for what? However, the major very warmly welcomed me and shook my hand, then told me that the paperwork had come through promoting me to chief warrant officer two. Congratulations. My platoon leader was there, and the crusty company 1st sergeant, and they both shook my hand and said congrats. Then the major did a little formal ceremony of pinning my CW2 bar on me. With that act, my new rank was chief. Imagine that: CW2 Denny. So there I was, my shining new CW2 bar and only a little more than three weeks left in Vietnam.

The whole promotion exercise took about two minutes, then I was out of there, quick and clean. There was no ass-chewing for anything, so I breathed easier. That new CO and I were getting along wonderfully when I compared him to the old one. In fact, he'd been friendly to me since we'd flown together for our Laotian adventure. Well, a promotion certainly perked me up a bit, put a new little spring in my step, and I felt pretty good about everything in general until I heard what the orderly room clerks were saying: "The Hornets are going back to Khe Sanh!"

We were officially on standby and would be given as much notice as possible when the 101st Airborne Division wanted us to come, maybe this week, maybe in just a few days. Either way was too soon as far as I was concerned. Damned Laos had looked like nothing but trouble to me the last time the Hornets were there, and I hoped we wouldn't go back.

That night, some of the guys took me to the Americal Division Officers' club. We had some actual food, and it was wonderful: a steak, a baked potato, and a ceremonial Scotch whiskey toast.

39

THE KHE SANH SERIES: LARGEST ARMADA

The anticipated call came from the First Aviation Headquarters down in Long Binh: "Get to Khe Sanh as quick as you can. Take every pilot you've got and every chopper you have that'll fly."

The first shock of our sudden trip up to the north country by the DMZ came when we landed and parked the Hornets' 116th Assault Company helicopters on a hillside at the refueling area on the south side of the Khe Sanh airfield base camp. A solitary 174th AHC Shark C-Model gunship sat on the crest of the gradually sloping hill, turned sideways. Its haloed profile was silhouetted against the stark white sky, and it was perched there like it was royalty elevated high on a pedestal looking out over its hillside meadow kingdom, which was filled with scores and scores of sister U.S. Army helicopters that had come to join the fight in Laos. A group of our Stinger gunship pilots was gathered in conversation near the solitary Shark, its toothy Shark grin painted red and white across its nose front, chomp, ready to bite, ready to fight.

With our helicopter crewmen gathered around us, our company commander (who was flying as pilot on my ship for this Khe Sanh deployment) and I listened to some stranger tell us, "That C-Model up there: that's the last surviving Shark gunship. The Dolphins and Sharks are wiped out. Gone. Not their men, although they've had a bad string of battle casualties. Wiped out means that all of their helicopters are gone, either shot down and destroyed or shot to shreds to the point that they were no longer flyable. That one and only last Shark helicopter and crew are temporarily joining the Hornet Stingers until their company gets put back together as soon as they get some replacement aircraft."

I stood there and let those words sink into my brain, which put a darker tint to my vision of the reality of our current situation: "Dolphins and Sharks wiped out." Wiped out! Our Hornet Company had flown with those guys many times on joint combat assault missions around Duc Pho down south of Chu Lai, and our gunships often worked together with the Sharks. Had flying around Laos been that bad? Hell, we came up here together with the Dolphins less than a month ago, and now we just learned that they were wiped out already. Just since then? Wiped out in less than thirty days? That was certainly sobering news to the Hornets, and instantly started everyone talking.

A guy wearing a First Cavalry patch whispered to me, "There's nothing unusual about the Dolphins. They're just examples of what's been happening in this fight to control Laos. The U.S. Army tried to use helicopters as weapons in a conventional warfare setting and Huey helicopters proved to have very short lifespans in an intensive antiaircraft environment like Laos. The A-A fire in some of the most contested spots is comparable to flying low-n-slow over downtown Berlin in WW II. Those damned LZs on the northern line, the ones closest to the DMZ, were like flying into the steel teeth of a meat grinder, and if you entered their firing envelope, then Boom-Boom-Boom, it was bits-n-pieces time, and you had practically no hope of getting out of the situation alive."

Hummm, that was informative to hear, something we sure as hell needed to know.

I accompanied our CO as he headed to the 101st Division command bunker to find out what was going on and what the Hornets' job was going to be. We walked by the Shark gunship and I rubbed the old girl's nose to get some of her luck and give the gunship some of mine in return. Then we went down into the Khe Sanh trenches and headed to the meeting we were there to attend. Our timing was just right since they were only getting started, and a very big crowd was already packed in the space.

A lt. colonel from the 101st Screaming Eagles began our preflight briefing. In a big and loud voice, he boomed out, "Gentlemen: listen up. Tomorrow morning we will fly the largest combined combat assault flight ever assembled in this war. We'll go deep into the heart of Laos to take our primary objective, LZ Hope, the end of the line located smack-dab on the damned Ho Chi Minh Trail. Next, we will take the town of Tchepone located next to Hope, the town that's the heart of North Vietnamese Base Area 604. I can't tell you the exact number of helicopters that will be in the assault flight because things are still being pulled together, but it will be the largest armada of helicopters ever assembled and flown in all of our years of being engaged in this Vietnam War. The South Vietnamese Army's seizing control of Ho's supply route will go down as the distinct turning point of this war: this will be the decisive beginning of the end for this long conflict. In the whole history of rotary wing aviation, this will be a singular event of major lasting importance in the annals of modern combat. It will be something you can proudly tell all of your grandchildren about, that you were a part of the biggest combat air assault ever."

The guy next to me said, "I've heard it'll be over 200, maybe 250 Slicks, something like that."

That primary briefing went on for some time, then everyone broke up into smaller subset group meetings to go over individual companies' roles in the mission. The Hornets' CO major and I were pulled aside to join one of those subset meetings. By the time it was over, everything we had been told had my head swirling and buzzing. To begin with, the last thing on earth I was prepared for came up as a stunning surprise to our CO and me: the Hornets were assigned to fly as lead flight company of the combined total formation. The 116th Hornets?

I thought, *Holy Cow! Really? The Hornets, leading all these helicopter companies, instead of one of the 101st Airborne Aviation Group Screaming Eagle Companies? Reestablishing Khe Sanh and the whole damned invasion of Laos were 101st operations. So why wasn't one of their outfits leading this ultimate assault?*

A guy must have been reading my mind, because he whispered to me, *"The 101st doesn't have a single Company left that can put up even a skeleton Flight of Helicopters. They put their whole Division's Aviation Assets into this Invasion, and now they're mostly gone, just like the 174th Dolphins, gone from the Southeast Asia stage before the last act even begins."*

As the senior aircraft commander in our company, I knew that it fell to me to be the flight leader of the Hornets. We had a full company flight of two combat assault platoons, the Yellow Jackets and the Wasps, for a total of 18 troop haulers we would put up, plus our Stinger gunships flying as our cover escorts. So, equipment wise, the Hornets were perfectly capable of doing the mission as the flight leaders, and we had enough able-bodied personnel ready to go. But on what basis did the 101st decide to put the Hornets in the lead? Why the Hornets? We certainly didn't know the area of operations very well: we had flown there only those two days that started this whole campaign and we never got all that far into Laos those goddamned two days. Someone at a pay scale that was higher than mine knew why the Hornets had been chosen, but it was a mystery to me.

I guessed that some bean counter had looked at how much combat assault time we'd had over the past year and compared our combat causality rates and decided we were up toward the top: the highest level of combat assault hours combined with the lowest personnel and equipment losses or something like that. As for my being the Hornets' flight leader; that was just a coincidence of my seniority and being an instructor pilot. It had nothing to do with anything about me personally. If Smitty had won that coin toss instead of me that first day when we were going to our units—if it had been him to stay with the Hornets—he could have been standing there in my boots instead of me and I would've been the unlucky one who drew the short straw and got blown all to hell that first day.

In our preflight briefing we studied everything on the big map: the entire flight route, the POL refueling station we were to use, the staging area we were to use, the specific flight pattern we were to fly for starting the formation, picking up everyone as we departed Khe Sanh and headed west following Highway 9 into Laos and, most important, our flight's ground track on the south side of the highway and the Tchepone River that flowed through the valley. The airspace was supposed to be a lot safer for aircraft on the south side. Over on the north side of the highway and river we could expect to find a high concentration of heavily armed Bad Guys. We studied maps and things for over a half-hour, did it all over a second time and then a third time.

The Hornets were going to lead this LZ Hope and Tchepone deal, this final objective of Dewey Canyon II or Lam Son 719 or whatever they were calling the invasion of Laos in our briefings! As long as I had been with them, the Hornets had never led the attack on a target that had its own special campaign name. Damn! That sounded like a big deal, Lucille, a damned BIG DEAL! My assigned pilot for the mission was to be a 101st Airborne man, an Airborne colonel, a full-blown bird colonel. I wondered if the 101st colonel was bothered that he was having to fly with the Hornets to get in on the tip of the spear for the coming assault? Evidently the 101st Division's people and helicopters had been expended as *acceptable battlefield losses,* chess pieces used up for an eventual victory in the end. There was so much happening it all left my head swirling and buzzing.

At least at that briefing no one brought any poster boards showing the forecast of *basically acceptable losses* for aviation equipment and personnel. I didn't think anyone wanted to see that sort of information written down. The recent past history showed that in some of the hottest LZs as many as 75 percent of the helicopters had sustained major damage going in and coming out of the LZs and the associated crew casualties had also been high. Everyone at Khe Sanh knew what the losses could be: it could be catastrophic for our side if the North Vietnamese chose to vigorously fight the helicopters.

After the briefing ended, the 101st Airborne guys fed us from a chow line. I recall beef stew with vegetables served on metal army mess kits. It beat the hell out of our usual diet of C-Rations. The major and I spent that night in the command bunker: some of that scene was a sort of helicopter geeks' slumber party combined with a fervent rumor-swapping fest.

All of us pilots were like fleas that lived on this giant elephant: everyone had a fractionally limited view of the total big picture of what was happening overall with the elephant (or the Vietnam War). The Hornets were a flea that lived and fought on the elephant's knee, but they used to live and fight on his shoulder, and they were experts in their particular situation. Some other helicopter company might live and fight on the elephant's big ole wide ass. Everyone knew a piece of the total big picture, but no one had any clue what a whole elephant looked like, and being an "elephant ass" expert didn't necessarily give you any particular insight into the best practices when operating in the deep folds of the "knee" territory. So that night we heard war stories from pilots who were normally stationed all over South Vietnam. Naturally, after each new story someone would call out, "Oh, I've got one that'll top that story." So, needless to say, the bullshit got pretty deep as the night wore on, and there was plenty of laughter at some of the more preposterous assertions.

The pilot's rumor mill was gushing over about the situation we would be facing the following morning. I'd been shocked to learn about the Dolphins, but that was nothing. The whole 101st Division's Aviation Group, for all practical purposes, had been destroyed in only the month since the Hornets had last been at Khe Sanh. People were saying the 101st had lost virtually all of their helicopters shot down and destroyed or shot to shreds. The 101st Airborne Screaming Eagles were the *Poster Unit* for the U.S. Army in Vietnam: the Paratrooper Heroes of D-Day and the French beaches of Normandy back in 1944, the same unit that told the Nazis "Nuts" when the 101st Division was totally surrounded and the Germans demanded their surrender at Bastogne during the Battle of the Bulge. But the NVA had done what the whole German army had never been able to accomplish: they had effectively eliminated the 101st Airborne Airmobile Division from the battlefield.

The past month, the U.S. had lost over 150 helicopters a week, with many crewmen wounded or killed. There was a problem with the whole concept of a fast-moving U.S. airmobile army. The air mobility concept, the very centerpiece of that war, looked seriously flawed. The weak link was the Huey helicopters we flew: they could be shot down too easily with ordinary infantry weapons or the most minimal antiaircraft weapons. The army needed to come up with a helicopter that was armored like a Patton tank. The invasion of Laos had proved that necessity to everyone. The only reason helicopters had ever worked very well as offensive weapons was because of the culture of the pilots, "When getting shot at, just take it. There's no place to hide anyway. I know, sounds insane. There's nothing else to do. *Just take it!*" Our old platoon leader, 1st Lt. Sparks, had this stuff figured out long ago. To fly combat helicopters, you had to join the legion of the crazy. People were right. Helicopter pilots were crazy.

The consensus opinion among the lower ranking pilots (like me) at the command bunker tilted between the grim side of things to full-blown nightmares about the coming assault. Apprehension levels where whipped to a peak by the knowledge of what had been happening to helicopters in Laos so far. The next morning it could be raining down choppers blown out of the sky if we put hundreds and hundreds of them into one giant push.

All night I tossed and turned and could hear distant explosions from somewhere in the area, our American outgoing artillery, I assumed. I finally fell asleep thinking that the next morning's mission would probably turn into a pure shit storm and I would have the privilege of being in the best seat in the house to see it as it played out. By that point in my tour in 1971 I had been the Hornets' flight leader for hundreds of combat assault missions, and no Hornet had ever been killed or wounded on one of my assaults. But I couldn't see how that record would last more than a few minutes the next damned day. With only about three weeks of flying left before my tour was finished, I dreaded the thought that in this giant assault into Laos I would be leading unknown numbers of pilots and crewmen to certain death, maybe a hell of a lot of them and maybe myself. Probably myself. I guessed that everyone had to die sometime, but I doubted that when we were cranking up our helicopters to go take LZ Hope that I would be pounding my chest and telling everyone, "This is a good day to die!"

In the morning, I was out at POL getting our helicopter refueled to the very top. I stood out there with my camera, taking photographs, turning around in a circle, and I took pictures in every direction, because all you could see was helicopters in every direction as far as you looked.

While I was photographing the amazing panorama, a guy approached from the Cobra gunship that was parked behind our old Huey. At first, I didn't recognize him, not there, not at Khe Sanh—he was too out of context. He called my name, held out his hand: "Eddy, is that you? Eddy Denny? El Paso?"

I shaded the sun out of my eyes and took his hand. "Johnny Hummel, is it you?"

What a surprise of seeing a friend from my hometown, from El Paso, Texas! Johnny was an old college friend from UTEP. We had been roommates for a time, had an apartment we shared with another friend, Brooks, during the '67–'68 school year, 3 and 4 years ago. Johnny Hummel. Damn, what were the odds of both of us being in Vietnam and both being helicopter pilots? Johnny: a Cobra Pilot. It was unbelievable.

Johnny said, "Yes, a Cobra pilot, aircraft commander of that gunship right there."

You could've knocked me over with a feather. I grabbed him in a bear hug and nearly kissed him. It might have been unbelievable, but it was so good seeing a friend from home, here in this godforsaken place. Memories of him flooded me, things we did, the apartment we had, and Brooks, our mutual friend. Actually, I met Johnny through Brooks. Brooks and I worked at the same motel, the Hawaiian Royal out on Dyer Street in northeast El Paso. We were both desk clerks evenings and weekends when we weren't going to college classes. Brooks and Johnny had been childhood friends since elementary school, had grown up in the same little old West Texas desert

Above and following pages: A series of photographs that together take in a 360 degree panorama of some of the approximately 250 Assault Slicks waiting in the staging area for first takeoff in the early morning stillness of Khe Sanh before the attack on LZ Hope and the town of Techepone.

oil-patch town of Barstow, about 10 miles east of Pecos. I'd actually been to Barstow with Brooks and Johnny and met their families, spent a weekend with them. We had some really great times together back then.

Seeing Johnny Hummel over in stinking Vietnam at all, but in damned Khe Sanh in particular, totally blew me away, "So, Johnny, what are you doing here?"

"I'm flying the lead ship of the Cobra gunship escorts."

Lead ship? Now, that did blow me away! I asked, "Am I dreaming this? Lead Cobra? No shit? That's what I'm doing. Lead ship of the Slicks. What on earth are the odds of that?"

What were the odds of old friends coming together in such a unique circumstance and so exactly paired? What were the odds that our helicopters would be parked right next to each other out of those hundreds of helicopters? Or that we would see each other at that moment, that exact time, not five minutes off one way or the other, but exact. Was it thousands of coincidences over three years that would result in our paths crossing there in POL in Khe Sanh, South Vietnam, that day, that hour, that minute, that mission, both commanding lead ships on a once-in-history mission? The odds had to be a trillion zillion to one. And any idea that seeing Johnny was a run-of-the-mill coincidence was very much short of the mark. Maybe coincidences never happened, not ever.

I was amazed that Johnny had actually talked. When I'd know him before, he was practically a mute. He never talked except on the rarest of occasions. Then it was two or three words, maximum. Brooks always did Johnny's talking for him. If you asked Johnny a question Brooks would answer it. Even around women, especially around women, Johnny would never talk.

One Saturday night, Brooks, Johnny, and I went over to Juarez after I got off work. It was about midnight when we arrived on the main drag in downtown Juarez. After a couple of brief stops, we found a little nightclub where we could hear the rock band playing as we walked up on the sidewalk. We went in, and there was a pretty girl dancing up on the bar and singing. She wore a miniskirt that had worked up where the whole crotch of her panties showed, and by the way she was dancing, she knew exactly what she had on display. Two other nice-looking girls on barstools provided the backup vocals. They were singing a Doors song, "Light My Fire." Then when the dancer saw Brooks standing there, obviously madly in love with her at first sight, she sang an open invitation straight to him: "Come on baby, light my fire. Try to set my panties on fire. Try to set my pantieeees on fiii—rrre." She rubbed herself very teasingly on the thigh near her crotch.

Light my fire, hell. This girl had the whole bar in a three-alarm roaring blaze. These three girls weren't hookers or anything. These were El Paso girls gone fully Wild Thing! The lead singer was a pretty Latina fireball, but the other two girls were Anglos, and they were already more than plenty drunk. The situation looked perfect to a bunch of knuckleheads like Johnny, Brooks, and me. I ordered up a round of rum-n-cokes. The song ended and Brooks extended a hand and helped his songbird down off the bar, pulled her into his arms and his waiting kiss, and they got started just that fast. He asked her if the girls wanted to go back to our place in El Paso and party, sing, dance, and drink all night.

The Latina girl looked Brooks in the eye and said, "Making love all night sounds better."

Well, *OoooKaay*, that sounded like a perfect plan! Brooks had the three girls up and headed for the door as our drinks came. I paid the tab and gulped down three fast drinks. Merely seconds after we came in our apartment door, Brooks and his Latina fireball made a beeline to his bedroom. It was funnier than hell, but Johnny's girl didn't talk any, either, and she was as silent as he was. I never heard either one of them say a thing, but Johnny and his girl were just as quickly in Johnny's shared bedroom along with Brooks and his songbird. I had my girl nearly fully undressed, only panties left, but she stopped me and said it was her time and she hoped I understood but we couldn't go any further because of her period, sorry.

Johnny's girl didn't talk, but my girl was exactly the opposite. She never shut up at all, and I had to ask her to wear a bathrobe to cover up if she wasn't going to put out, damn her little round ass. Eventually, in her stream-of-consciousness style of conversation, she told me that the three girls had each claimed to be spending the night at the other's house, and they all lived at home with their parents, and they were all only sweet 16 years old.

"Hey, Brooks, hey, Johnny, time to finish up and take these girls back downtown to get their car so they can be going home."

In her style, my girl also told me that Brooks' girlfriend, Sunny, was

Suelita Barrera, the little sister to Roberto "Bobby" Barrera, and that was bad. I knew Bobby Barrera. He was basically the top hood in Northeast El Paso, and he would break Brooks into small pieces if he ever knew some Gringo-Cracker had seduced his innocent younger sister.

"Hey, Brooks, you had better ask her how old she is and who her big brother is."

I would tell him the other worrisome news after the girls were sent on their way.

All of those memories of Johnny flooded in, filling my head with an instantaneous overload. As we stood there silently staring at each other, I laughed and asked, "Remember?"

Johnny said, "Yeah."

Same Johnny as always: one word conversations.

For clarification, I said, "I was remembering those girls we met once over in Juarez."

"Me, too," he said.

I noted, "They were too damn young, but they were already full-blown wild maniacs."

John laughed, said, "Yeah, they were that."

I added, "The girls you and Brooks had were Screw-Monsters."

He nodded.

I said, "I've never known many girls who were such damned total nymphos like those girls. Not often. Like never."

He nodded and said, "That's why I'm gonna look up my girl when I get back home. Guess I'll ask her to marry me."

I looked for the nearest rock to crawl under. I felt like such a fool: running my mouth about those girls and then to hear that John was planning to marry one of them. It seemed to me that a guy usually didn't get many young women if you didn't talk any at all. Talking was generally required. That girl was surely the first one John was ever with, the first girl he slept with, so he probably had a good plan to grab that one and marry her.

Seeing Johnny Hummel at Khe Sanh was the last thing I ever expected, and him talking so much was even more surprising, although a very pleasant surprise. But a Cobra pilot: *Johnny*, a *Gunship-Killer*. I could've never pictured that, not ever. Quiet John, waking up every day with killing on his mind, running up damned body count in Vietnam. None of that whole scene seemed to be reality to me. Quiet John talking. Quiet John a lead Cobra gunship aircraft commander. Damn, I'd seen everything then. Being in the army had certainly made Johnny blossom socially.

We would be taking off soon. John and I shook hands and embraced one last time and he went back to his menacing-looking gunship. That brief exchange we just had left me shaking with cold chills running all over me. I had this horrible feeling that Death was screwing with me one more time. Seeing someone from back home in El Paso right there at my helicopter in goddamned Khe Sanh had to be Death's way of letting the Real World say good-bye to me just before Death would finally do its will with me. This whole thing was just so strange that I knew the entity of Death existed and was present with me at that very moment. Everything that was happening had some meaning to it. These were steps being taken to the final end, till it was lights out, till Death took me. Everything I had experienced in Vietnam all led to this place in time: Khe Sanh and Laos and this assault mission. Everything I'd experienced that was tied to death filled my thoughts: the times I had been on paths leading to death but was pulled off and other men died in my place, or when I'd stared down the barrel of a rifle and watched the bullet coming out or found myself in a broken helicopter falling out of the sky dead weight to crash into the jungle out in the mountains or all the times I had screwed up and nearly crashed my helicopter into the jungle or the side of some damned mountain. So it appeared to me that I must have been spared all of those times when I could have been snatched up by Death so I could be at Khe Sanh to keep an appointment with Death that very day somewhere in Laos. All sorts of crazy thoughts of death were swirling in my thoughts because of seeing Johnny Hummel, and that couldn't mean anything other than that seeing an old college roommate was clearly a death omen for sure. If this mission was to mean my death coming in only a few minutes, I didn't want to keep thinking about it. And I laughed at myself for having become such a short-timer who was becoming paranoid about buying the farm at the end of his tour. I watched Johnny climb into the cockpit of his Cobra. His helicopter was certainly a damned good-looking machine. He put his helmet on, and I knew that seeing him had to be an omen, that fate was letting me watch what was coming for me. It was fascinating to see it all unfold.

I looked all around; so many helicopters. I would never see anything like that again. None of us there that day would see such a sight ever again. That was unique. That was history concentrating itself, funneling into a single point in time for a single event that morning at that place. That day would obviously be the peak of my tour in Vietnam. Hell, it would probably be the peak of my whole damn life. The Hornets were leading a flight of maybe 250 helicopters. I didn't know how many, but that was probably about 15 whole damn assault helicopter companies, and I got to lead the Hornets as a kid of only 24 years old. Damn. Two hundred fifty Huey Slicks at $600,000 each would be a lot of money, about one hundred and fifty million dollars. Would I ever have the opportunity to lead anything else that added up to that sort of money or would I ever lead a collection of men who would even hold a candle to 500 helicopter pilots and 500 crewmen? To try to keep calm, I kept telling myself that all I had to do was lead the Hornets and all the others would just follow the Hornets. I was sure I would never see anything to match a fraction of that gathering of helicopters at Khe Sanh. And anyone who was not there to see that spectacle would never get to see anything in the future that would ever come close to that day.

The 101st Airborne bird colonel flying our right seat arrived out at our helicopter, and he looked like he was sent straight from central casting: all of his flight gear looked brand new, including his flight suit and spit-shined paratrooper combat boots. I imagined that I'd flown more hours in the past week than he had flown in the previous year, but he was just one promotion step away from being a real live brigadier general, and if the 101st Screaming Eagles wanted him flying in the lead helicopter, the Hornets' only choice was to salute, smile, and extend their warmest heartfelt welcome to him. If the NVA had a clue he was flying in our bird they would do everything in their power to shoot us down: every damned gun in Laos would be blasting away trying to blow us out of the sky. Salute. Smile. Be nice. Extend the colonel the warmest possible welcome to the Hornets.

The Hornets weren't leading that mission as any sort of an honor. Plainly the 101st was simply reaching down deep into their standby reserves in the First Aviation Brigade to find an intact assault helicopter company. And Johnny Hummel leading the Cobras; he wasn't with the 101st Airborne either. No, Johnny's shoulder patch was First Cavalry. So, I guessed all the 101st gunships were all gone, too.

Start time for the assault on LZ Hope was upon us, and we were loaded with troops for takeoff. Radio chatter was short, crisp, and intense. All the pertinent players had established their commo checks. Everyone was ready for the word from the air mission commander to take off, begin the attack.

Twenty-something years later, the Dallas VA doctor wanted to know how I felt about our mission that morning and the two large forces arrayed against each other: all of the ingredients were in place for a massive clash of wills that could erupt into a giant ball of mutual death and destruction at the point of full engagement. Yeah, that was basically the situation. I recalled waiting to go and being tensed up as tight as a spring. The buildup to where we were, all the wild rumors and talk in general, had apprehension levels up to their maximum. And the thing I dreaded most was the possibility that this assault might end in a massacre for us, and we would take massive casualties, but I would survive the whole damned thing and then be haunted by it forever. How would I ever be able to live with that memory? Our pending thrust into the heart of the Ho Chi Minh Trail was like every other stinking combat assault mission: you damn well had to goddamned take it. I certainly hoped for the best, but I certainly expected the possibility of flying into a nightmare killing-field situation of NVA hot lead filling the sky.

No matter what I thought, everything was set. We were going to do that

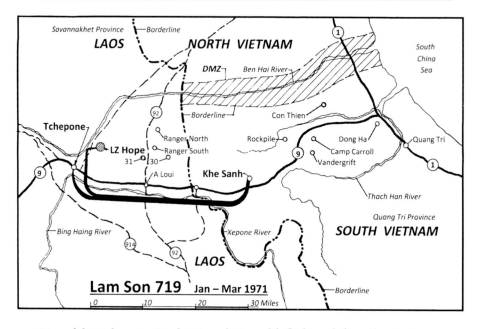

Map of the Helicopter Combat Assault Armada's flight path from the staging areas at Khe Sanh to LZ Hope and the town of Tchepone. The attack armada was called the largest combined helicopter force in the whole Vietnam War by the preflight briefers of the 101st Airmobile Division, the Screaming Eagles, the Commanders of the U.S. Army Aviation Assets gathered at Khe Sanh.

assault into Laos, no question about that, and all the decisions had been made. This was a very large operation that couldn't be easily stopped or altered, so I just focused on the details of doing the job at hand and tried not to think about the bad outcomes we might all face. I was very aware that I was in a position where I had no control of anything. That freed me to just fly my helicopter, lead the Hornets, and go where I was told by the air mission commander. Everything else would fall into place behind us. We would know soon enough how things would unfold for us that day when we actually flew our first lift into LZ Hope. Finally, the order came over the radio for us to depart and the agonizing waiting was over.

We came up out of Khe Sanh and circled around in the prescribed traffic pattern in a semicircle east of the airfield and helicopter company after helicopter company came up to join the combined assault formation. Our helicopter had South Vietnamese Rangers on board, the most highly prized of all the ARVN soldiers, their very top dogs. They looked picture perfect, all clean-n-shiny and they all wore little yellow ascots at their throats. They were escorted by two Americans who displayed no unit patches or name tags, no rank, no emblems, nothing that said America. They were just good-looking young officers, lieutenants, or captains maybe. And they were unarmed, no pistols or M-16s.

We circled west of the base and turned to a westerly heading at Highway 9, still climbing higher (highway was a comical name: it was nothing more than a narrow one-lane, red-clay dirt cow path that had been washed out in very many places). I got my first look at the parade of Hueys following along behind us and it was stunning! Company after company for as far as I could see. It was sobering to think the U.S. could amass so many helicopters into one hardened fist and smash it hard into the face of the North Vietnamese Army. We were flanked on each side by lines of gunships: Cobras on our right and Huey C-Models to the left, with formations of Huey Slicks in the middle. We headed straight toward the Laotian border. We were going to the *End of the Line* for that Vietnam War! One damned way or another.

The American top brass thought this was the battle that would turn the war permanently in the favor of South Vietnam and show that the ARVN could fight and win a major operation toe to toe against the North Vietnamese Communists, both sides with major forces fighting it out in open country, army standing up to army. That was what the U.S. brass had hoped when they first planned this invasion, but from almost the beginning of Operation Lam Son 719 everything got stalled out because the ARVN sat on their asses at Firebase A-Luoi as soon as they went into Laos. They were finally on their own and were unbothered by pesky U.S. Army advisers. So this big LZ Hope airlift was being flown three weeks behind the original schedule! Three weeks! The South Vietnamese Army could have belly-crawled from Khe Sanh to Tchepone and back again in three weeks.

North Vietnam had been given ample time to maneuver plenty of their units into position. Guesses varied about the true nature of our situation, but everyone agreed about one thing: the whole damned deal looked tuff for the aggressors (which happened to be the U.S. Army). Estimates that I had heard ranged from 25,000 to 40,000 NVA that had taken up positions in Laos to confront the South Vietnamese. Most of the big thinkers thought the NVA forces would come from the north, and all the brass thought they'd take more time. But to everyone's surprise, two divisions of NVA had come from the A-Shau Valley, which was southeast of Tchepone or Khe Sanh. Three divisions did come from North Vietnam. Altogether, five full NVA divisions waited for us, and if they wanted to turn on the chopper-grinder they could surely destroy every damned helicopter that was in the air that day. No one on the American side wanted to admit that, but that was what the real truth was.

When we crossed into Laos, I was scanning the flight ground-track in front of us, and everything was clear, with no visible muzzle flashes or tracers, not yet. We were cruising straight and level at 5,000 feet, doing 80 knots, and everything was developing normally. The weather was high clouds and hazy air. A long solid chain of Cobra gunships flew parallel to us about a mile north of our flight route, shielding us from the DMZ borderline, which was very near. We could clearly see all the mountains of North Vietnam beyond that.

I hated our flying altitude because I disliked height and always had, but beyond that, a person on the ground could see a helicopter pass overhead for at least three or four times longer if the aircraft was flying at 5,000 feet instead of 1,500 feet, the Hornets' usual cruising altitude. I might have grumbled a little about our height, because the colonel told me that flying in Laos needed to be that high to avoid shoulder-fired antiaircraft rockets the NVA were using called "Stingers." (It was funny that someone had chosen the same name to call their AA rockets that our gunship platoon had long ago chosen for themselves.) The Stinger AA rockets had an effective height range of about 4,500 feet, and that was the reason for our 5,000 minimum height. It might have been nice if someone had mentioned goddamned antiaircraft rockets in our preflight mission briefing the night before instead of my first hearing about that little fact right after we crossed into Laos.

As I was scouring the terrain looking for the slightest signs of enemy hostilities, there was the sudden smoke trail of some sort of a missile coming up as fast as a damned rattlesnake strike, and it sure looked bigger than anything that could be shoulder-fired. The missile hit its target with a massive explosion, *Kaboom!,* which caused a secondary explosion of fuel and ammunition that blossomed into a fireball that became a roiling cloud of white smoke that dropped tiny fiery pieces of debris down everywhere over a desolate patch of Laos.

So much for the idea that 5,000 feet was a safe altitude.

Then the reality of what I'd just seen hit me like a load of bricks! Goddamn it! That was John Hummel's Cobra turned into an expanding cloud of smoke! The instant it happened, I was absolutely coiled so tightly that I shuddered all over when I saw that missile explode, and I'm sure the helicopter I was flying jumped around the sky. I was watching when my friend had just died. We'd been visiting and talking only a few minutes earlier. Seeing him had made me feel less alone and filled me with memories of true reality, the true reality of a Real World back home in the States, where everything was normally sane and where insanity was the rare exception.

The Dallas VA doctor, a PhD psychologist who had exclusively specialized in PTSD treatment for over 25 years with the VA, certainly perked up with his questions when I told him about seeing Johnny Hummel blown up into nothing but smoke. Naturally, the doctor wanted to know about the feelings I had as things happened at the time back then, the ones I could still remember.

Well, after the missile blew up the Cobra, for a short time I was just mesmerized seeing everything. My first thought was that this couldn't be happening and my lying eyes couldn't be seeing what I saw, but that didn't make the cloud of smoke go away. So I thought maybe that wasn't Johnny's Cobra, maybe that was some other lead Cobra instead of Johnny's. The next flash was that if the NVA had the missile launchers (and obviously they had) and were going to use them to shoot down helicopters, then we were all totally screwed and were flying into certain death because there could be only one outcome when things became our helicopters opposing guided missiles.

I held my breath and watched the spot where that missile came from and waited for the missile launcher to swing around in our direction and fire again. We were getting farther away from it only so damned painfully slowly. The radios were all buzzing with the static caused by multiple people trying to all broadcast at the same time, and my brain felt like it was sizzling inside from the adrenalin and the state of absolute fear as we moved across the sky deeper and deeper into Laos. Tick-tock, tick-tock. Time had slowed to a crawl as our line of helicopters that stretched all the way to the horizon flew into whatever the NVA had ready for us.

What the hell were we going to accomplish that day that was worth John Hummel's death? If he had to die, why didn't he park his Cobra back in refueling at Khe Sanh a few spaces away from me where we wouldn't have seen each other? Knowing who flew that Snake changed things in a very profound way. Seeing that gunship vaporized wasn't something abstract to be rationalized. There was a person there, two people, pilots. My life was entwined with one of them. Hell, I had met his mother. I had been in his family home where he grew up. I would someday have to visit his mother and tell her what had happened to Johnny in goddamned Laos. That was if someone didn't have to visit *my* mother.

Not one word was spoken in our helicopter. The colonel and I exchanged looks and shook our heads, meaning *that was a bummer.* And it was, on so many different levels. If the NVA had SAMs for killing helicopters, we were going to lose every such exchange, and not just some of them or most of them. We were going to lose 100 percent of those fights.

All we could do was keep going, hope for the best, and *Just Take It.* But I sure was hoping that first missile was merely a one-time deal, some foolish yo-yo NVA mistake. It seemed to me that any missiles they had were intended for use on the fighter jets flying our escort air cap, and some low level NVA officer had just gotten overly trigger happy. At least that was what I tried to convince myself of, but that didn't stop my butt-pucker meter from being pegged by what had just happened. If I had not been scared enough before, seeing that Cobra gunship turned to smoke sharpened my focus on the reality that we could be heading right into a total hell before things were finished that day. And I found myself fully baptized in the concept of living like you're already dead and the total acceptance of the self-awareness of your own eminent death, be it in moments or in fifty years

I felt the boney fingers of Death's grip tighten on my shoulder. Johnny Hummel being killed was a little show put on by Death for an audience of one. Johnny and I were both leading that damned assault just so I would have a front row seat to see him die. Death was screwing with me on the most personal level possible. Of all the things I had experienced in the Vietnam War, Johnny's death was completely beyond being a mere coincidence more than anything else that had ever happened to me, and I had faced far too many goddamned "coincidences" already.

I asked the colonel if he'd like to fly and then collapsed into my seat as soon as he took over the flight controls. If we were opposing SAM missiles, it wouldn't matter one bit who was flying at the time if an antiaircraft guided missile blew us up. I put on the Saigon Armed Forces radio station and turned it up loud. Waylon Jennings sang, *"Someone's gonna get hurt before you're through/Someone's gonna pay for the things you do ... just to satisfy you."*

Yeah, no shit, someone's gonna get hurt. I wondered what "acceptable battlefield losses" number the generals placed on that most important operation of the whole damned war? Was it 10 percent, 20 percent, maybe 50 percent, or could it be even more than that? Somewhere someone knew how many aviators the generals were willing to sacrifice chasing a victory at Tchepone to achieve their long-venerated dream of cutting off the Ho Chi Minh Trail.

If we'd been sent on a martyrs' errand that morning, despite the roaring music I imagined that I heard 1st Lt. Sparks hollering in my earphones crystal clear, "You'll do your job, and you'll not stop for a damned single second. If we're getting shot at, just take it, damn it! There's no place to hide anyway. I know, sounds insane. There's nothing else to do, *just take it!*"

We still had about another 20 minutes of flying deeper into Laos to reach our destination, and getting back out of there alive would take just as long before anyone could take a normal breath again. We were like World War I infantrymen who had just come rushing out of their trenches and were racing across no-man's land just waiting to be met by withering enemy machine-gun fire. The adrenaline rush I had at the time had slowed the tick-tock of the clock to a painfully slow pace, but we proceeded on to LZ Hope with no visible muzzle flashes or tracers, not yet. Still, I had myself braced for our end.

Wasn't this the "The Charge of the Light Brigade" all over again? *"Not tho' the soldier knew Someone had blundered.... Theirs not to reason why, Theirs but to do and die.... Cannon to right of them, Cannon to left of them. Cannon in front of them.... Boldly they rode and well, into the jaws of Death, Into the mouth of Hell...."*

That's where we were, flying our Hueys around in the mouth of hell, and our progress seemed to be infinitely slow as we passed over terrain where the U.S. had already had innumerable helicopters shot to pieces over the past month. Finally our air mission commander told us that we were one minute from our turn onto the base leg for our approach to LZ Hope: start descending out of 5,000 feet to 1,500 feet to prepare for final approach to the LZ.

I was absolutely amazed that we had gotten that far without being fired on (with that one exception of the single Cobra the NVA had taken out). We made it as far as we had by some sort of a miracle, but that miracle could end in a big bang at any time. I figured the anticipated shit storm was just about to get started as we made our descent into the LZ. Sit up straight and fly right. We were going in to deposit our ARVN Rangers. Hold your breath and hope. My whole body felt like it was quivering from absolute dread of what was waiting for us as we turned on final. I looked back at the swarm of helicopters coming behind us, blotting out the morning sky. Man, what a stunning and awesome sight to watch! Roger Walker would have loved to have filmed that display of helicopters, but Roger was back somewhere in Texas, I guessed. I wondered what my colonel would have done if I had told him that he had the controls and then started to climb out onto the skids like ole Roger had done to me during the assault back at Kham Duc. Guessed the colonel would have soiled his nice new flight suit. Damn. I wished I was back somewhere in Texas instead of flying over the Ho Chi Minh Trail right then. It felt like Death was hanging right there in our helicopter to take me away just any time, that the NVA were going to open up on us just any second and that in a wisp it was going to be lights out for everyone of us. Tick-tock, damn, we were moving so painfully slowly.

Spread out in front of us was a beautiful LZ. It was giant, many wide-open acres, flat and grassy, with the nearest tree lines far, far away. A couple of smoke ships were laying down a smokescreen on the north side of the LZ. Three screaming fighter jets made a low-level pass over the LZ doing at least 600 MPH. On the ground, there were Pathfinders waiting, giving hand signals with paddles and doing everything exactly by the textbook, like back in flight school at Fort Rucker. A smoke-grenade at the Pathfinder guy's feet pumped out purple smoke clouds that swirled around him. Our approach felt like we were coming in to an aircraft carrier. We touched down, soft as a baby's ass.

The colonel was talking up a blue streak on the radio, offering a colorful running narration of our progress. I couldn't very well tell him to shut up and stay off the radio, keep the channel open in case someone made an emergency mayday call. But it did sound good to hear him calling LZ Hope COLD so far. I thanked my lucky stars. I was stunned. There hadn't been a single shot fired at us that I knew of, and that was a total surprise to me. I wondered how on earth we had gotten so lucky, but I still felt as if Death was hanging heavy over us and this was Death's way of torturing us, to drag things out like they were going. I was just glad that the rest of our Hornets hadn't heard all the gossip that was flowing in the command bunker the previous night about helicopter companies sitting in an LZ when the NVA would open with barrage fire with a zillion guns firing simultaneously. Finally, the radio call came that the Hornets' Slicks were empty, and I immediately pulled pitch and we were gone and still not a shot fired at us. A miracle.

That initial lift was the first of many to come, and we still had all day to go, but to my amazement, we had made it into LZ Hope our first time without getting shot totally to hell. On the return trip to Khe Sanh to pick up more ARVN troops, I was astounded to hear each of the companies following us report that LZ Hope was still COLD as they came out of the place. Except for Johnny Hummel's Cobra gunship being blown to smithereens not a single other helicopter took any enemy fire of any kind either in the landing zone or en route to or from the LZ. Something strange had happened so far that morning: the entire area from Khe Sanh to LZ Hope and Tchepone had gone totally nonhostile at a time when we knew the NVA had five divisions out there waiting for our big helicopter assault. We'd been told that they even had eight to ten full antiaircraft battalions dug in all over the western section of the Laotian operations area that had 23mm, 37mm, and 57mm AA guns that were 100 percent effective when used against our slow-flying Huey Slicks.

Indeed, something strange was happening. The sky was crowded with helicopters concentrated in a single place like it had never been in the whole Vietnam War. There had never been another instance even remotely similar to what we were doing: the largest armada of helicopters that would ever be assembled was freely flying over the battlefield and all the NVA guns were being held stone-cold silent so far. I assumed that the North Vietnamese were making last-minute adjustments to their final battle preparations once they learned our exact landing zone location, and they would focus their attention on that spot and bring down the sledge hammer on us during our subsequent lifts into LZ Hope. Every passing minute seemed to be infinitely slow and pure mental agony as we waited for the NVA to start blasting us. But the second lift into LZ Hope went just like the first: everything was just as cold as the North Pole, and not even one shot was fired at us by the NVA. Very strange.

Just how long might our luck hold out or how long before I had a damned fatal coronary caused by waiting for the shit to hit the fan? But for lift after lift the NVA held their fire. By late in the morning everyone must have felt like we were experiencing some sort of a Major League Miracle. I know I did. My date to leave Vietnam and the war was only three weeks away, merely 21 days, so I had only a couple of weeks of flying left. I knew I'd be making it back home if I survived that day in Laos. Tick-tock, tick-tock. Just how much can time slow down? How long can a day take?

Finally, finally, finally at the end of the long day, fueling up back at Khe Sanh, lots of guys were out of their helicopters, talking in groups. They were so pumped up by the release of pent-up anxiety that everyone was literally giddy and filled with disbelief. We'd done LZ Hope, every bit of it, then assaulted the village of Tchepone. In the waning afternoon we did some resupply missions at the western-most Laotian firebases. Everyone was saying, "By far, the best day yet in Laos—only one Cobra shot down the whole day. That was actually 'acceptable battlefield losses' for a change."

Visions of the missile hitting John Hummel's Cobra had repeated continually in my head all day. So, no, nothing about our losses that day was *acceptable* to me except for the fact that I had survived it unhurt. The fact that the NVA didn't fight the American helicopters that day could only mean that our army had given Ho Chi Minh's army everything they wanted. Everything. We had brought thousands upon thousands of South Vietnam's best troops deep into Laos and plopped them down where they were surrounded and outnumbered by at least two or three times, so our helicopters were doing the NVA a favor. But I figured that the NVA's free pass for the American helicopters was just for that one day.

The North Vietnamese wanted the U.S. military to leave Vietnam as soon as possible, and the last thing they needed was to cause the Americans to lose face with a major defeat and the loss of many helicopters. That would simply prolong American involvement in the war until the U.S. could exact revenge for any perceived disgrace because of any major combat defeat during Lam Son 719 in Laos, especially if premier army aviation combat units were the forces that were defeated. That would mean that the U.S. Air Force would just bomb Hanoi and Haiphong that much longer and harder until our military strength and superiority over little North Vietnam had been reestablished in the eyes of the Western World. No, inflicting major damage on our aviation units wouldn't help North Vietnam any. It was the ARVN they wanted to defeat and totally humiliate in the eyes of the Vietnamese people. They wanted the American-controlled puppet-rulers in Saigon to be the ones to lose face, appear to be stupid.

Hauling ARVN troops to the battlefield in Laos was one thing, but hauling essential supplies to sustain them through an extended fight was something else altogether, and the NVA would use all their means to stop any flow of supplies and ammunition. The next day, combat for our pilots would start again, full on, and the prospects of flying back and forth into a battle in Laos that could last for a few months looked pretty grim. And that was what all of us pilots thought the plan was: occupy Tchepone and interdict the Ho Chi Minh Trail for as long as possible, at least until the next monsoon weather began, maybe six months or more. The war was entering a new conventional warfare stage.

But that next day the Hornets were safely away from Khe Sanh and Laos and were back at the Hornets' Nest in Chu Lai. Since the U.S. had lost no transport Huey Slicks in the assault on LZ Hope and the town of Tchepone, the 101st Airborne brass had more helicopter assets left over than they had been planning on, so they sent the Hornets back to Chu Lai to resume their duties there. I guessed the Airborne big thinkers had not included the 116th AHC Hornets beyond the first day of the invasion of Tchepone in their planning because they had figured we would be wiped out and used up that first day. We probably would've been if the NVA had pulled the trigger on us. But some miracles were apparently of the giant-size variety, and on my mental calendar I scrawled a giant-sized *X* on day number 21 left on my Vietnam tour. I had survived the day the Big Battle of LZ Hope never happened, so, by God, I was officially a Short-Timer in my mind. I thought, *Screw Laos, and screw Vietnam and its stinking little war of attrition and body count.*

Back at Chu Lai I got word to report to the CO's office. He said there were some items to discuss now that I was nearing my rotation date. There was a limited-time army career program for warrant officer helicopter pilots that had just popped up. The war was winding down, so the army would wind down, too, and they wouldn't need as many pilots as they had. Here was the army's deal: I would have to sign a "Voluntary Indefinite Enlistment" contract if I wanted to stay in the army, or when I returned to the United States I would be discharged from the army right then, immediately. I needed to let them know within a couple of days; they had paperwork that required some time to get done, one way or the other. It had to go up to the First Aviation Brigade and get approved and then come back. So think it over a day or two but no longer than that.

I left the CO's office. Two days, hell! Two seconds was enough time! There was nothing to think over. Before, I had still owed the army three more years on my enlistment, but then out of the blue they were offering me a 35-month early discharge? I stopped and went back in the commanders office and said, "I'll take the discharge and get out of the war business, sir. I still have to finish college."

There. That was done. In three weeks, I would be out of the army and unemployed. All the little plans I had for my near future just went out the window. Who needed a damned paycheck? But, Lord, it felt good to be unemployed. I couldn't remember ever feeling better. I had gone to Tchepone and survived, and—did I dare think it?—it appeared I'd survive my tour of flying helicopters in Vietnam.

40

WATCHING THE FLY-BY
FROM THE DECK

My last couple of weeks of flying around the Chu Lai AO went by uneventfully. I was floating on cloud nine after the army gave me the chance to get out of the military as soon as I returned to the United States. For the first time since I had become an army combat helicopter pilot I knew for certain that I would never have to serve a second tour in the Vietnam War, and that knowledge put me in a relaxed and carefree mood. I felt like a huge weight had been lifted off my shoulders. My whole world suddenly looked bright and sunny for the first time in more than a year. The army's ultimatum sounded crazy to me: sign on to an enlistment that said I would stay in the army *indefinitely*, because any word that had *infinity* as its base sounded like it probably meant a very, very long time. There was no way I wanted to be in the army a whole career. I wasn't lifer material. Instead, the idea of getting discharged 35 months early sounded totally fabulous to me.

So I was able to fly with an unburdened mind, relaxed, and I could even reflect on the good aspects of what I had been doing for the past year. First and foremost, I had worked with a bunch of good guys I had learned to trust totally, guys I knew always had my back no matter how bad things might get when unexpected crap was coming fast and furious. Second, Uncle Sam had given me access to a stable of some fabulous $600,000 Huey helicopters and let me hot-rod them to my heart's content all across the Vietnamese countryside; and if something broke on a chopper the maintenance guys simply gave me another bird and turned me loose to go again. That was more than most people would ever experience in their entire lifetimes. I had gotten to do all that flying and it wasn't costing me a dime. Instead they even paid me to do it—maybe not much but something.

At last even those last few flying days were done. No more flying for me. I was done with the damned war in Vietnam, and particularly done with the damned war in Laos. I felt loose as a goose and in a party mood. A bunch of us from my Wasp Platoon went up to the Officers' club at the hospital for some hell-raising as my little sendoff hootenanny.

We were just beginning to get warmed up, the booze flowing, when a runner from the Hornets Company came busting in the front door of the club with a message, "Listen up, all Hornet Pilots. You've gotta go immediately to the flight line. There's been an emergency call, and everyone's gotta go now. The whole company is taking off as soon as possible, and that means right now, tonight. The Hornets have been ordered to fly to Khe Sanh tonight, soon as everyone is rounded up, so hurry up, hurry up, all Hornets gotta go now!"

Well, exactly what was that about? Didn't know—they just said "emergency and come NOW, tonight, not in the morning, come now." I started for the door with everyone else, but the messenger-runner kid stopped me and said it didn't mean me—going to Khe Sanh didn't apply to me, so just relax, Three-Three. So there I stood and watched as my platoon mates left without me. That was my ultimate proof that Ed Denny's War was over. OVER. Really over. The only thing left was a ride on that big ole jet airliner, then it was home to El Paso and my wife. I guessed I would live to see my next birthday after all. Within a week I would be searching the want ads looking for a civilian job.

With the Hornets gone, there was a bunch of nurses left with only a little handful of men in the club, at least three nurses for each man. Most of the hospital men had stayed away. They weren't interested in being at a Hornets party.

But all I could do was worry about what was happening and what was so bad at Khe Sanh that the Hornets had to go at night. That was unusual as hell. Helicopter companies didn't just get up and move out in the dead of night unless there was something very important going down. The runner-kid had said Khe Sanh didn't apply to me. I was finished flying and wasn't a Hornet anymore when it came to being called to combat. *The Senior Hornet*: that was really what didn't apply to me anymore. That airfield at the boundary of hell—sorry, Khe Sanh—there was no way on earth I wanted to go back there ever again. Still, I felt like crap that my guys would go and leave me behind.

Captain Bobbi Sue Wolters, the operating room nurse I had known for a long time and had become good friends with, came up and asked, "You feel like an old fire horse? The firehouse bell rings, you gotta jump up and go racing off to a fire?"

I admitted, "Yeah, feels real damn odd not answering the bell at all and then feeling being cast aside like an old worn-out shoe."

"Does it feel like that? Don't you think it's simply that you've done your time, finished your part of the war, and it's time for others to do theirs?"

"No, what it feels like is my family of Hornet brothers just left me behind here in this frigging bar, and I'll probably never see any of them ever again. Before they can come back from Khe Sanh and Laos, I'll already be long gone for home on the Freedom Bird. I've waited a whole year wanting only to have the chance to leave here alive, and now that it's here I would rather fly off with the Hornets one more time than have to see them go off like this and then worry like hell about what stupid shit might happen to them. If any of them go up there and get themselves screwed up, I hope I never learn anything about any of that, because I sure won't want to know if it's anything bad."

A couple of hours later the captain and I were outside on the club's deck looking over the cliff watching the ocean. We had both put away enough Scotch and waters to have a serious buzz going. I wanted to watch our helicopters pass by. They would fly up the coastline feet wet, flying just off the shoreline, free of the possibility of any nighttime ground fire. Sure enough, I heard the familiar *Whop-Whop-Whop* of rotor blades coming, then the First Platoon, the Yellow Jackets, started streaming by, passing just above us, one by one, and it was an enthralling sight. Then the last Yellow Jacket ship passed us, and I could see the big white Hornet painted on the nose of the next Helicopter! A Wasp. My platoon, and they flew low, at the same height as the deck where Bobbi Sue and I stood. I saw them clearly. They had their cockpit lights burning brightly, so I could see their faces that night as they passed by us. The first aircraft commander gave me a little wave "howdy" and a crisp little salute, and it was my buddy, Larry Hood, leading the Wasp Platoon off to the unknown. But Larry had been excused from combat flying a while ago and became a maintenance test pilot because he had already been shot down while flying combat way too many times, probably more than most every crazy Loch Hunter-Killer Pilot in Vietnam. Hell, his ass had been shot out of the air over a dozen times, but I guessed no one could keep him away from making this emergency trip up North! Larry was a real piece of work. He was due to be going home himself in just two weeks. There was no way he should be going to Laos, but I guessed he was a fire horse as much as any of us and he was just stepping up to accept his role as the senior Hornet.

Each Wasp helicopter passed by in turn, and I saluted all of the aircraft commanders a last good-bye: Bob and Ken, Mr. Miami, Bill Shobel, and Steak-Sauce Woody, followed by Lt. Oklahoma and others. There went MY Helicopter, number 340, named "God's Country," with my crew chief flying off with someone else. Hey, Heavens, you take care of yourself young man. Then the Hornets were gone off into the black night, headed up north. Next came the Stingers Gunship Platoon, followed by a couple of maintenance ships, off into the night, flying into who knew what. But it couldn't be anything good, and I figured it was something more serious than just plain ole bad.

The ultimate battle of the Vietnam War was playing itself out since we had put the ARVN into Tchepone, and I suspected that the poor South Vietnamese Army wasn't doing well, probably getting itself ripped up. I stood there and listened as the sound of our helicopters faded away slowly to nothing, then there was only the relative silence of the sea waves breaking on the rocks below and, faintly from inside the Officers' club, Janis Joplin screaming out her song about trying *just a little bit harder.*

It was a driving, hard-beat, fast song, but Bobbi came into my arms to waltz: slow, so slow, half speed of the song. We danced to her pace, very slow, steady, and damned close. She came next to me, pressed to me and half sang, half hummed softly along with Janis, and we danced, Bobbi's head on my shoulder, her heart next to mine. Clean. God, she smelled so clean and sweet, and the piercing smell of her perfume filled me.

Our music rolled over, and screaming Janis went away. A song I knew well from another woman started, "Angel of the Morning." Captain Wolters leaned up to me and gave me a kiss. Well, nothing like that had ever happened between us before in all of the instances we had spent any time together. And it wasn't a brother-sister kiss. It was a woman-man kiss of the soulful and heated variety. My heart instantly skyrocketed and my brain exploded into Fourth of July fireworks. Her mouth tenderly on mine, she said, "I'm a virgin, and I won't give that up, so mark that down and understand that before you say anything. But if you want, you could stay here at the hospital with me in my quarters tonight. I'll take tomorrow off. We'll have breakfast in bed, then we can spend the day sunning out on the beach and go swimming in the ocean. But I won't screw you tonight, so don't even think about trying anything like that. Be completely sure you understand that, okay."

That didn't take any time to decide, none.

Normally I didn't get up to the hospital's Officers' club because I was always down at the Hornets' operations shack doing scheduling at night, but I had been there six or eight times. Bobbi Sue and I always seemed to gravitate to each other if she was in the club, and there had been an undeniable instant chemistry between us from the start, but nobody had ever done anything about it. I was married and she was engaged to a doctor who was back in Cincinnati and that was that. Anyway, when we first met, she had told me in very clear language that she was NOT looking for a man to get involved with: period. So, we got a little bit drunk together and danced, and that was all that had ever happened between us. She always played the perfect lady part, and I was always the perfect officer and gentleman, though maybe a little tuned up from the Scotch. And I guess the fact that she outranked me by a few notches also helped me remember the part about being a gentleman.

I said, "Yes, ma'm, I'd appreciate nothing more than spending the night and going swimming."

When I thought about it, I realized that there was no way I wanted to go back to an empty Hornets' Nest Company Area that had only maintenance people left behind there, and then have to go to bed in my empty hooch with only my thoughts filling my mind. If I did that, I knew I would be awake the whole damned night and probably worry myself into a total emotional fit. Laos had scared the pure crap out of me, but the thought that my Hornets were having to go back there without me scared me to the same degree but with a different kind of fear. It was the fear caused by being totally useless and totally helpless. Yes, Bobbi Sue, I would very much appreciate not being alone, and if there was ever a case of wanting someone to help me make it through the night, man, that night was it.

She kissed me again. So our deal was sealed, and it would be on her rules.

"Angel of the Morning" playing from inside the bar faded out and only the lonesome sound of the crashing waves remained as we headed for Captain Bobbi Sue's private quarters. Okay, I would try a one-night stand that did NOT include any screwing. Anyway, it had been so long since I'd been with a woman my thoughts about sex had long ago dissipated and withered away to nothing.

Nurse in White Satin

S poiler alert: my night spent with Bobbi Sue Wolters never evolved into a sexual conquest or a conquest of any sort. She had made it clear where the red lines were all drawn, so I never tried to push her boundaries, not even the slightest amount. She was the one who originally invited me to stay with her, so the whole deal was totally her show, and I accepted the role of being the passive and obedient follower of whatever she was prepared to do romantically. To start with, she further made it clear that she let me stay with her that night because I would be going to Cam Ranh Bay in only a day or two to catch that jet airliner to return to the States, and she would never be bothered by me coming back around every chance that I had and hounding her like some horny old mutt dog trying to climb on her bones. Our little adventure together was purely a one-and-done sort of experience, and that was what she required of our night spent together.

That night was a single point in time: it was a fleeting spontaneous combustion that would live only for that moment. But for that time, since I was forbidden to act out any attempt at seduction, I was able to be simply me, with my layers of protective façade temporarily abandoned and I felt like Bobbi Sue exposed her unedited self as a woman in her purest form. She wasn't an army captain and she wasn't an operating room nurse anymore. She had laid all of her different uniforms aside, and her military officer's tone of voice and head nurse's bearing melted away. She existed for a while in a pure void that offered no context for her other than her natural beauty as a female human being that greatly exceeded anything of a merely sexual nature. She was a warm and sensitive person who was opening her soul to me and asking mine to join in a brief union with hers. She was offering an intimate weaving of two human spirits that I had never experienced with any young woman before.

That night my thoughts and feelings were like winds of a hurricane blowing in every which direction all at once. First, I felt like I was finished with the Vietnam War for good—I was 100 percent done, hot damn, and that made me euphoric; but that also meant I was finished being a pilot and would probably never fly again, which was a depressing reality. I was as alone as I could ever be: my helicopter company had flown off to some battle in Laos and left me behind, and that made me feel helpless and worthless. But at the same time, there was no way I ever wanted to go back to Laos, so I accepted staying behind. Just the thought of Laos made me realize that I would never again have to land in a goddamned hot LZ and grit my teeth and *Just Take It* and hope like hell I didn't get my young, dumb ass shot completely off, which was a wonderful thought. But I was also giving up my persona of being a warrant officer and a pilot (of which I was proud). So naturally my army income was ending, and that was bothersome. Hell, I was going to be job hunting within the next week.

My wife, Jane, would have been less than pleased to know that I was climbing into a nurse's bed to spend the night, and there was no way to ever make her understand that everything was totally innocent, that Bobbi Sue's and my night together was not as a woman taking a man into her bed, but rather, things were more like I was an injured animal that she had briefly taken in to care for and attend to like a young girl might help a puppy that had gotten hit by traffic. I knew no other woman I would ever meet in life would know (or even suspect) key parts of the inner core of me that involved my experiences in Vietnam that Bobbi Sue simply intuitively knew. She had been immersed in the heart of that war as thoroughly as I had, but she had done it much longer than I had: three years straight through. That was three Christmases, three birthdays, three of everything. Three years being in Chu Lai working at a hospital had to seem like forever, and I imagined she occasionally must have been as lonely as I had often felt when I got down.

She and I were such a total cliché: two people who had each been alone for too long, getting by only on letters and memories and hopes of some Future where we would join a loved one. But that night we just needed to allow ourselves to take a companion for a short time to hold us as we fell asleep. Nothing that night ended up being about screwing at all. There was nothing that happened between Bobbi Sue and me that I would have been ashamed to tell anyone, but as things happened over the years no such subject came up in conversations.

Bobbi Sue's hospital-staff quarters seemed like a VIP suite at the Waldorf Astoria Hotel compared to the poor digs to which I was accustomed. To start with, she had indoor plumbing, glory be to the Modern Age! There was a counter with a two-compartment kitchen sink with hot and cold running water right there in her room. Plus, her very own personal bathroom was attached to her apartment, with an actual Real-World flushing commode and a big, shiny bathtub and shower.

I waited for Bobbi Sue while she was in the bathroom doing her girly routine to get ready for bed, and I occupied myself over at her bookcase looking through her record collection.

"Ahem. Ahem. Say, AAAhem." Bobbi Sue cleared her throat to get my attention.

I turned. There she was, framed in the bathroom doorway, one arm raised, resting on the door jamb, and her other hand on her jacked-up hip. There she was, all right, nurse in white satin. The record I was holding and looking at was perfect: the Moody Blues. So I put it on her record player and fired it up and the orchestra's sound filled her room with "Nights in White Satin."

She was a vision, silhouetted by the bathroom light haloed around her from behind. She had on an ankle-length, white-satin, open robe and matching shorty pajamas, made translucent by the back lighting, the line of her body showing clearly, like she was standing there all but naked to see. Damn, this was really all of her that she was presenting to me. She was stunningly beautiful. If I had been a renaissance painter, seeing her glowing in that light, haloed so, I would have painted her as one of heaven's exquisite angels.

I had heard of people who claimed to be each other's soul mates, and I knew that could've been Bobbi Sue and me. But soul mates would have had to be in some other universe, at some other time and in totally different circumstances: we were both already all tied up in existing relationships with other people and neither of us was free to become anyone's other half. Anyway, dwelling on what could have been or what could develop had no role in our one-night fling.

It was then that I felt something was very wrong with me. I could have been lying naked somewhere in a roadside ditch, naked angels dancing everywhere, offering themselves to me in batches, but my overarching depression was so absolute and I had been crushed down for so long I could have lain there in the ditch with every trace of sexual desire and aggression leached out of me while the naked angels danced all around a Dead man.

Bobbi Sue's rule about the virginity issue must have been her single prohibition, because evidently she was showing everything else that was permitted. In those circumstances I would have normally expected to become aroused at the first sight of such a scantily clad young woman and experienced an instant erection. But to my surprise, despite the charged sexual situation I found myself in, I felt like my normal emotional and physical responses were very flat—and not because I was holding myself in check. Something was wrong with me. I remained cool and waited for Bobbi Sue to take the lead when she came to me and kissed me as she settled into my arms, and we danced to "Nights in White Satin" for the whole long song.

The next morning, I woke up all alone. Bobbi Sue was gone, and the bed felt very empty without her, but a note was there: "Shower is still hot if you want. I'll be right back with breakfast."

When I came out of her bathroom she had returned to her room and had a big breakfast spread out. She told me that she'd scheduled herself off for the day and got a Jeep from the motor pool. How tough was this—the whole day for us and nothing we had to do except have a little holiday.

I made a wild guess at it, and asked about her fiancé back in Cincinnati. "Isn't he a Doctor?"

She laughed and said, "Thoracic surgeon, you know, Chest cutter, lung-n-heart things."

There didn't seem to be anything to lose in inquiring, so I asked, "Guess with his knowledge of anatomy, he might notice a missing hymen, if he checked for it?"

She laughed again and poked me in the shoulder and replied, "Yeah, I imagine he'd be able to tell. But I don't know if that would be a big deal to him or not, because we've never really discussed anything about that subject. I don't know what he's expecting from me, but I am pretty old for your average virgin, and he and I have never been in a situation for him to know one way or the other. Our romance budded and blossomed after he left here, and our courtship has all been conducted through the U.S. mail. The virginity thing was a promise I made to myself when I was young: I would save myself for the one special man I will eventually marry. None of the virginity thing is about anything he might expect; it's about what I expect of myself, because I just think it's the right thing to do. Guess that sounds old fashioned in 1971, but that's how I feel about things."

Well, okay, if that was how things stacked up, there was no way to argue with anything she'd said to me. I was just glad that after we cleared away the breakfast things she cheerfully stripped down to her panties again and jumped back into bed and held out her arms for me to join her. We passed the rest of the morning away in each other's embrace letting our passions heat up to a very hot simmer but never a rolling boil we couldn't control. I held myself in check as much as I could and just tried to focus on enjoying where she was taking us and everything she was doing for us or letting happen to her. But after spending the night and the following morning in her bed, I felt crazier than hell for ever telling her that I would not try to take her all the way. My episode of stunted sexual arousal had passed, and I was living exclusively in the moment—there was no thought of any future, not even as soon as the next few days. There was only that moment, and I found myself wanting to be with the woman I was with right then, and I didn't care anything about right or wrong. But I was still playing my assigned role in Bobbie Sue's game, and things were under her control such that I could take only what she offered. She let us hang on the verge of consummation many times, but she never allowed us to bust through into the final conjunction and blending.

With the morning gone, we got up and went out to lunch, then took Bobbi Sue's Jeep down to my Company Area, the Hornets' Nest, to my hooch. She changed clothes there, out of her fatigues, and put on a tiny yellow bikini and a short terrycloth cover-up robe. She wanted to lie out by the surf on our sandy beach, work on her suntan some and maybe go in the ocean for a swim.

I could have packed up my things that day and grabbed a plane to go to Cam Ranh Bay, but there was no way in hell that I wanted to wrap things up with the good Captain Wolters yet. Being with her had stopped all of my onslaught of random bad thoughts and feelings, and I was truly unworried and relaxed for the first time in many months—since I had been on R&R in Hawaii—so I wanted to steal away whatever time I could to spend with her. Cam Ranh Bay could wait one more day, then I would start my trip back home to my real life and my woman I had waiting for me.

With our flight personnel gone, the Hornets' Nest was a ghost town except for the ground personnel and the maintenance grease monkeys. Bobbi Sue looked like a movie star there on the Hornets' beach, such a pretty woman and such a beautiful body. Before long there were a dozen guys standing on the sand dunes gawking at her, drooling. A fabulous round-eyed woman, nearly naked, on our beach: nobody had ever seen anything remotely like that around our Hornets' Nest before! When I sensuously rubbed suntan lotion on her then made a big show of kissing her deeply, it sounded like I heard guys passing out and falling in the damned sand!

Bobbi Sue and I were playing around and joking and having a good time putting on our little theatrical show for our audience of spectators. Then a friend of mine, a captain from maintenance, came out to us there right next to the breaking surf and said he needed me to help him right then. He had a helicopter he needed to ferry to damned Khe Sanh right away, that afternoon, so he had to have another pilot fly up there with him and he couldn't find anyone else. Would I go with him? Apparently, I was the only pilot in the Company Area other than him. It was important! The Hornets were up there flying four choppers that were just about over their flight-hours limits, if they weren't already, and properly they should've been Red-X'ed before they were ever allowed to go in the first place. But the Hornets' instructions had been to throw the book out of the window and bring anything that could fly, regardless of their flight-hours status. I guessed that whatever emergency they had at Khe Sanh was that bad. So my buddy wanted to take a helicopter that was just coming out of its regular 100-hour service and swap it out with one of the over-hours birds that was working at Khe Sanh. He would never forgive himself if something catastrophic happened to one of the over-hours choppers and he had a good bird to replace it with but didn't get it to the guys flying in combat.

"We'd just zip up to Khe Sanh and then right back, and we'd return to Chu Lai before dark."

He looked at Bobbi Sue in her little bitty bikini, then he looked at me and knew full well he was asking a lot of me to leave her right then and go flying to a damned place like Khe Sanh, of all the stinkholes in Vietnam that I hated most. And he knew damned well that I'd finished flying in that war. By every right, I was finished. The stinking war might still be going on, but by God I was finished with it and was finished with the army in general in my own mind.

"If you're planning on being back here before dark, you must be ready to go?" I asked.

"Yeah, just as soon as you can be ready," came the reply and a big grin. He knew he had me.

I caved in and said, "Okay, let me get my gear on one more time, but this will be the last time, no matter whatever other bullshit might come up."

His big grin said he knew I'd never tell him to get lost, that I wouldn't go with him.

Bobbi Sue and I returned to my hooch to change out of our wet swimming stuff. First thing, I removed my cutoff blue jeans, and stood there in front of Bobbi Sue to show her that despite her rules or my being married, I wished that we'd made love fully last night or even that morning. I was being as aggressive as I could be under her rules: but all I could do was show how I wanted things to go.

Bobbi Sue came into my arms and whispered, "When you get back, I'll be in my room, if you want to stay overnight with me again."

We shared the last kiss we would have until I could get back to her, and then she silently turned away and left. As I put my flight suit and guns on, I listened to her Jeep drive away and I was painfully aware that I was alone once again.

Sorry Khe Sanh was definitely a big pain in my ass right at that moment, and I knew I was going to feel resentment about the role the damned place had played in my Vietnam experience for the rest of my life if it caused me to fail to consummate a sexual union with Captain Wolters. And I was pretty damned sure Bobbi Sue was right on the verge of jumping on my bones and screwing the hell out of me right there in my hooch that very afternoon *if* no one had come around turning my little world upside down and asking me to go to that sorry place with them. I hated that place. I even hated just thinking of the name of it. The touch of Death hung thick in the air there, saturating the atmosphere for miles in all directions with its creepy feeling. So, my attitude about the place that afternoon was, "Hey, Khe Sanh, screw you, and screw the war you rode in on!"

42

THE KHE SANH SERIES: MACHETE-MAN

My maintenance captain buddy, Tom, waited out in his Jeep for me to get dressed. Tom was an original good ole boy from somewhere down south: Tennessee, I figured, based on his thick, hillbilly twang. He was always in a joking and fun-loving mood with an infectious laugh, so it was almost impossible to be down in the dumps for very long around him. Despite his country-cousin personality, Tom was actually all about business, getting things done the way they should be; therefore, I was sure that if he felt the need to interrupt my afternoon on the beach it had to be for a reason that was very important to him. Letting a Hornet crew fly a helicopter that was overdue for required maintenance probably seemed like a mortal sin to him. He was going to owe me big time for this favor (not that I was going to be around to ever collect), but he still owed me, damn it.

Ole Tom was a sly dog. He knew damned well that if given the choice between spending the afternoon with a round-eyed nurse or unexpectedly having the chance for one last afternoon of playing in the sky with a nice olive-green U.S. Army Huey helicopter, I had no actual choice, particularly since I knew it would be the very damned last opportunity I'd ever have to take the aircraft controls in my own hands. Tom knew that same thing about every single Hornet pilot: to the last man, they all loved flying those dang helicopters and probably would have done it for free, no pay needed at all.

With ambivalent feelings (torn between a bird of one feather and a totally different bird of a totally different feather) I started putting on my things and felt like an old matador preparing himself to go into the bullring to face the toro bravo one more time. I thought I was done with that ritual forever and I'd never do it again: but there I was, one more time, strapping on my guns and ammo. First, a good trustworthy .38 caliber 6-shooter revolver in a western holster, worn hanging low, like Billy the Kid, then a 9mm semiautomatic pistol, a 15-shot + one, in a shoulder holster (with six ammo clips).

I tightened all my shoulder straps and made sure everything was working properly by pulling a couple of quick draws in front of a mirror. All was well. Then, I put on my flight jacket and aviator-type sunglasses. Last but not least I grabbed my helmet and chicken-plate, then I was ready. I studied myself in the mirror and thought, *That's what an army helicopter pilot should look like.* And that would be the very last time seeing myself dressed up for that warrior role. In about four days, I was going to cash out of the army at Fort Lewis, Washington, and walk away as a proud U.S. civilian, so salute good-bye to being a pilot and a warrant officer. Attennn-tion! Salute! Hell, yes, now let's go fly a mother-humping helicopter. We'd take a short joy ride up to Khe Sanh, then be right back. No sweat.

The song playing on Saigon radio when I turned it off as I left my hooch was completely perfect, "Born to Be Wild," and I certainly felt like the past year had lived up to that rock-n-roll sentiment. Every helicopter pilot I had met and flown with must have been born with an exceptionally wild hair up the ass, every insane one of them.

Out at the flight line we got airborne quickly and were soon hot-rodding our helicopter up the Chu Lai beach low-level around 110 knots, about 125 MPH, when we passed the hospital Officers' club at deck height. Bobbi Sue was standing out there and waved at us as we roared by. I waved back to her and made a mental promise to myself to return to her ASAP. Hell, time to be with Bobbi Sue was rapidly running out on me, so I needed to hurry if I intended to see her again, ever.

We eventually landed in Quang Tri, alongside Highway 1 near the coast, to refuel. We'd been scorching the I Corps countryside flying at low-level the whole trip, and we pulled in there in record-breaking time for a trip from Chu Lai. When we departed the Quang Tri POL, we headed straight out west to Khe Sanh to find the Hornets, wherever they were, and deliver our fresh chopper to them, swap it for their red-X'ed helicopter, then ease that old girl back to the Chu Lai maintenance shop.

We landed at the dusty red-dirt Khe Sanh POL station. There was a cluster of helicopters parked at the edge of the hill, and we saw the last Shark gunship sitting there. Tom headed over to talk to them, and I headed to the command bunker. Down in the trenches again, and that always gave me a cold chill and the shivers. I was going to find which radio frequencies the Hornets were using.

When I entered the place the scene there was complete chaos: six guys were hollering into different radios and a big crush of other guys were yapping at each other, everyone talking over the next guy. I tried to get the info I needed, but as soon as I made them understand I had a Hornet chopper to deliver, actually had a helicopter in good running shape, they really got excited and immediately were all over me. To bring me up to date on the status of what was happening at that moment, they told me that the Hornets were busy, way out in the boondocks. It would be at least an hour before they came back in. But right then they had a hot emergency situation to take care of. They already had one bird refueling in POL, but they were needing a wingman to go along with him to medevac two whole injured helicopter crews, a total of eight wounded people. The pick-up zone was real close by, easy to find. Just take a few minutes: we'd be back before the Hornets ever returned from the field.

Another warrant officer pilot spoke up and said he knew exactly where the place was, he could easily guide me, and he was ready right then to go with me. But we needed to hurry up and catch the other chopper in POL before they took off and tried to do this Dust-Off mission alone.

"Time is the difference between living and dying. You gonna help get these people, or not?"

When that hotshot young mental midget said that, I thought, *Hey, Professor, you bigmouth dumb-ass, when you spout only clichés, that tells me you don't know shit. How long you been here in Vietnam, sonny, three whole weeks?* I thought that, but I bit my tongue and didn't say anything. Pilots normally never said insulting crap to another pilot in front of others, but this kid had just done that.

What I did say was, "If there's anybody out there who is really near to dying, time probably won't matter anyway, and nobody can do anything about that sorry circumstance. But if you think time might make some sort of difference for anybody who might live, then we'd better hurry up."

We trotted through the trenches back out to my Hornet aircraft and saw our maintenance officer, Captain Tom, back at our helicopter. I told him I was going to do a real quick little medevac run with this other pilot flying with me who knew the territory and the pick-up zone. We'd join this other bird refueling there in POL and just hop over the border and then be right back.

We got all coordinated with the other helicopter crew, radios set, maps marked, and we took off. Captain Tom stayed behind at Khe Sanh POL. The Professor was an absolutely manic Chatty Kathy, telling me ALL about what was going on around there: the South Vietnamese ARVN were in a full rout, trying to run away from the battlefield in an across-the-board retreat, a completely out-of-control stampede. The invasion of Laos by the South Vietnamese had disintegrated into a total defeat, and things had turned into an absolute massacre for the ARVN. A well-fought retreat executed by a well-organized army could be done with a minimum of casualties, but the ARVN were anything but well organized. Hell, they had never been organized worth a damn the whole year I had been there.

All the ARVN's northern firebases had been overrun, and the same with the western-most firebases: Lo-Lo, Liz, Sophia, A-Louie. At least half of the ARVN soldiers had been killed in the different fights, and the remaining survivors had panicked and rioted. They killed all their own officers and NCOs, then cast off their own weapons and ripped off their uniforms. They tried to make themselves *NOT* look like soldiers. They thought that if they presented no threat to anyone, then maybe the NVA would take pity on them and not kill their poor helpless South Vietnamese brothers. That didn't turn out to be the case. So the South Vietnamese were running for their lives on foot as fast as they could go, trying to escape, get out of Laos, back across the border. But whenever the northern brothers could catch up with them they mowed them down like dogs that had no dignity or honor for being such worthless cowards on the battlefield.

U.S. Army helicopters, flown by American crews as always, had been trying their very best to airlift out all the South Vietnamese troops they could, but they lost horrible numbers of choppers evacuating the ARVN firebases as they were being overrun. There'd probably been 10,000 South Vietnamese killed already in this huge debacle, maybe as many as 15,000, and things were still far from over. There were still plenty of ARVN running around in their damned underwear trying to make good their escape. What we were doing in the present was mopping up different pockets of retreating troops when we could get them to stop long enough so we could pick them up.

I was glad that I'd come up there with Captain Tom so I could get a first-hand look at how the goddamned Vietnam War was ending, because after what had happened to the ARVN in Laos it was sure damned clear that the North Vietnamese had won the war. They only needed for the U.S. to make their face-saving final exit and everything would be finally settled. America just needed to quickly declare victory and get the hell out of damned Vietnam.

Soon we crossed over the Laotian border and could see our target hilltop marked with smoke, yellow and red, two smokes. Roger that. We were on approach, following the other ship, flying in his five o'clock position, up real close. We were somewhere in the general area where Johnny Hummel's Cobra had been blown out of the sky, and my thoughts kept flashing on him. From a distance, we could see the pick-up zone and there were maybe 300 or 400 people there, a big mob scene. Some men were pushing them back, creating enough open ground for us to land our helicopters. I could see what I assumed were helicopter crewmen on three stretchers and other crewmen sitting on the ground, their arms behind their backs. That seemed odd.

Almost all of the Vietnamese were stripped down, most with no shirt, some wearing little sleeveless undershirts, most not, and nearly all of them wore just undershorts and did not have ARVN uniform pants on. Many of them had dried mud smeared all over their bodies, and who knew what the hell that was all about? Was that supposed to be some kind of protection from mosquitoes? The sun? Or just crazy wild men? With a few brush strokes of red war paint, they would've looked like Montagnard tribesmen if they'd had some aboriginal spears to chuck. And as we neared the PZ, everyone started raising their hands in welcome to the helicopters and wildly jumping up and down in joyous anticipation of our arrival. After loading our injured American crewmen first, we wouldn't be able to load too many others, and everyone left behind would just have to wait until some other helicopters came for them.

On the ground, the people keeping the mob under control and out of our landing spots were doing a good job maintaining absolute discipline. Hell, they even had a couple of guys acting in the Pathfinder role, guiding the helicopters toward our eventual touchdowns with hand and arm signals just like they knew what they were doing. So we were approaching on short final and everything was going normally for the overall extreme situation that existed right then.

Now, 45 years after the events, except for my VA shrink back in 1994, and after that a few close friends, this is the first time I've ever really told the story of what happened on that hilltop just over the Tchepone River at the Laotian border. And the personal memory of it is far worse than any ordinary nightmares. The unexpected flashbacks the recollection of those few minutes has triggered over the years brings the smell of burned gun powder flooding over my senses, the taste of absolute fear in my throat, and the feel of hot blood spattering on my face. Over and over again during my year in Vietnam, Death had toyed with me and let me escape, usually by a narrow margin. But at that place, at that particular time, Death was not playing around anymore. Death loomed there, waiting. That hilltop looked to be the place I was going to die, and the stupidest damned thought that kept racing through my mind was, *Are you having enough fun on your last helicopter flight, Hornet Three-Three?*

Thank goodness, there have been periods of multiple years at a time that went by when I never had a single conscious thought of going to that damned little hilltop, and that certainly suited me just fine. My mind was doing an excellent job of blocking that particular shitty memory for years at a time. Then, for no identifiable reason, perhaps an odor or a particular sound, totally out of the blue, maybe when I was in an important business meeting with a dozen other people and we were haggling over million-dollar items, suddenly I would feel myself flying my helicopter once again and approaching that same goddamned hilltop—all the same sounds, smells, tastes, colors, tactile feeling of the helicopter controls in my hands, and naturally the damned fears. Everything down to the smallest frigging detail, such that I would feel like I was having an out-of-body experience and had been transported through time back to that exact shit-hole event. I would be totally gone out of my business meeting, gone to Laos and that hill, until I would hear my name being called by someone, probably for the third or fourth time, before they would pull me back to what was happening in the meeting and I wouldn't have a clue about what was being discussed in our meeting at that moment. That didn't happen very often, and luckily I was generally able to cover for it somehow. But I certainly didn't want to be the architect who was known for being a crazy head-case Vietnam War vet.

Maybe my conscious mind was doing a great job of suppressing any thoughts of that day for extended periods of time: years and years could go by. But my subconscious mind was cutting me no such slack. The nightmares of that hilltop came on an all too frequent basis. I would wake up in the middle of the night, drenched head to toe by a cold sweat, and for just a second or two I could recall the particulars of my dream before everything would all slip totally and quickly out of my mind and be gone like smoke in the night. That particular dream was only one of about two dozen recurring dreams I've dealt with for 45 years now. Usually the dream has just been a straight replay of that day's events, but often it would take a twisting turn and become even worse than what really happened. On those occasions, it became a dream of exactly what came so close to actually happening.

People say that you can't dream about actually dying. If you're dreaming about falling, you never actually hit anything. You just fall and fall but never hit, never die in your dreams—or so I've been told. I've died on that hilltop way too many times in my nightmares, but my brain refused to stop working and I watched everything all unfold from outside of myself, saw myself being killed, until everything finally ended when I got dizzier and dizzier until my thoughts were sucked into a swirling whirlpool of blackness that became a totally quiet and featureless void and nothing existed there other than my ultimate question: *Is this all there is? Then make it stop.*

I saw my Dallas VA shrink in private sessions a couple of times a week for a few months (plus a weekly group session), then the one-on-one visits were reduced to once weekly (in addition to the ongoing group). But it must have been at least a year that I was seeing him in 1994 before I finally told him about my last helicopter flight in the Vietnam War and making that quick trip to the hilltop in Laos to rescue those downed fellow aviators. I had long thought that the whole story sounded so unbelievable that he would think I was just trying to blow massive amounts of war-story smoke up his ass. I mean, come on: who could believe any BS about sleeping with a beautiful VIRGIN nurse, a captain at that, and then being called away to take a last joy ride and winding up in Laos were you landed in a huge pile of shit! Well, if I had heard such a line of crap, I would have been looking for my wading boots, because the bullshit was really getting seriously deep. Anyway, a beautiful

American woman who had kept her virginity intact for three years in stinking Vietnam was about as likely as running across a centaur eating an ice cream cone while he was talking to a unicorn! I bet every pilot he had ever worked with told the shrink a good nurse-story, and everyone had a combat-story about flying into some goddamned total hell on earth at least once or twice in their Vietnam War adventures. But you had to admit that the unexpected "Last Flight" gimmick made for an interesting twist to an otherwise typical bullshit yarn. Well, regardless of whether he believed it or not, I told him about that day in the clearest, most detailed description of what I could remember. I didn't notice him scribbling on his notepad, *Bullshit, Horse-shit, Chicken-shit.* But that would probably have been my reaction to hearing such a whopper of a tale, if I didn't know it was true, and that I was very ashamed to be telling anyone about it. Ashamed. Ashamed AND guilty. That was what I had felt all the years since I'd been in that sorry PZ on the 23rd of March in 1971. Ashamed, until 1994 when I met the understanding VA shrink. Now, I'll hereby lay down the rest of my personal burden of feeling ashamed and guilty by revealing to anyone who gives a good goddamn about the horrible things I did.

Here's what happened. As we neared touchdown, the American crewmen on the ground I was watching had their heads down to avoid the flying rotor dust, but things didn't look right. American's with their arms behind their backs; that situation was wrong. We were on a very hot approach, coming in fast and fully committed to a full touchdown landing instead of stopping at a hover. When the first helicopter got within about five feet of the ground, coming in hard to land, the surrounding mob that circled his landing spot suddenly rushed the chopper and instantly swamped his ship. It happened in a fraction of a second. The helicopter was simply totally swallowed up. It was like a humming bird being captured by a roiling army of rampaging stinging ants. Captured. The helicopter and crew were captured by the mob in the blink of an eye. I couldn't believe what was happening. None of that could be happening on what was supposed to be my last joy ride flying an army helicopter! But it was.

Our helicopter was still maybe fifteen feet in the air, but we were rapidly descending to the ground. When I yanked the collective past full max power to reverse our descent, we managed to stop at about a two-foot hover and started to go back up into the air, but hands seemed to grab us from every-where and things rapidly became a stalemated tug-of-war as we came to a stop at about a six- or seven-foot hover, unable to gain any additional altitude because of all the weight that was dragging us down. At least we were still flying and weren't completely pinned to the ground, but we weren't getting away from there any, either. We hung there in a brief equilibrium, and time had suddenly slowed down so much that it seemed like we were stuck there forever with our engine screaming out its last horsepower and the rotor blades slapping the wind with thunderous claps. We were high enough that any additional Vietnamese who were trying to catch onto us were having to jump up for us, but some were succeeding and soon their ever increasing combined load would pull us to the ground. We were in the shit about up to our necks. It was totally clear to me that I was surely going to die very soon.

As we hung there struggling to escape I was seeing all sorts of random things happening on the ground all around us, but I was stunned wordless to witness a shockingly sickening sight. Out of the blue, a big shining machete hit one of the Americans who was on the ground. It chopped him on the back of the neck and cut half through, then quickly, there was another goddamned whack, and a head rolled in the dirt and was kicked by some thoroughly *Insane Machete-Man*. What the hell, that crazy goddamned son of a bitch just cut that guy's frigging head off! The headless body flopped forward into the dirt. I saw the river of blood that poured out and the red puddle blossoming there in the dirt. A second cutter started on a stretcher patient, wildly swinging his own nasty machete, hack, hack. A second head was kicked like a ball!

A glimpse out of the corner of my eye showed that the first chopper's crew chief and gunner had been pulled from the aircraft and were being passed over the heads of the mob. Machetes slashed chunks and bits out of them, sending blood spurting and flying. At the same time, some Vietnamese guy ran around the rear of the helicopter and ran full blast into the spinning tail rotor. Instantly his head was gone in a spray cloud of bright-red blood mixed with brain-matter gray. In the cockpit of the downed helicopter, I could see machete blades slashing toward pilots and I looked away as fast as possible. If that was beginning, I sure as hell didn't want to watch the obvious outcome. No way did I want those sorts of pictures frozen in my brain the rest of my life.

In our helicopter a big knife blade was hitting the floor by my legs at the bottom door jamb, and arms and hands were reaching inside my open doorway, searching for any purchase to grasp and hang onto. Our helicopter was the terrified mob's only expectation of salvation from the prospects of looming Death, so they were all desperate to get on board, and they didn't understand that they were only crashing us. Their fear was tangible, palpable, and it immersed them in its total control.

Over the intercom, I yelled the obvious: "Shoot! Shoot them off our damned skids!" But I looked in the backseat area and saw that both the crew chief and door-gunner were fighting hand to hand, trying to fend off machete-armed men who were obviously North Vietnamese, so our crewmen couldn't get on their M-60 Machine guns at that particular moment. I pulled my .38 pistol, and that bastard whacking at me from the ground with his machete was going down. Struggling to hold a hover with the cyclic between my knees I didn't hesitate, didn't vacillate, just fired at the machete swinger on the ground as quickly as I could and shot him in the face, *Boom,* and he dropped like pure lead. I wished him a speedy trip straight to hell, the sorry son of a bitch trying to chop my leg off.

With the immediate threat to me dealt with, I twisted around in my seat, took aim and shot the guy the door-gunner was wrestling with, two shots straight through him and in the process I blasted the hell out of the door-gunner, with my bullets hitting his chest armor and blood and crap sprayed all over him. The gunner must have thought I'd just killed him. Damn, getting hit like that must have felt like a mule kick. From the look on his face, he looked like he was sure he was dying right there.

I screamed at him and said, "Toss his ass out and get on your 60. Shoot the damn door-gun or we're all gonna be killed right now!"

Cocked my .38 pistol again. There were others who had climbed onto my skid and were trying to come in my door, reaching in, grabbing at me. *Boom, Boom.* Two fell away like big bags of potatoes. My pistol had been inches from their faces and blood spatter sprayed back all over me, particularly my face. I could feel the wetness of the gore on me. Needed to wipe out more. Two were not enough.

At such a crazy time as right then a flash of a memory took me momentarily back to when I was gazing down the barrel of 1st Lt Sparks's pistol when he said he would kill me. I'd always thought he meant he *could* kill me if I ever did anything to get the guys in the back hurt. Now I knew he was telling the truth. If need be, he *would* have killed me or any other pilot he thought needed killing, and he would have done it with no hesitation or vacillation. What I had thought at the time had been just a little private school lesson from Sparks was actually exactly what it seemed to be, a straight-up simple promise spoken in very plain English. I guessed Sparks's flight training methods had stuck with me because I was fighting as hard for the sake of the guys in the rear as I was for myself. But I needed some damned help from the rear compartment. And why weren't the door-guns starting up? I saw why no one had started a door-gun yet. More hand-to-hand fighting was going on in the back, but by then there were even more Bad Guys joining the fight.

So many things were happening all at once around me so damned quickly, but seemed to be taking such a slow tick-tock of time, that everything seemed to blur together. I was flying the helicopter with the cyclic between my knees, had both of my pistols in my hands firing away, and the pilot I didn't know, my new professor friend, was wrestling with me on the damn controls, trying to take over the helicopter while American aviators on the ground were getting their heads severed simultaneously with Bad Guys getting shoved out of our aircraft and our wingman's helicopter starting to disintegrate and throw off parts following some sort of main rotor strike on the tail boom or something. My .38 pistol was out of bullets almost as soon as I started firing it, but I kept pulling its trigger just the same while I fired the 9mm with my left hand. My doorway quickly emptied of the Vietnamese I shot, and I could feel our helicopter inching up ever so slightly higher with each shot person who fell away. Soon, to my great relief, those damned maniacs in the stinking PZ couldn't reach us as easily as earlier, not with their wild jumping or their filthy little hands or the bloody machetes some of them had. But we were still in a stalemate. The only thing going in our favor was the fact we had not been pulled all the way to the ground yet, and we were actually getting a small amount of distance between us and the rampaging Vietnamese. We were making our getaway an inch at a time.

Finally, I heard a single M-60 start firing, beautiful music straight from heaven, the best music ever. *Rat-a-tat-tat-tat-tat...* Nearly naked Vietnamese immediately started falling off our skids, lots of them, and our helicopter began a lurch skyward. Oh, shit! We were not climbing straight out: our damned helicopter was rolling over onto its heavy side. Shooting those guys off of just one skid had caused us to become very asymmetrically loaded— one side of the helicopter was loaded a lot heavier than the other side—and that certainly wasn't a good situation. I barely caught our chopper before it totally flipped over and managed to stabilize us in a very lopsided hover. We hung there in the air like the severe helicopter version of the Hunchback of Notre Dame.

But all of our violently sudden and drastic aerial gyrations of the helicopter had thrown all the North Vietnamese Army scum with their damned machetes to the floor so that our two crewmen back there in the cargo compartment with the little bastards could start kicking the intruders out of our Hornet helicopter, since none of them had a written invitation to begin with. It was NOT socially acceptable to get on a man's helicopter without prior approval: everyone knew that. So those five stinking NVA gentlemen got to try some low-level skydiving. At least, none of us shot any of them. But both of our M-60 door-guns were up and ready to go, so there was some shooting done, just the amount that was needed to get us to a flyable weight and that weight distributed in some rational fashion. I directed the gunners to clear our skids where I wanted it done, and that involved shooting some people, which I ordered to be done. Then, yes, we were actually starting to slowly pull away from the ground! We were flying. Maybe just minimally, but we were in the air and not back there in that damned pick-up zone.

The first question I asked myself when we got away to a somewhat safer distance was, *Why hadn't everyone on our helicopter been shot dead back there?* There had been at least a dozen times people had been close enough to me to put their hands on me—close enough that I put the barrel of my pistols

up to their foreheads when I shot them. If they had used guns we were
screwed, hanging there in the air completely immobilized. If they'd had guns
they would've shot us, so obviously no one had any guns in that mob. That
was the craziest thing I had ever heard of in a war, but it must have been
some mob rule: NO GUNS ALLOWED. The ARVN had thrown all their
guns away, and I guessed they wouldn't allow anyone to hook up with their
mob and keep a gun. They didn't want to give the NVA any reason to open
up on them if the NVA saw any guns anywhere. There had to be a reason
why the ARVN had disarmed themselves and thrown away their guns, and
I bet that there had been psych-operations done by the NVA that said safe
passage from the battlefield would be granted to unarmed noncombatants.
That was the only explanation I could think of for why we were still alive.

So what was the deal with guys running around with machetes? The
machete-dudes were obviously NVA. Their uniforms were mostly gone, like
everyone else's, where they could mix in and disappear among the mob. Guns
would have made them obvious to everyone and dangerous to everyone
because the presence of guns could have gotten the mob fired on. Machete-
Man, the lead beheader, wore enough of a uniform that he was easily recognizable as an NVA soldier, probably of some officer rank, because he seemed
to be in charge. If you flew combat assault helicopters, beheading might not
normally be your biggest worry but it was that day. I had seen the Americans,
the ones on the ground wearing flight suits the same as I wore, and I guessed
that they all had their heads chopped off. I'd seen Machete-Man take some
unfortunate pilot's head off, watched him during the entire hideous ordeal,
and then I saw the injured man on the stretcher beheaded. There were others
I had glimpses of, but I looked away from them whenever it was possible. I
did not want to see anymore of that kind of insanity than I had to see. But I
knew there were multiple severed heads. I saw four of them stuck on the ends
of machetes being paraded around through the dangerous, chaotic mob and
other heads kicked around like damn soccer balls out on some kid's schoolyard playground.

We still had more than a couple of dozen people hanging from our skids,
but we were shedding them as they fell off, one after another, falling into the
sky, needless to say, with no parachutes. Thanks for flying with U.S. Army
Airways: hope you enjoyed your flight, especially that last hard-landing part.
Crew chief wanted to know what to do about the situation: "Should I shoot
'em, or pull 'em in?"

I answered, "Pull the good ones in, but if they have any kind of damned
machete with them they're lousy NVA, so shoot every one of those dangerous
sons of bitches before they can get in here and start whacking everybody."

Our crew guys managed to get twelve pulled in. The others fell, gravity
taking them away, and our crewmen shot two NVA who had machetes hanging

from their belts. We saved twelve men that medevac run: twelve men plucked from the pit of Hell. Sadly, they were not the injured American aviators we went out there to get but twelve others. Still, any twelve lives had to be a good thing. But it was accomplished at the cost of twelve for twelve: twelve American army aviators being killed in that PZ, eight who I guessed were technically POWs, plainly murdered in front of everyone, mercilessly and pointlessly beheaded by the NVA. There was no rational reason for them to do that other than just general evilness. Then there was the four-man crew of the first helicopter, lost on a mission where they thought they were doing the right thing, doing the best they could do in the circumstances. I didn't know what finally happened to the two pilots. I didn't see that. But the two crewmen's heads were stuck on lousy machetes and were being paraded around.

Actually, those twelve American flyers were murdered by the U.S. Army, because they were nothing but damned *basically acceptable losses* that had been accounted for when the U.S. Army first decided to take over the Ho Chi Minh Trail and the pitifully inept ARVN held that ground for only one goddamned day. ONE DAY. I sure as hell felt like all the American aviator lives that had been pissed away in exchange for taking Tchepone for a single day amounted to nothing less than murder, plain and simple. And army aircraft crews were still paying for that damned one single day with their lives, just like our first helicopter crew had done that day and just exactly like my crew and I almost had done.

After we got back to flying within specs and with more reasonable load capabilities, I banked our chopper back around, and we went back to that hell hole and parked ourselves in a high hover, sitting smack over that shitty makeshift pickup zone. Machete-Man and his NVA buddies were dancing in a blood frenzy, displaying American pilots' heads stuck on machetes. God, it looked like some primitive scene out of the Dark Ages or the Holy Land Crusades. And from the looks on their faces at that moment, our Hornet helicopter was the last sight anyone in that PZ was expecting to see hovering high over them. But the Hornets had a rule of their own: *Shoot at a Hornet, you die: Hornets' promise.* I figured that possibly getting your head chopped off pretty much equated to being shot at.

Being in an emotional frenzy also described my condition at the time. My heart was racing, trying to escape my chest, pounding so fast I was panting like an exhausted old dog. I was feeling totally out of my body, floating at the ceiling of my helicopter, watching everything as it happened. I knew exactly what we were going to do, and I had zero doubts about anything. I kept thinking a single thought, over and over: *Bring a knife to a gunfight, even a goddamned machete, bad mistake, asshole! Things not going to end well, not for you, not here, not now! Time for you to meet your very own version of Mr. Death!*

Over the intercom I told the crew chief and door-gunner, "Fire! Fire at will!" I figured that order would probably put me in jail for the rest of my life. I was ordering my men to do the same sort of shit that the Americal troops had done at My Lai. There might have been moral and ethical differences, but the ruling principle of My Lai and that PZ were the same: *Kill the bastards and let God worry about sorting them out, the bad from the worse.*

Our twin M-60 machine guns began singing their particular duet of death. Both guns simultaneously blasted Machete-Man and cut him down hard. Both guns kept locked on him until they beheaded him, in the sense that whatever was left on his shoulders resembling a head was pureed. Then it was his NVA friends' turn: anyone with a machete, door-guns shot 'em down and dispatched them right to hell!

Bring a knife to an unarmed fight, any evil you get away with will come back to you in spades.

If any ARVN bystanders were shot by accident, mark that as *basically acceptable battlefield losses.* Those guys shouldn't have been standing around in their boxer shorts so close to any of our primary targets, the NVA, because that made those ARVNs *collateral damage.* There was always plenty of that but none of them was innocent anyway, because standing around was all they did while our American aviators were frigging murdered in front of the eyes of other American aviators who were helpless to do anything about it at the time. But payback could be a real deadly bitch when you were messing with the Hornets. The 116th AHC took all this shit very seriously and very personally.

By then, my machine guns had gone silent. They were both out of any remotely viable NVA targets. In real-time terms the guns had been working only a relatively short time, 20 to 30 seconds at the most, but in perceived time on the scene things seemed to go on and on and on. I had ordered my crew to shoot, so I had an obligation to watch everything that was happening. I had stopped counting at a dozen different areas in the mob where we had shot people. There were only a few more, about five or six. At each of the locations, there were a few bodies down.

I hovered over to Machete-Man and looked at the corpse. Our machine guns had screwed him up royally. I noticed he was wearing a necklace made out of little yellow ascot handkerchiefs tied together into a chain, but they were redder from his blood than they were yellow. I had wondered whatever happened to those South Vietnamese Rangers I had carried out to LZ Hope on that day of the Largest Armada, the ones who wore bright yellow scarves. Machete-Man's body gave me that answer, at least about some of them. Their war had ended. The necklace around a dead man's body showed that. And then his war had ended, when he met a Hornet. The circle was closed. Machete-Man was bad: a Hornet was worse.

The last thing we did in the PZ was check the other helicopter. It was sitting there still running with the rotors turning at idle speed. No one was in the cockpit or the cargo compartment. About a third of one of the rotors was gone, there was a big gash across the rear of the tail boom, and the tail rotor had one of the blades broken. Every system that normally turned was drastically out of balance, consequentially the helicopter was shaking like a very old lady with very advanced Parkinson's disease and severe palsy. It was obvious she would shake herself to pieces before she ran out of fuel, and a damned fire would probably start sooner rather than later. The old girl was dead but had not yet finished all of the various parts of the dying process for helicopters. It was a sad sight for a pilot to see.

Making the short trip back to Khe Sanh, I turned the flying over to the Professor. I never got that guy's name: he was always simply the Professor in my mind. I had the shakes too bad to fly. While it was happening, when the shit had hit the fan full bore, I was able to take care of business, function automatically. But afterward, I felt sick—not puking sick but the curl-up-in-a-dark-corner-and-sleep-for-three-days-straight sorta sick. If the damn world was going to be that way, where anyone remotely like Machete-Man existed, chopping off heads just out of meanness, then count me out of that sort of stinking world. I'd go live on some deserted island instead.

My new buddy, the Professor, had been a motor-mouth Chatty Kathy at the beginning of our mission, but by the end of it he had clammed up completely, like everyone else in our helicopter. When we landed at Khe Sanh POL, the Professor jumped out of the pilot's seat and raced around to the rear of our chopper and threw up under the tail boom. Then he took off toward the command bunker in a trot without saying boo to any of the rest of us. I guessed he needed to run and tell all of his 101st Airborne bosses exactly what had happened out at that PZ. I imagined him blabbing to the brass: "Americans' heads chopped off with machetes, and the other helicopter we were with was overrun by panicked men and crashed and the crew was dragged away by a crazed mob and I got our helicopter out of there only by a miracle and then the aircraft commander, Hornet Three-Three from the 116th Assault Helicopter Company, ordered his crewmen to fire their machine guns into a big crowd of hundreds and hundreds of unarmed South Vietnamese Army soldiers, killing no telling how many of them but it was a whole hell of a lot. Doesn't that create a big problem for the 101st when word gets out that a big bunch of ARVN have been killed by an army helicopter? Won't the Screaming Eagles get blamed for this mess when it should be the 116th? Aren't the Hornets from the Americal Division? So shouldn't this all be the Americal's fault?"

It was possible to picture how the Professor might have seen things that way and gone all tattletale on me in the 101st Airborne command bunker, and I might need to expect the big hand of the army to snatch me up and plop me down in front of some 101st honcho colonel who would holler at me and want to know exactly how big was the goddamned brain fart I'd had out in that PZ over in Laos? And it's possible to picture how I was after the Professor went trotting away. The two crewmen and I sat in the doorway of the cargo compartment of our Huey and just quietly rested for a spell. I was exhausted, and I was sure they were, too. So we tried to decompress from our totally wired state and catch our breath. The Hornets hadn't returned yet, and Captain Tom was still over by that old Shark gunship with the engine cover opened up. He had climbed up in the engine housing all the way to his ass, so he was busy. The two crewmen who had been with me were neither a crew chief nor a door-gunner. They were just two mechanics from our maintenance shop who thought they were getting the rare chance to go on a helicopter joy ride all afternoon instead of having to work all day in the shop back in Chu Lai. No one expected anything to come up like the hell of a rodeo we had just been through. No one expected anyone would be dying that day or anyone would have to kill any enemy that day or my two novice Gunners would get so damned much on-the-job training in effective door-gunning. I had to give them an A+ for being such quick learners.

When I could talk, I told them, "If any questions come up about what has happened today, I am the commander of this helicopter and anything done on this aircraft was done by my orders. Here is what happened out there: I ordered you to fire your door-guns on hostile North Vietnamese Army troops who were at the time attacking and killing American airmen on the ground. That will be easy to remember because it's true. The second important thing is this: there were NO ARVN troops on the battlefield that we saw anywhere, and the only people on the battlefield other than the NVA were mutineers who had killed their officers and NCOs and deserted the battlefield and discarded everything that could possibly identify them as part of any military. They attacked two U.S Army helicopters and crashed one of them, and they were a direct threat to kill us if they could. That is also true and accurate. The third thing: There were no good people out at that place. They were all murderers and totally insane savage wild animals, and none of them got anything they had not already earned, probably many times over. So remember: you shot NVA troops and any other casualties were the minimal possible collateral damage. They were acceptable battlefield losses. Remember those exact words, because if anyone asks about any of this sorry deal, that's the kind of bullshit they love to hear and they'll suck it right up. And the last thing: you two guys saved all of our lives out there. We were completely good as dead and you two pulled us out of it somehow, so I want to say thank you for saving my life and saving each other's lives. I'll never forget what you guys did for me. You guys are real live heroes. I mean, tonight in the hooch back at the Hornets' Nest you can tell everyone how you fought NVA in our helicopter hand to hand, way outnumbered, and you won. You beat every one of the little bastards in a true life-or-death struggle, and you two being alive proves that as a fact. I'm going to put you guys both in for medals for today, and I hope they give you something real nice. Now, I better get up to the command bunker and find out exactly which piece of my ass they think they're going to kick over this deal."

I started to walk away, and one of the guys said, "Wait, Three-Three, you can't go in there looking like that. You're a mess. Take your helmet off. You've still got your helmet on, and it's got blood-spatter shit all over it. Give it to me."

I looked at my flight helmet. It was all speckled up, my damned leather gloves were redder than they were gray, and my Nomex shirt sleeves were all spattered below the elbow. It seemed to take every ounce of strength I had left to pull off my gloves and roll up my sleeves, so I flopped back down in the Huey's doorway. The two mechanics performed a pit stop on me. One guy made me wash my face and hands, and I was amazed at how sickly pink the running canteen water turned. The other guy asked where my guns were. He found them on the floor deck under the aircraft commander's left seat, and he got .38 bullets and a 9mm clip out of my survival vest and loaded my pistols for me. He said it made me look more senior and serious to have my pistols in my holsters. "You know, a little more of the mad-dog chief warrant officer look." Then he told me to carry my helmet. A pilot carrying a helmet always looked like a man on urgent and important business, and he gave me back my freshly cleaned up helmet. While they were picking at me, they invited me to their maintenance EM hooch that night, and we could all get stoned out of our heads together. We deserved a party after that day, and it didn't matter that I was an officer anymore since I was going home. They had all heard I was getting out of the army as soon as I hit Stateside. So I could be just a regular Joe and not a stuffy old officer with a stick up his ass for just one night and share any of their weed I wanted.

Then, out of the blue, the fashion consultant said I had held a damn pistol to his head one night after there had been a fragging at one of the Wasp's hooches. He was the guy I had shot in the chicken-plate just a few minutes earlier. Did I remember that night of the damned fragging? The pissed-off Wasp Platoon Pilots came busting in their EM hooch with guns drawn and scared the holy shit out of everyone in maintenance. They all walked on eggshells for a while after that, afraid that some fool might do another fragging and all the Wasp pilots would come back with guns blazing. I didn't remember him from that incident in particular, but I sure remembered that sorry night. A lot of things about Vietnam had been screwed up, but that goddamned fragging incident was by far the most screwed up of all. A damned good warrant officer was blinded that night, his eyes blown out. It was a damned good thing that there had not been any more throwing of hand grenades around the Company Area, because I really didn't know what Dick Salmond might have done if that situation ever came up again. He did tell them the Wasps would come back and kill them all. Dick had seemed totally serious when he said that, and it didn't seem wise to doubt that captain's warning. I would have walked on eggshells, too, if I'd been in their shoes. I guessed that when Captain Salmond had been killed the maintenance guys felt like they could relax a little about that item.

I appreciated their offer of honorary membership into their EM pot fraternity, but I told them I had a prior commitment for the evening. They laughed and said they had seen her on our Hornet beach and they understood perfectly, they wouldn't trade an evening with their bunch for a tumble with a beautiful round-eyed American nurse like her, either. I wanted to tell them it wasn't like that, but that was way too complicated to explain to them, particularly since I didn't understand any of it myself.

They had me as cleaned up as well as they could get me, and they were still like two old women. The fashion consultant was straightening my pens and code book and maps and ammo clips and emergency walkie-talkie in the pockets of my survival vest. He said their party would last all night and I could drop in anytime if plans changed, and they would just absolutely love to have me come over and join the fun. And then the lightbulb over my head turned on real bright, and I realized that this maintenance guy, whose name I had forgotten the second I first heard it, was as gay as a goddamned goose, and I hadn't seen it until right then. Fiddling with my goddamned survival vest contents, he had started absolutely swishing to an exaggerated extent, such that I was sure he was making it plain to me what the REAL him was all about: a secret homo. I didn't yet know if he was wanting to screw me or have me screw him, but it was clear he was wanting somebody to screw somebody. I looked at the other one. I figured that birds of a feather flocked together. Shit. Two gay guys had just saved my skinny ass from certain death. And if I'd had two brothers, right up until then I felt like I would have wanted them to be exactly like those two clowns; that was the depth of a bond I was feeling for them both at that moment. The swishing and limp-wrist shit, I could have done without. But if my brothers had to be what they had to be, I could have accepted that with no problems. I'd never been come-on to by a man before, and if the fashion consultant was giving me a pitch he was barking up the wrong tree. My cup of tea was more like Bobbi Sue Wolters than some Brucie-Fudge-Packer. The most I had ever thought about homosexuality was to ask myself if there would ever be a circumstance where I'd kiss another guy. My answer to myself was always *Yuck—just that idea would cause a gag reflex, and I couldn't get my head wrapped around anything more than that. Yuck—was it.*

About as quickly as it had come up, the sudden girlyness miraculously vanished and everyone was back to acting like boys again. Goddamnit. How could that day get any stranger than finding out that we had homo Hornets in our company working on our helicopters?

Well, it sure the hell could. When I went dragging my ass into the command bunker fully expecting a ton of bricks to come crashing down on my head, the place was spooky quiet. The "Professor" from the 101st Airborne was over in a corner squatting down on his heels, rocking back and forth with a wet towel draped over his head. When he first saw me the 101st captain who was running the show came quickly over to me and started profusely apologizing to me for sending us out to that horrible PZ. He said he thought the mission was going to be a simple and straightforward Dust-Off of some wounded American flyers and would be easy in, easy out, no sweat or problems since it was right on the border and all. He had no idea at all that the situation was what we found it to be, and sure as hell he would never knowingly send anyone into that sort of a deal. My pilot over there in the corner had told everyone what had happened out there. The captain again apologized at great length and said he hoped everything had just been a misunderstanding and he would totally understand if I was really pissed off by the whole damned thing. He knew he would have been if that shit happened to him. But my pilot, he was the one everyone in the command bunker was upset about. Did I know his name or what company he was in? I told him no on both counts. He must have told me his name in the beginning but I instantly forgot it, and I never heard anything about what company he was in. Didn't he belong to the 101st like his shoulder patch showed? Didn't he belong to the captain?

No. No one knew who he was, and no one had really seen him before that day. He obviously was from one of the 101st companies, but just which one nobody knew. But he sure was screwed up by what he'd been through. He had told everyone in the command bunker what had happened in the PZ, and the concerned captain I was talking to wanted to know how I was holding up—and my crewmen, how were they?

Then—and this was the freaky-as-hell part—the captain said, "He told me that you had to let go of the helicopter controls so you could shoot your pistols to lighten your helicopter's overload, you know, get some people off of your skids if you were ever going to get a chance to get out of that pickup zone. So he took the controls and was flying the helicopter when you were busy shooting, and he was praying harder and more earnestly than he had ever prayed to God before in his whole life, because he knew you were all dying at that very moment. And God answered his prayers, and he knew exactly the moment when God sent Jesus to your helicopter to take over the stick, because he could feel Jesus's hand through the cyclic, moving it to fly the chopper, even when the pilot kid was fighting against the divine inter-vention, because at first the kid didn't understand what was happening, didn't understand that Jesus had taken the stick and was saving you all from dying. So he totally relaxed his hold on the cyclic and watched the stick moving around without his input like it was churning buttermilk or something. He watched as Jesus flew your helicopter and got you all out of Death's grasp, and he said at that moment he gave his life to Jesus with absolute belief in his heart since Jesus had just given him a born-again new life, when he was so certain that he was irretrievably dead. Then he broke down crying and fell to the floor and started praying, I guess to thank God for giving him such a miracle. And he's been there on the floor ever since, just like he is now, and he's been freaking the shit out of everybody here in the command center since. I need to get him out of here and into a bed. Shit, man, I think maybe he's had a nervous breakdown and his brain could be really fried, poor kid."

Oh, man. The Professor evidently hadn't mentioned anything about our door-gun work, not yet at least. I wondered if he'd been so zoned out that he was unaware of everything that had gone down out there. Maybe I wouldn't have to explain what had happened to some 101st colonel after all. Maybe the Professor had been mentally transported to a wilderness to visit with Jesus for a little spell, have a pleasant and profound conversation with him while our door-guns were working out so hard cutting down those NVA soldiers, the damned Machete-Man and his cohorts. Maybe. Maybe. How much could I rely on a *maybe*?

I told the captain, "Jesus didn't fly our helicopter today. I imagine he was a little busy with more important matters than getting distracted by another crazy chopper that got itself into a mess."

Then I pulled out my Zippo lighter and fired it up and lit a cigarette. I cupped my left hand around the lighter while I lit it with my right hand, and said, "I guess our young friend over there isn't a smoker, because when you're lighting your lighter in a flying helicopter it takes both hands to do the job, so you have to learn to fly with your knees controlling the cyclic stick. Hell, I can fly from here to Da Nang right now using only my knees."

The captain laughed real loud and said, "So you're the kid's Jesus."

"I never told him out there in that PZ that he had the controls. I felt him fighting me on the controls, but that was a lesser distraction at the time because I was dealing with more important issues right then, like fighting off assholes trying to climb into my cockpit and chop me up."

"Should we tell him and bust his religious balloon?" The captain asked, still laughing.

I shook my head and indicated a no to his question. If the kid had some-thing bigger than himself and that damned war to believe in, something watching over him and helping him and possibly protecting him, then he was better off than most of us over there. Anyway, if he believed, it wouldn't do any good to tell him anything to the contrary. He wouldn't buy it or even listen. Plus, I very much wanted him to ruminate over his personal "Jesus Miracle" until I got the hell out of Dodge and made it to that waiting Freedom Bird down in Cam Ranh Bay. It was best to leave that sleeping dog lie. If our door-guns hadn't come up in his conversations, they must not have been a problem even if he was aware of all of that shit happening. I was just going to keep my mouth shut and hoped the Professor did, too. I recognized my exit cue and immediately booked for the door.

I wanted to be back at Chu Lai, back in Captain Bobbi Sue's hot shower with her scrubbing Death's disgusting filth off of me. I felt like I had been swimming in it all day, had been baptized in it. I'd probably killed a lot of people I had personally shot: some close range, some straight in the face, blood spraying back onto me, the slimy filth. I didn't want to go back into my memory to recall each of them, one by one, to count them, because I didn't want to know any total. I've never wanted to know. Then there was the other part. I ordered the door-guns to fire, and I had no idea how many that gunfire killed but I felt good riddance to them. I didn't know what all the ramifications of that day were to be. Right then, I just felt totally numb and dazed and wanted all that trash swirling around me to get out of my head.

The captain's hot shower, her wonderful hot shower, I focused on that. It was what I needed right then. However, we never made it back to Chu Lai, not that day and not that night. No hot shower. No pretty nurse washing my back, then taking us to bed. I would never see Bobbi Sue Wolters again. She'd been an interesting woman to get to know a little bit, and she'd been a needed angelic and innocent comfort through a long and hard night. Being with her didn't feel like it happened last night. That couldn't be, because it seemed like an infinitely long time ago when that happened. And there was no way in hell she and I had been playing in the surf just a few hours ago, and I held her locked in an embrace and took her warm kisses in my hooch just over three hours ago. That was impossible and completely unbelievable. I didn't know it yet, but the only things Bobbi Sue and I would ever share were already done. All that existed of Bobbi Sue ever again were just the memories we had made that single time we spent together.

Captain Tom's plan that we could fly a red X-ed helicopter back to Chu Lai didn't pan out. The Hornets exchanged a shot-up bird for ours, and we were going to take the used-up bird to the helicopter depot at Da Nang, turn it in, and get another in exchange. That wouldn't happen that day before dark. It would take Captain Tom at least a couple of days to get that all done when you figured in the fact that the army had their usual paperwork involved. I was screwed.

What I planned as my personalized alternative: go on to Da Nang with

Captain Tom, then hitch a ride south from there, and I might make it to Chu Lai that night before it got too damn late to see Bobbi Sue. That plan fell apart when we started flying our shot-up bird and every damned red warning light in the helicopter lit up, and we had to make an emergency landing at Quang Tri. I got stuck there. Quang Tri was not at all on my list of favored places, but I spent the night sleeping on the floor out at the operations shack, tucked in a corner. My night of bad dreams was particularly vicious that night: a whole new batch of nightmares joined the pantheon that already had taken up residence in my darkest places.

I finally got to Chu Lai the NEXT night, after midnight, a day too damn late and too late at night to go see Captain Wolters. The clock had totally run out for us. Game over, with no overtime.

My Hooch was totally dark black when I walked into it and turned the light on, and it was silent as a grave. There was only the faint sound of the breeze coming in off of the South China Sea. I imagined the men who had lived with me in that hooch who had already preceded me in their exits from Vietnam. I recalled that long, tall Texas cowboy, Austin Scarborough, and that Dallas madman, the modified stock-car racing Roger Walker, and his best buddy, the Green Beret, our instructor pilot before me, Leon Richards, and Dennis Plumber with his skinny legs and giant handlebar mustache and Sherlock Holmes smoking pipe, and our very own Hornet Company Philosopher, Gary Newton. Maybe I'd earned a place to be included on that list of men I had come to respect. I felt I had. I'd always tried to do my best, and I wasn't ashamed about anything I'd done during my tour in Vietnam. Their ghosts hung heavy in the air of that musty place, along with the ghosts of too many dead men. I didn't care to see any of the dead ones. They all came around in my nightmares much too often as it was.

I packed up: all my things stuffed in a duffle bag. Travel clothes laid out, tropical worsted khaki, with just the barest of basics. No award or decoration ribbons, just rank, CW2, and my silver wings, freshly polished. Just rank and wings. That told the whole world anything they needed to know about me and who I was: I had been a chopper pilot once. I would dress up like a toy soldier for public consumption one last time. I finally got into the damned shower about 1:00 a.m., a cold one seemed fitting, the last cold one. I finally got to wash away the dried and caked-on two-day old Death that coated me all over. As I shampooed my hair the water turned pinkish from the dried blood I was washing away. I was finally washing stinking Vietnam off of me, and I scrubbed myself a very long time. But I knew in my soul that I'd never get it all off.

I fell onto my bunk. Since yesterday afternoon up at Khe Sanh, I'd been in an absolute state of shock. I hadn't spoken to anyone, not one word, about what had gone down at that PZ! I was beyond being exhausted.

I was totally wrung out. I gave myself up to sleep, and evil dreams started again.

The next morning I signed out of the Hornets. My job in that shit-hole place was all done. The Vietnam War was finally over. For me, it was over. Out at the Americal Division headquarters, while I was getting a flight pass for Cam Ranh Bay, I was pleased to see the full Hornet Company landing in all of their normal splendor. They'd returned from Khe Sanh, so I guessed that deal was over. I trotted over to the Hornets' Nest, to the chopper revetments parking area, looking for Larry Hood. But my long anticipated C-130 touched down right then, and I needed to get back over there; that sweet C-130 wouldn't wait around long. Larry wore a distinctive helmet that had some reddish spray paint on it, and that was what I was looking for. His helmet wasn't there. No Larry. I had to get over to the C-130: there was no more time for anything. I had to run. New passengers were lined up, getting aboard. In the Americal Division offices I kept an eye on the plane and used a nice army secretary's telephone to call the hospital. Bobbi Sue was in the OR, couldn't come to the phone, so I left a message someone took down for me: "Sorry, Captain. My apologies. Wanted to get back but couldn't: en route Cam Ranh. Good luck selling flowers back in Cincinnati. Hope you have a wonderful life. Hornet Three-Three."

Cam Ranh Bay, finally made it! In the Officer's Travel Club, whiskey shots, doubles if you please, playing nickel slots. Getting a little bit tipsy as quickly as I could, on the way to being blasted drunk. Blot out everything that was swirling in my brain. Vietnam, Cambodia, Chu Lai, Khe Sanh, Laos: was the insanity all just in my imagination? No dreams tonight, take care of that, shooting straight whiskey. No dreams except sweet-dream-baby, baby tonight. Went over to the juke box, laughed out loud. Dropped a quarter down the slot and played the same song five times in a row. Laughed: wouldn't you just know it, the danged Moody Blues singing "Nights in White Satin."

> That last Medevac run into Laos, that goddamned Machete-Man PZ,
> Let's make that just another bad dream,
> Some very nasty ugliness that never happened.
> Wouldn't that be a better World?

The Moody Blues said it right: *"Just what the truth was, they couldn't say anymore."*

JET AIRLINER:
CAM RANH BAY, VIETNAM,
TO FORT LEWIS, WASHINGTON, USA

Rolling down the runway, the Flying Tiger Line's DC-8 jet airliner got to transition speed, then we rotated and left the runway, wheels went up, and we were finally flying! Wild cheers filled the plane: our *Freedom Bird*, soaring into the sky, everyone going home. Someone behind me shouted, "Vietnam don't mean nothing!" The cheering was back and raised to a crescendo, with the addition of chanting: "F-T-A, F-T-A," the draftee enlisted men's rowdily vocalized opinion.

I remained quiet. Everything was a blur. I was hardly aware of where I was or exactly what was happening around me. I was naturally happy that I was alive, but I wasn't as jubilant as I had always thought I would be. I couldn't get the thoughts out of my head of those I'd met in the Hornets whose last rides home involved being in a casket. Back in the early stages of my tour in the war, when we lost two helicopters to enemy ground fire in less than ten days and all of those guys died, I thought my whole year would go that route. I'd done the math and forget two ships in ten days, I said two ships in six weeks, the amount of in-country time I had back then. That would have totaled nearly twenty helicopters the Hornets would lose in my year. If our losses were going to be like that, hell, almost all of us Hornets were gonna die. Twenty birds shot down would mean 75 to 80 dead flyers. So I'd spent my whole time under that perceived level of threat, and sitting there on the Freedom Bird I felt a huge sense of relief that things hadn't turned out that badly. Not even a fraction of that. We'd had only eleven men killed. Only eleven men. I guessed that if you had been one of those eleven, then you might not have used the word *only* to describe what had happened. As our Freedom Bird climbed out to higher skies, those eleven dead men were what occupied my thoughts and I couldn't get them out of my mind, no matter how hard I tried. Eleven men. Eleven caskets. *Pin my wings on my chest. Tell my Momma I did my best.* Eleven didn't sound like many until you recalled each of them individually, one at a time, and my pounding head didn't want to do that anymore. I reclined my seat and closed my eyes. Immediately, the faces of the two warrant officer pilots I had met at Khe Sanh and flew with into that Machete-Man PZ in Laos jumped into my head. They were dead. Don't forget them. In the whole year of flying, until that last damned flight, no one who flew with Hornet Three-Three or in his formation ever got hurt one little bit, not until that ship was taken down. Don't forget them, or that guy from the first day that you tossed a coin with, Smitty, or that Dust-Off guy you met up at Tay Ninh—he was good as dead and was by then for all you knew, or your friend from El Paso, Johnny. So, it was more than eleven dead aviators loitering in my head, painfully more than a mere eleven. Hell, I saw a whole dozen aviators killed at the Machete PZ.

Had three days passed or was it four? To be honest, I'd still been woozy from the previous night's drinking when I got up that morning and got on the Freedom Bird, so I didn't really know for sure when all that Laos crap happened. But if I hadn't been arrested yet for door-gunning those ARVN over the Laotian border, then that meant I'd just made good on my getaway. I had already decided that no one would find out about Laos, probably, unless one of the four guys who were there ever told the story to somebody who mattered, I very seriously doubted that would happen. I told myself that all of that Laos head-chopping crap was something that happened in the past. I could never do anything about it then, so put it out of your mind. And that was what I did as much as possible for a very long time.

A major who was sitting next to me introduced himself; then he opened a satchel and pulled out a bottle of old Scotch, some that was as old as I was: 25 years, Chivas Regal, and it cost over $300 a bottle. He opened it, took a big long draw, and then passed it over to me. It was strong, jolting, a shock to the system. We kept passing it back and forth until the whole damn bottle was totally gone. And totally gone also described me and the major.

He asked, "Well, Daddy-O, what'd ya do in the war, as if the wings don't give it away?"

I think I slurred something like, "Top to bottom, east to west, want the best? All IV Corps, DMZ to the Delta, Cambodia or Laos, or out at ugly Khe Sanh. Need the best, who ya gonna call? Those son-of-bitching 116th Hornets! That's who. We put the original ass in combat assault."

That Chivas made a wonderful anesthesia. Wake me up when the war's over. I'm gonna take a little nap now. Since Laos, three or four days, whichever, all my sleep had been full-time nightmares: John Hummel's Cobra turned to smoke or hearing *Chasin and Denny shot down* or the M-60s driving Machete-Man to ground or *Happy birthday, Daddy* sung by little boys. The crap just rolled on nonstop. Seemed I was stuck with the large industrial-sized assort-ment of shit-dreams.

Woke up and my new buddy, the major, drunk as a skunk, was loudly singing marching songs: "Used to drive a Cadi-llac. Now, I hump it on my back. Ain't no use in looking back, Jody's got your Cadi-llac. Ole Jody's got your girl and gone. You get a line; I'll get a pole, honey. You get a line; I'll get a pole, babe; we'll go down to that fishing hole, honey, honey, oh, babe of mine,"

The good major had another bottle of Chivas Regal 25 out. Rolling Thunder was still rolling full blast. Must not have been drunk enough, not yet: "Used to date a Beauty Queen, now I date my M-16. Ain't no use in feeling blue. Jody's got your sister too"

Jet airliner stopped in Japan. Changed flight crews. We were flying on a Flying Tigers plane, and I thought Flying Tigers were from back in World War II, not Vietnam. Stewardess looked like the twin sister to Gomer Pyle. Then the one that got on in Japan, twin sister of Lee Marvin—another one, Charles Bronson. We flew on, went by the northern route over Alaska to Fort Lewis, Washington, up by Seattle. Back in the USA.

Hit the processing center around 3:00 a.m. Round-the-clock service, the time didn't matter. The whole process at Fort Lewis was generally a wham-bam, thank-you-ma'm sort of a deal. There was nobody greeting us upon our arrival. No army rep saying, "Welcome home, soldier. Thank you for your service to your country." No bullshit like that.

Those taking a discharge were separated as a bunch, culled out, herded like cattle into a different processing line and rushed along as fast as possible through the little stations, given a medical looky-see by low-ranking enlisted nonmedical personnel. I got my physical from some spec-4 yahoo. On the scales: my weight 116 pounds, same as my unit, the 116th Assault Helicopter Company. Then he asked what my weight was when I went to Nam. I told him 150, and he wrote that down on his form. The weight going to Vietnam? Not the weight returning? He wrote 150 pounds instead of the 116 pounds I actually was! A difference of 34 pounds. What was that screwy army bullshit about? Why intentionally put down the wrong info? Obviously the army thought they needed to screw me some way or another, but I couldn't figure out their game right then. I'd figure that out when I applied for VA services. To his credit, the guy did say I should go to a dentist because I had problems with my teeth and gums. No shit! You think living on C-Rations nearly a year might tend to cause problems like that?

Bunch of papers stamped with rubber stamps. Then, drum roll, please: "You're discharged from the army. Now move on." Go to the paymaster: last stop. There was a loud scene going on at the pay table, lots of cussing, slam-ming the table, and there were some big MPs there trying to cool things down. President Nixon had imposed a military pay freeze for discharged military members. There was a $600 maximum amount you could get at discharge. You had anymore coming, file a claim. You say you'd put your money into an army savings account, most of your paycheck every month, take this form, file a claim, but $600 was all you'd get right then, period, nothing else, period.

"Hey, Mac, you'll get it someday. I guess. I don't have nothing to do with that. You wanna complain, call the president, see if he'll accept your call and chat with you. Take the form. File the form. Then hurry up and wait. That's all I can tell you. NOW, MOVE THE HELL ON, MAC."

Based solely on my one experience doing it, I concluded that when the army was done with you all politeness went out the window. They basically put a boot in your ass and gave you a stiff shove out the door. There I was, a chief warrant officer 2, busted down to a *PFC*, a *Proud Friendly Civilian* (the version to use around kids), and I finally heard those beautiful words: "You're discharged. Now move on, buddy." That sounded much sweeter to me than "thank you for your service to your country."

The army didn't care a bit about thanking anyone for anything; they had the draft. You could serve in the military or spend your time in jail. Frankly, the army didn't give a damn which you chose. Anyway, the Vietnam War was winding down, and they no longer needed more people, which was more than fine with me. Getting a three-year early-out was great for me. Thanks, Uncle Sam.

They were nice enough to provide a bus that took us over to the Seattle civilian airport. They put us on the curb sometime before dawn. My travel orders qualified me for a standby ticket home to El Paso. Stood in line, got my ticket, first available seat wouldn't be until middle of the morning, Seattle to Denver, then change planes and go on home. Be there around 6:00 p.m. I had the ticket!

Most people I'd met in the army were pretty good people—they'd share their $300 Scotch with you. But the army as an entity in Vietnam, that sucked, and if the army ever looked in any history books, they would have noticed that *outside occupiers lost every damn time!* When the dust settled, Vietnam was gonna be *"same crap, different war,"* with the usual outcome.

But America's *acceptable battlefield losses* weren't going to be very acceptable when seen in the light of a total and humiliating defeat of the South Vietnamese military and government, when those losses were judged as purely wasted: tens of thousands of American lives spent for a losing cause. But that was not what happened in Vietnam. I went there opposed to the war. I left there certain that I'd been right all along. It was nothing I ever wanted to do again, but I was glad I had that experience, scary as it was. I didn't like the war, but I was proud that I'd been a Hornet. I was proud that

I'd been a warrant officer and a combat helicopter pilot. I didn't like the war, but I was proud to be an American and a Texan, and I felt like I had to obey my call of duty.

What really happened in Vietnam was that the Americans won every major fight we had, and we gave a hell of a lot better than we got. We would get out with honor because the North Vietnamese would let us go home because they knew we had never really begun to fight. They also knew that if we had been turned loose on them, the U.S. military could make all of General Curtis LeMay's sweet SAC dreams come true. We could have turned the whole damned country of North Vietnam into one big smoking hole any single day we wanted to do it. And if you bought into that idea, you probably agreed that if we took out North Vietnam with nukes then we would need to take China at the same time, drop the big ones on them just to show Russia we shouldn't be screwed with. We could've gone Doctor Strangelove on them any day, so the North Vietnamese tippy-toed around us and just gave us enough trouble to make us take our *"Proportional Response"* approach to warfare and go home. Yes, sir. We were winning when I left.

And not one man I knew about "died for nothing" that I ever heard about, because they all went down fighting to protect their brothers fighting on each side of them. They should be recalled that way, honored for that, and respected for that. It might have been okay to dislike war, but America should have respected the warriors who were just doing their duty as instructed by the brass. Hey, it was war, accept it—*some people died!* That was the nature of war, and all you could do was just take it! *"Just take it, I know, sounds insane. Getting shot at, just take it, damn it! There's no place to hide anyway. Resist your natural reflex to duck away. Just take it, I know, sounds insane!"*

Would I ever forget those unvarnished words of my first Platoon Leader, 1st Lt. Sparks? Would I forget Dick Salmond's appropriated Jeep? Or Steve Chasin's Zen-of-Helicopter-Flying? Or all the Agent Orange I sprayed or the blue jeans Serna and Larraga gave me or Johnny Hummel's Cobra or Smitty's coin toss or those two pilots I met in the Khe Sanh POL? I could only hope so, but I knew it would be impossible.

44

JET AIRLINER: DENVER AIRPORT, I'LL BE HOME TONIGHT, BABY

The trip from Seattle to Denver was mostly eventless. I just watched Rocky Mountain scenery out my window and listened to a song that another soldier sitting right in front of me kept playing on his little cassette player, over and over. I recognized him from the Ft. Lewis Discharge Center. He was playing an old Chuck Berry song, "Back in the USA," and I thought that was funny. But a stewardess came over and told him he was disturbing other passengers so he would have to quit playing his music if he didn't use earphones. A polite argument ensued. Another Stewardess Lady came over and asked what the problem was. She said she knew how to take care of that. She asked the young soldier to let her see his cassette player and then proceeded to remove a battery from it. She said it was clearly defective so she would get him a fresh one from the galley, and she walked away with his battery.

I was thoroughly pleased to have such mundane things to keep my thoughts occupied. The garbage that kept trying to bust into my brain was nothing I wanted to deal with right then, so any distraction from that was more than welcome. The funniest part of all that: the damned Chuck Berry song kept playing in my head and sometimes it rolled into other Berry songs: Maybelline just couldn't be true, but Johnny was Goode as ever.

So the beautiful Rocky Mountains, the same mountains that ran through El Paso, and that old rock-n-roller kept me from feeling that I was going out of my head, kept me feeling calm and in control of myself, because I was wanting to jump up and yell and grab a bottle of whiskey and a stewardess's hat, put it on, and do a Chuck Berry duck-walk dance move up and down the aisle, playing my air guitar, while I sang "Back in the USA" at the top of my lungs. That other soldier and I could've done a fine duet act instead of sitting there trying to behave like we were back in Sunday school class.

Finally the airplane touched down at Stapleton Airport at Denver, Colorado—needless to say, in the USA. I was then officially on the last leg of my trip, with hardly more than another hour of flying time to go. Just had to get to a different gate down the concourse, a relatively short stroll, and then wait out a couple of hours of layover. I had lost all track of time by then: it was maybe 30 or 36 hours since we left Cam Ranh Bay, or maybe more. Hell, I didn't know. We'd been through so many time zones and the international date line, I wasn't sure what day it actually was, maybe Tuesday or maybe Wednesday. All I knew for sure was, I wasn't sure of anything right then.

I was exhausted and wearing the same wrinkled-up 4- or 5-day-old clothes I'd traveled in and was walking pretty slowly in the fast-moving crowd. I must have looked like a walking-dead zombie, zoned out, with big dark bags under my eyes. Then I noticed three cute young sorority-sister types walking toward me, talking, laughing. As they neared me, they veered straight at me, and the middle girl coughed up a great big juicy honker and spit it on me. Laughing, giggling, they scampered away. There was additional laughter as they ran into the crowd, which I assumed came from people who agreed with the sentiment expressed by the three little foxes, the stupid goddamned young bitches. Yeah, that was funny, real goddamn funny, girls. Back in Vietnam I'd heard of such crap happening to people who'd been in the States on R&R and never thought much about it, because it was getting to be an old joke already and not funny to most people by 1971. Felt like I wanted to scream at them, "What if I'd counterattacked you by reflex, you stupid skanks—zap, zap, zap in a split second, then laid you down dead, calmly, peacefully, on the floor, totally dead? Then, two more seconds, laid out your sorority sisters, equally peacefully dead, forever-n-ever dead. Doubt you'd find that so funny, you ignorant assholes."

What a trite little cliché that was: almost predictable, if I'd thought about it a second. But what had my attention was my emotional response that instantly grabbed me the moment that spitting crap all went down. Kill. Kill her. Kill the piece of shit. Go off on her like a goddamned bomb hitting her. My head was instantaneously flooded with visions of killing that girl and her friends, and the pictures I was seeing were ugly to the max. However—the terrifying part of everything that was happening—I was fully able to do all of the things that existed in my head, and I had wanted to explode on her for a tiny heartbeat and had only barely stopped myself.

If I'd had my guns on, I'm afraid that the little giggler would have been shot, because I would have automatically drawn and fired without any conscious thought or hesitation the instant her spit hit me. I had just stepped out of a different reality that existed in a place far, far away where I'd been given the power of life and death. It was fully within my power to decide who lived or, more important, who died. And killing was perfectly okay and normal, entirely accepted as a central point of everything, part of the daily social system. Killing was celebrated and glorified, and good killers were elevated to positions of honor. You just had to do your killing within the few rules the army imposed, and as long as you adhered to the killing rules you were totally free to kill everybody you wanted. No sweat.

I still felt raw all over from the killing I had done less than a week ago, and I'd been as tensed up as a coiled rattlesnake ever since then. It was pure luck I'd been so tired and worn out from the trip I was on that I was really just moving through the airport in slow motion and I had made no response to those girls in any fashion. I just stood there with girly-spit dripping off my face and let them get away.

What on earth was the matter with me? Killing someone? That thought wouldn't have occurred to me a year ago, before Vietnam, not in a million years. In Denver it was my first thought, and it erupted up out of my sub-conscious mind, not the product of some rational thought process where you weighed all the aspects of a situation and then decided to take some particular action. No, this was instant, automatic, and the worst part was that it was purely instinctive—an overwhelming urge to kill. Goddamn it. That had never been in me before, not that I'd ever been aware of. Yeah, I had felt the urge to kill plenty of times, just like I did last week in Laos. But I thought those times were caused only by the heat of battle in a combat situation. Apparently it wasn't just a combat deal. Apparently this was a generalized deal. Apparently Vietnam had brought out the killer part of me. So since it seemed that I had an aroused killer instinct raging in me, and being back in the USA, I was going to have some readjusting to start on now that I was nearly home.

As the people just passed on by, I wiped the dripping girly-spit off my face: looked down and saw the main sputum hanging there, dangling from my aviator's silver wings. Oh, I bet that girl's sorority gave extra points for a premium hit like that one. A pilot's wings: come on now, that had to be bonus-point territory. Looked for a men's restroom, found one and put my head under the faucet, then ran hot water for a damned long time. Washed my wings an equally long time. After I dried my face and combed my hair, a man in a business suit approached me and started talking.

What the hell now? Gonna get some old gay guy's best pick-up routine?

He bashfully said, "Saw what those bad girls did. Can I get you a drink to apologize for them?"

We sat at a little food court and got a couple of Cokes. He opened his briefcase, took out a flask and offered it over. "Wild Turkey, Kentucky bour-bon at its best. Those wings. Helicopter pilot? You coming home? I was with 1st Cavalry in Korea. Makes me a vet. How was your time, see any action?"

Before I could get away from him I thought those damned college girls were going to have him crying: he was so upset, apologizing for the disrespect they showed me. He seemed to be a nice man, and he made me feel better.

But I still felt like ripping into that girl. However, for that trip I was still an army officer and even by war rules the army frowned on killing silly college girls at the airport.

Got my wife, Jane, on the telephone. "I'll be home tonight, baby. Be arriving El Paso at six o'clock, coming in on a plane from Denver. They've already called my flight. Gotta go."

MY WIFE, OUR APARTMENT, BACK IN THE WORLD

I came out of the door and down the stairs of the last airplane ride of my long trip back from the war in Vietnam at the El Paso International Airport. Maybe it was because the plane we had flown in on was a little regional jet or because the airport had so many planes already at the gates, but for whatever reason we exited our plane a good distance from the terminal out on the tarmac and walked into the airport. That walk seemed like something out of some World War II movie, and I felt like a made-up fictional character that I wasn't comfortable playing. I didn't know how I was supposed to act, how I was supposed to be feeling. But what I was feeling was simply being void of any feelings. I felt completely numb and oddly two dimensional, and I was putting one foot in front of another only because I was being carried along by the other passengers. I was really home, but I felt stunned. The entire scene was unbelievable and distorted like I was moving through a liquid atmosphere in slow motion and was very unconnected from everything going on around me. Still alive. What more could I have asked for? I was feeling a little bit tight from all the booze I'd had on my trip. That 25-year-old Chivas Regal Scotch the major shared with me had me totally blasted for hours, and then those drinks on the plane from Seattle, and that old guy in the Denver airport with his Kentucky bourbon, and the drinks on the plane from Denver. So the alcohol in my system might have had something to do with how I was feeling right then. Probably.

As we approached the terminal building, through a big plate-glass window I saw Jane, my wife, waiting there with my mother and father: my welcoming committee. I was relieved to see them. I'd been waiting a whole year to see that very sight, undoubtedly the single most important sight I'd ever seen in my whole life up until then. I'd made it home, and I wasn't in a damned box. But I felt absolutely flat, rift of every normal human emotion as things were unfolding.

As soon as she caught sight of me, Jane was springing up and down, her loving arms ready. My last few steps she ran to me and grabbed me in a giant hug and a honeymooners' kiss. My mother joined in a big group hug, and I felt as weak as a rag doll and thought I might pass out from being so dizzy. As I stood there limply in everyone's arms, I felt as though I'd been shocked by a cattle prod. My vision filled with the sight of Johnny Hummel running across the same tarmac I had just covered, running to his waiting extended family: mother, father, aunts, uncles, cousins, and his girl. But they were all crying and sobbing as a flag-draped coffin was rolled up and presented to them and the running Johnny melted away into smoke before my eyes. I felt like someone had just hit me in the face with a shit-pie, and I watched as Johnny's Cobra exploded before me. I had just experienced another damned flashback where I reexperienced every emotion and physical response I had felt at the time of the event actually happening. It felt as if someone had thrown a bucket of ice water on me, and a sudden coldness instantly shot through me to my bones.

Looked out the windows, saw my Franklin Mountains. Whenever I'd been away and returned those mountains always made me feel back at home, back where I belonged, where I fit in. Those mountains said I'd really made it back, pressed that feeling into me more than anything else. I was home. Problem was, exactly who the hell had come home? Damned if I knew, but I felt totally changed.

Concerning Jane, she and I were going to have to start over from the beginning as strangers, because Eddy Denny was dead, irretrievably gone. He had become someone else in Vietnam. For a seemingly infinitely long time, no one had even called me by the name Eddy. Hornet Three-Three or simply Three-Three or the last name of Denny had been my only names. Jane, my mother, and my family knew only Eddy, but he was dead. Eddy was gone. Only a week ago Eddy was killing people, shooting people point blank in the face, emptied two pistols, and if Eddy had more pistols, he would've emptied them, also. But Eddy could never have done that: Eddy always said he was an antiwar pacifist, and Eddy would never have shot anyone that way. That was not possible. It was Three-Three pulling the trigger, experiencing it, and Eddy was nowhere to be found. Eddy was gone and had been for a long time by then, gone off to some other dimension and time, forever. It was obviously a straightforward case of *Invasion of the Body Snatchers*.

We made our way to baggage claim, then out to Jane's car, her Camaro that she loved so much, and she asked me to drive. She knew that was something I'd missed so much. We took my parents to their house, and my mother wanted me to come in, stay a while and visit for a couple of hours, but Jane said she had something she had to show me, a big welcome-home surprise, and we'd visit all day tomorrow, all day long.

She gave me driving directions over to the Eastwood end of town, her life-long stomping grounds. She led me to an apartment complex that looked very nice. We parked under covered parking in a reserved and numbered space. She let me look at the buildings some and the beautifully landscaped and carefully manicured grounds. A few buildings were one-story units, and for apartment buildings in El Paso in 1971 everything was very, very upscale.

I was sure that she knew my paychecks had stopped as of that day, and I was unemployed starting right then. My warrant officer's paycheck might not have been a lot, but I was sure it was more than a motel clerk's paycheck, and that's what I'd been before the army: a motel clerk and a college student. I doubted there were any jobs around for helicopter pilots who didn't have a civilian license to show a prospective employer. I was a helicopter pilot only in the goddamned army.

Laughing and giggling, Jane seemed to be very excited and happy with the game we were playing. She made me cover my eyes and led me into an apartment. When she said to open my eyes, it was a truly impressive joint. There was a large living room, for an apartment, filled with beautiful modern furniture. We went in the dining room, also nice, with a big wooden table and six chairs, a china hutch, and a butler's pantry. There was a fancy, large eat-in kitchen with a table and four chairs. The place had two bedrooms. The master bedroom had a big king-sized bed, with a big dresser and large chest, an attached bathroom with twin sinks and separate tub and shower, terrycloth bathrobe hanging on the door, new house slippers by the shower. Everything was totally plush and totally brand new. A large walk-in closet was full of clothes. She showed me another walk-in closet. The other bathroom was just as nice as the first. The second bedroom was smaller than the first but ample. It just had a rocking chair over in the corner but no other furniture.

Jane said, "When the time comes: our nursery."

For an apartment, the place was huge and furnished very nicely. I hated to question how she thought we could afford this model apartment we were looking at. Then it hit me and I wondered, so I asked her, "Is this a model rental unit?"

She squealed, jumped. "No, it's going to be our home."

My good wife was thinking Cadillac style all the way if she thought we could afford such a place. It had to cost a fortune at rent time. I'd always known that Jane was a little bit of a spoiled rich kid who had been raised from a young age by her well-to-do grandparents, so money had never been an issue in her life. But we would never have a budget that would allow us to afford anything like that place if I was going to be going back to college to finish my last year and get my degree. But Jane was clearly excited, totally jumping for the place, and I didn't want to disappoint her, not right then, not in the first couple of hours I'd been home after being gone so long. I tried to be as diplomatic as possible and quietly mentioned that maybe we should look up near the college for a student apartment.

She immediately and firmly said no. She had already rented this apartment.

I was flabbergasted and asked, "You've already signed a lease and everything?"

Jane answered, "Duh, yeah! Or how could I move all our stuff in, all of our furniture?"

"What furniture?" I asked.

"This." She waved all around. "All of this. Oh, I understand, you thought this was a furnished apartment. That would probably be too expensive. No, that's my surprise for you. All of this is ours. We own it! I bought it all to set up our home. Isn't everything so beautiful, don't you love it? Welcome home, baby, to your fabulous home!" She jumped more and squealed, "I love it, everything we have!"

I took her in my arms, kissed her, hugged her tightly, and said I loved her. When I told her I loved her, I was telling her about my intellectual thoughts, not my emotional feelings, because right then I was totally numb, had no feelings, and you could've knocked me over with a feather. I was numb from stupid Vietnam and stupid Khe Sanh and stupid Laos and stupid killing people, and I was numb from sectional sofas and king-sized beds and kitchen appliances and I guessed all the damned curtains on the windows, the art on the walls, and the damned robe and house slippers in the bathroom.

At our old Officers' club back down in Cu Chi, over the bar, there was a pilot's guidance: *Pilot, change what you can, accept what you can't, and be smart enough to know the fu**ing difference. So, don't ask for damned bar-tab credit, 'cause we don't do that. Cash talks. Bullshit walks. End of Story.*

Didn't ask about the rent or how much was left of our savings or what the hell everything cost. Knowing those particulars right then wouldn't change any of it. That bar sign kept yelling at me: know the difference between what you can change and what you can't. And heaven knew I sure didn't want to come home and start any problems right off the bat. From the way she obviously loved what she had done, if I started talking about returning furniture to the damned stores that would have certainly hurt her feelings and probably pissed her off royally. Things were done, and I didn't see how they could be undone without driving a big and unneeded wedge between us right from the damned start of us trying to pick up the pieces of our lives after being separated so long by that worthless Vietnam War.

Had to admit she'd put together a BIG surprise for my return. That was sure, that was dang sure!

Had to admit she had picked out some very nice stuff, whatever it cost, obviously a lot.

Had to admit I wasn't going to do anything to spoil my first night home with my lovely wife.

Had to admit the covered parking was really nice, pure Cadillac style.

Had to admit she had me hog-tied right then, and that was going to be our home, our new little second honeymoon home, except it was anything but little and I was sure the same thing would apply to the damned rent whenever I discovered how much that was going to be.

Had to also admit Jane knew all of my hopes and dreams and plans for what I wanted to do with my life, which meant both of our lives since we were married, and she had known all of that in detail since before we ever decided to get married: finish my degree, teaching job, architecture school at night, then architect. With that all done we could settle down into a comfortable and secure and stable life and raise our family together. And she knew full well I would feel that everything she had done here directly flew in the face of all of that. But she did it, anyway.

Had to admit I wished we had talked all of this over before she'd done anything, but I suspected that was the last thing she would have wanted to do. It looked like Jane was jumping us way ahead to the comfortable, secure, stable lifestyle and just blowing off the nuisance parts like college degree, architecture night school for another degree, maybe two, architecture apprenticeships, and so forth. I guessed we would get around to talking about those things after we had spent a few days catching up on our lovemaking.

Told her I probably smelled like a hog and I needed to get those filthy clothes off and get a very long hot shower. Oh, my God! It just sank in. I was going to have access to my very own shower once again. I was going to be able to start living like a civilized human being again. Oh, my God! A real, honest-to-goodness flush toilet. No more crapping in sawed-off oil drums and then later smelling the burning brew of diesel fuel and a communal pile of everyone's combined turds. That had been a key feature of our lives back in Chu Lai, that and not having any place to get anything to eat. Seemed that then I was going to have TWO damned flush toilets at my disposal, as well as TWO showers, hot ones, since I was back home with my wife.

Jane said a shower was what she had at the top of the list of her to-do items. She'd join me, scrub my back, then she'd cook me a real home-cooked meal, since I'd written her that we were living on C-Ration crackers and peanut butter most of the time over in that place I'd been. How about a nice salad, a juicy steak, and a baked potato and asparagus for a start? Then we would make love. Anything I wanted. She wanted that night to be perfect for me, for us; one neither of us would ever forget.

In the shower, the water could be turned on to be hotter than anything I could stand. I loved that. The days of cold Vietnam showers were finished, and never again for me, never another cold shower, not even if I lived to be a damned ripe old age of 105.

My loving wife was pretty, naked, and in my arms. Oh, that had been a long time coming, and there had been many nights when I ached all over from missing her so much. My young wife, the agile dancer, standing flat-footed she could do her patented Rockettes high kick and throw a sculpted leg over my shoulder and made it look so easy. Those fine West Texas women standing up beat all the others lying down. Jane totally lived up to that myth, if she didn't actually exceed it. Being connected with a woman again was as good as I had remembered it to be. Man, if someone could capture that feeling in a little eye-dropper bottle, they could have sold it for $1,000 per bottle. But at the exact moment of union and the onset of my feelings of ecstasy, stupid shit flooded my brain. Johnny Hummel couldn't ever have this again. Steve Chasin, Dick Salmond—okay, okay, the whole damned rogue's gallery living in my damned head had gathered into a knot and were waiting to get recognized. My choice: I could stop what I was doing right then and fall down onto the shower floor and curl up into a fetal position and let the hot water beat on me while I moaned about dead men, or I'd just have to take it and try to ignore the thoughts I was suffering with at the moment. There was no choice to be made. West Texas women standing up beat all the others. Well, you know how that saying went.

While she was frying up some steaks for us, Jane said she knew I'd always held back in my letters, never told her the truth about what was really going on around me in Vietnam, but now that I was back I could really tell her the truth about what it was like over there, what happened.

Oh, man, where to start? Okay, might as well start at the beginning. First thing, told her about the Long Binh Replacement Center, then the helicopter ride to Chu Chi, assigned to the Hornets, and seeing this guy from flight school I knew slightly. We rode on the same helicopter, me to Chu Chi, him to Tay Ninh, called Rocket City. We'd had this coin toss to decide which of us went where. His name was Smith. After a few weeks went by I was up at Tay Ninh and asked about him but nobody had ever heard of a Smith. I found out he'd been killed... Whoa, cowboy, she stopped me right there.

"Oh, no, awful, someone you knew, killed! Baby, you have to put those awful things like that out of your mind, totally out. That's all in the past now. You must get those things out of your mind. Forget about any bad things like that. Thank goodness, all of that is behind us."

"You didn't let me finish, the coin toss..."

"Oh, honey, baby, just erase all that stuff from your mind. You're home with me, safe-n-sound. That's all that matters. We have our lives to live now, starting tonight in our bed. Thank goodness, you're out of the army and Vietnam is now totally in the past. I should've known better than to ask. That's awful about your friend, and I'm sorry, but just wash those bad thoughts out of your head."

That was the only time Jane asked about Vietnam. If I tried to ever bring it up she stopped the conversation and nixed that topic; she wanted no Vietnam talk. That was the past, so forget it! She was totally right. Okay, all I had to do was erase Vietnam out of my mind. Now, why didn't I think of that? Tell me where to get my brain washed out, because I had nasty stuff in there I was wanting to be rid of.

By the time I'd been home three or four days and searched the *El Paso Times* newspaper employment ads first thing every morning, I was not feeling secure about the local job situation. I couldn't take too much time about finding a job because we really needed a paycheck coming in. I had finally asked about our money situation. And as I feared, Jane had basically spent most of all the money we'd put away while I was overseas. I'd sent nearly all of my paycheck home every month, plus Jane had worked at a good job and lived at home with her parents. After a whole year of doing all that saving, I'd thought we would have plenty of money so I could finish my senior year of college, and get my degree and a teacher's certificate. Instead of having a nice, comfortable twenty grand in the bank we had about four grand and a rent bill coming up real fast and every month thereafter.

It was so damned funny I had to laugh to keep from crying like a baby. Jane had waited till I got home about buying a nice TV. She wanted me to get what I wanted. I think we settled on the Sony, a big console job with a remote control. They would deliver it to our nice big apartment with its covered parking and our personal reserved space. What was a few more hundred bucks spent for a TV? Might as well spend everything we had in the damned bank.

Now, here's where the crying part came into play. When I got my last-minute notice about getting discharged from the army, that was not at all what we'd been expecting. That whole situation came as a total surprise to me, right out of the blue. It was a welcome surprise but nothing we'd been planning for, so I wrote Jane a letter, told her all about my getting a three-year-early-out from the army. Told her it was great: a precious army discharge sooner than I had been expecting, so I could finish my college degree right away and start teaching. God blessed me: I was not going to have to go back to damned Vietnam for a stinking second tour of duty in that shit-hole.

She had received my letter BEFORE spending any of our savings money. It was all still in the damned bank. We couldn't discuss any plans through the mail because it took at least two weeks to exchange letters and we didn't have that much time available. The important thing was that I told her what my hastily revised plans had become. She knew all of my ideas. She might have known my ideas, but evidently she didn't agree with them and didn't wait to discuss things with me when I got home. She just acted on her own, totally went with her choices, even though they ran completely contrary to what I was thinking. She was sure when she explained things I'd see things her way, agree with her.

Which color TV did I want, Sony or Panasonic? She didn't think going back to college sounded like a good idea, be a teacher and lock myself into a lower-paying job forever. Anyway, nobody needed a college degree. Her father didn't have a college degree and he'd worked himself up at the Standard Oil Refinery from an entry-level laborer's job all the way to the top, to the manager of the whole refinery, and I could do the same thing. The sooner I got a job in some good company the sooner I could start moving up. College was just wasted days and wasted nights that generated no paycheck.

Jane told me, "Okay, now let's face the truth about things. You're going to be twenty-five years old in a couple of months on your next birthday. Architecture school would take years. You'd be at least thirty years old before you finished. For Christ's sake, are you gonna be a professional college student till you're thirty? Are we gonna have to wait that long before having our children? Until you're thirty or even older? No! We can't do that, I won't do that! I want you settled into a good job. Then buy a house and settle down and start a family, four kids, and be a family. That's what I want. That's all I've ever wanted, you and me, having our family, having our kids, my family."

Well, okay, it was best that we had all the cards out on the table, wasn't it? How come I had never heard any of that before? I had heard about us having kids, but FOUR kids. That was news to me!

She said, "I've had time to think while you were gone all this year, and I saw things a lot clearer than I ever had before. We need our family. Every minute you were over there I was worried to death that you might get killed and any chance we would have to bring our babies into the world would be gone forever. That idea drove me crazy the whole time you were gone, and it really made me think about what things were truly important in life, and our family always came out on top. So, I don't want us to wait until we're in our thirties to start our family. I want to get started while we're still young."

Well, okay. Jane had me boxed in. It seemed that her year of being closely attached to the Vietnam War had crystalized her life goals and aspirations, and they apparently were at direct odds with what I'd always had in my plans. She had become fixated on the idea of starting a family, and she wasn't talking about merely having a baby. She had it in her head that she wanted four kids and wanted them in rapid succession, like about a year or two apart each. Could you imagine dealing with four kids of stair-step ages of one, two, three years old, with a last baby making a total of four kids? What a crazy circus that would be. Imagine the times when all four of them would get to crying at the same time. What she was indirectly saying was that she didn't want to work but rather she wanted to be a stay-at-home mom and raise her little herd of angels. We were going to have to get that worked out and come up with something we could both agree on. If we did things her way I would have to simply forget finishing college, forget about being an architect, but that was the only thing I'd ever wanted to become since I was a little kid about six years old.

Vietnam had crystalized a few things in me, too. First, I felt like men had died in my place and I owed them something. I needed to do something with my life that would justify the fact that I'd been spared when others died. I needed to make a contribution to the world that would make it a better place, and being an architect probably was the only venue I'd ever have to accomplish something like that.

A couple of days later, after our new TV was delivered and set up, when I first turned on our new Sony, I swear, the evening news flickered on and bigger than hell there was a Hornet helicopter! My Wasp Platoon! The reporter was talking about how Firebase Mary Ann had been overrun by the enemy. NVA or VC sappers had gotten inside the wire, killing many people. Mary Ann: I'd sprayed Agent Orange there and worked out of there many times. That was near the damned tight-hover hole where I'd once torn up a helicopter's rotor blades chopping the tops out of trees, where a sniper had killed Kenny Koch. The TV showed grunts loading body bags, more than a helicopter could lift in one load. Guessed that some poor Wasp crew was having to fly the Graves Registration mission that day. Watched the TV, flashed back, smelled death, and was instantaneously there again that moment. A chill hit me, the coincidence, the timing. The very first time I turned on a TV since I had gotten home and there was a Hornet helicopter right in my living room. It was old man Death telling me plainly, "Don't come back or you'll die next time. Take my word for it."

Despite feeling like I had just received a clear death warning through my new Sony, I'd been thinking the only best option that Jane had left me was to go back to the army recruiter, tell them I had reconsidered, and sign up to go voluntary-indefinite. I'd go in for the whole army-lifer-bit, the 20-year hitch. I'd do my second tour in Vietnam, be there to turn out the lights when the war was over. In the meantime, I could make Jane happy. We'd start making babies, pop 'em out every year. I thought she might have wanted me to go back into the army. She liked being a pilot's wife, telling people all about her husband, showing photos of her very own warrant officer helicopter pilot: that's my man.

Change what you can, accept what you can't, and be smart enough to know the difference. Bullshit. I didn't think there were many things in life you couldn't change if you tried hard enough. I'd better look at those want ads again to see if I had missed anything or else plan on flying Dust-Off in Laos or Graves Registration again. I could always start to architecture school when I was 44 years old after putting in my 20 years with the army. I shouldn't have any trouble looking for a job as an architect's apprentice when I was nearly fifty or so. I would be old enough by then that I might look a little like a middle-aged Frank Lloyd Wright.

INDEX